THE
WISCONSIN
KRUEGER FAMILY TRAGEDY

16 Years

OF LETTERS FROM PRISON

THE WISCONSIN
KRUEGER FAMILY TRAGEDY

16 Years
OF LETTERS FROM PRISON

KAY SCHOLTZ

Trails Books

BOULDER

Published by Trails Books, a Big Earth Publishing company
3005 Center Green Drive, Suite 225, Boulder, Colorado 80301
1-800-258-5830
E-mail: books@bigearthpublishing.com
www.bigearthpublishing.com

Cover and text design by Ann W. Douden

9   8   7   6   5   4   3   2   1

Library of Congress Control Number: 2013937008

Printed in the United States of America

| CONTENTS |

| ACKNOWLEDGMENTS |

Before I begin a minute of writing, or you begin a minute of reading, I must first express a sincere thank you to Bill and Virginia Elmhorst for giving me the privilege and opportunity to make this book happen.

I've looked upon this project as a chance of a lifetime. As a lover of Clark County and Wisconsin history in general, I am honored to take part in this endeavor. I hope I have done justice to the story of Caroline, Ennis, Leslie, Louis, and Frank Krueger and helped give them the vindication they deserve.

Thank you sincerely, Bill and Virginia, for trusting in me.

I also want to thank my husband for the support, patience, and input he has given me in putting this story together. He has always given me the freedom to be myself and to pursue my dreams in our thirty-plus years of marriage. No one could be as unselfish as he, my best friend, and my rock. Thank you, Tom!

Lastly, I would like to thank my editor, Mira Perrizo, for the patience and guidance she has shown me. Her expertise has helped to make my words and the words of the Krueger family come to life.

| INTRODUCTION |

It is said that experiences in our lives make us who we are. That couldn't apply more to the Krueger family of Longwood Township, Clark County, Wisconsin. On September 14, 1918, near the close of the First World War, their lives were changed forever.

Their story, once common table talk throughout the Midwest and beyond, has nearly been forgotten. The intention of this book is to focus more on the life of the Krueger family in their struggle for freedom rather than the incident that caused their troubles. I was prompted to begin this project when recently given a large collection of letters exchanged between Krueger family members that span nearly sixteen years.

My goal is to let the Krueger family speak, using the original words they penned and penciled. In addition to their legal woes, I chose to include excerpts from their letters about life on their farm at Longwood and events in the surrounding community during the years preceding and during the Depression.

They now have a chance to tell their story, from their side of the fence. It is a story riddled with heartbreak, sadness, suffering, and questions that may never be answered. It is a true story, and it is a tale of how so many lives were tragically affected over a situation so poorly handled and out of control.

The Krueger story is also one of great strength and a mother's hope, patience, and determination to fight for her sons and what she always and unfailingly believed was their injustice. Let their story teach us to accept others when they have different beliefs than we do. Let it teach us to leave people and the scenes of tragedy alone unless we are there to assist and not escalate the situation. Let it teach us to have patience and the strength and courage to stand up for what we believe in, like Caroline Krueger.

Let me introduce you to the Krueger family and the tragedy that took place in September of 1918 in Longwood.

The Krueger family planted their roots in Longwood when Ludwig (Louis) Krueger, husband of Caroline Krueger, purchased forty acres there in 1884. His deed stated that he was to cut off all the timber suitable for saw logs or lumber and allow the former owner up to five years to haul it away. Ludwig was a farmer and carpenter. He died in 1910 from pneumonia, leaving his widow Caroline and their five sons. One son, Robert, died in 1913 at the age of twenty-six, in Carbon County, Utah, where he had been suffering for two weeks from pneumonia. He was employed as a locomotive fireman on the railroad.

On that life-changing day in 1918, family members consisted of widow Caroline Krueger, fifty-six, and her four remaining sons: Frank George William Krueger, thirty-seven; Louis Albert Edward Krueger, twenty-eight; Leslie Almond Arthur Krueger, twenty-four; and Ennis Charles Florian Krueger, twenty-one. They lived on the original 1884 homestead in their unique self-built farmhouse located 1.5 miles south of Withee, Wisconsin. The Kruegers were known by neighbors as prosperous, hardworking, and God-loving people, but they didn't always fit in.

The beautiful Krueger farmhouse was inspired by eldest son, Frank, several years after he returned home from attending college at Ashland, Wisconsin. The home was completed in 1917, replacing the family's primitive log cabin. It contained electricity, a flush toilet, hot and cold running water, a telephone, an elevator, a built-in ice box, a heating system attached to a windmill, and was considered one of the most modern rural farm homes in the area. The family increased the size of their property with an additional 200 acres of farmland in Longwood Township and a lot in the village of Withee.

In this day and age, the Krueger brothers would most likely be known as conscientious objectors. They, along with their mother, had strong religious convictions. They displayed an American flag over their fireplace and loved their country, but felt that fighting a war on foreign soil was something they should not partake in.

In the late summer of 1918, Frank and Ennis did not register for the draft when they were required to do so. Frank was in his late thirties, but the age limit for the draft had been extended and now included him. Ennis had just come of age at twenty-one. Leslie did register and took his examination that summer, but failed to show up on his scheduled date of entry. He was hiding out along with his brother Louis, who was called up for an exam but never showed.

On the Saturday afternoon of September 14, 1918, a carload of four men stopped near the Krueger home with plans to arrest Frank and Ennis Krueger for failure to register for the second draft on September 12 at Withee. Frank and Ennis were in a field husking corn frozen by an early September frost, about a quarter mile north of their house, when three of the men, two of them U.S. marshals, exited the car. They walked up to the woven wire fence and began shouting at Frank. As tensions built up, Ennis shot into the air with a revolver he frequently carried. The U.S. Marshals—Joseph Gantz of La Crosse and Cyril Marks of Madison—fired their guns as well. It is unknown who fired first as each claimed the other did. Frank and Ennis ran through the cornfield toward their house seeking refuge, while Peter Rasmussen, marshal from the Village of Owen, emptied his gun at the fleeing Krueger brothers. A bullet grazed Frank's leg. Gantz and Marks ordered the two local men, Rasmussen and Earle Kidd, driver of the car, to motor back to Withee and gather up reinforcement.

The situation escalated into a mob mentality that Saturday afternoon at Withee and the same continued back at the Krueger farm. Carload upon carload of men armed with guns—calling themselves a posse—lined the highway in front of the Krueger home and extended as far as two miles south. With more than 150 men at the scene, chaos was imminent. Tension was high well into the evening, until sunset ended the horrid ordeal. In the end, many rounds of gunfire took the life of one man, Harry Jensen, Withee depot agent, and left several others wounded.

During several episodes of shooting that evening, the Krueger farmhouse was riddled with more than four hundred bullets. Mother Caroline saved herself by huddling behind the large kitchen chimney in prayer. Son Frank hobbled from the farmyard where he had stood guard near the windmill. He made his way into the house where he sought refuge, bleeding profusely from a second gunshot wound to his other leg.

Caroline phoned for a doctor but no one would come to their aid. She waived a white rag from the door of her house and walked out into the darkness toward the angry mob, desperately seeking help for her bleeding son. She was arrested after a struggle and handcuffed. Robert Vater, a neighbor with whom the Kruegers were in good standing, came with his horse and buggy and loaded up Frank, who was no longer able to walk. Vater took Frank to his house promising to help him get medical care. No one else was bold enough to come to Frank's aid. Once at the Vater farm, Frank was arrested as well and taken away.

Ennis and Leslie escaped in the darkness that night by blending in with the crowd and running off into a wooded area to temporary freedom. Ennis, the youngest Krueger brother, was supposedly shot and killed a week later in a barn north of Withee, in Taylor County, by Joseph Gantz, one of the U.S. marshals involved in the original shootout. While in jail awaiting trial, Caroline Krueger was not allowed to attend the burial of Ennis. Stories evolved as time marched on and she became doubtful as to the actual death of Ennis. Leslie was captured later that fall near Crow Wing County, Minnesota, where he found work on a farm.

Frank and Leslie, now both in custody, denied shooting Harry Jensen. A Clark County jury found each of them guilty in a 1919 trial and a judge sentenced them to life in prison with hard labor. The Krueger brothers were immediately taken by railway to Waupun, Wisconsin, to serve their sentences at the state prison there. Caroline was charged with the murder of Jensen too, but was acquitted. She, along with all four of her sons, faced several lawsuits from Jensen's widow and others who were wounded in the shootout.

The homestead, or what was left of it after that dreadful day and those to follow, was never as majestic for the Krueger family as it once was. On September 16, their huge barn burned down after being filled with cans of formaldehyde. U.S. Marshals had hired a local doctor from Neillsville to orchestrate an attempt to gas out anyone who might be hiding in the barn. When the doors were opened, the barn—overflowing with hay and straw—unexpectedly burst into flames. It was a total loss along with contents, tools, and harnesses.

It didn't take long for the bullet-ridden home and outbuildings to be ransacked by neighbors and onlookers; the flag that adorned the mantel above the fireplace was even stolen.

Caroline returned to the farm alone in the late summer of 1920. Her son, Louis, was still on the run, Ennis was said to be in the grave, and Frank and Leslie were serving their life sentences at Waupun. Her letters to them expressed the great loneliness she felt and the trying times she experienced. One problem that infuriated Caroline was the continued passers-by who stopped to look at the homestead and take photos. For the most part, Caroline wished they would leave her alone. In May of 2012, I found myself taking pictures of the Krueger home and wondering what Caroline would have thought of me, too.

In the summer of 1921, when Louis returned after his capture and release on bond from the La Crosse County Jail, he and his mother attempted to make a life together alone on the farm, with little equipment left and few resources. Over the years, Caroline, then in her sixties, worked as hard as a man. She helped Louis saw firewood, milk cows, shock oats, run the sawmill and engine, and do whatever needed to be done according to season.

From Caroline's letters we learn that money was tight and life was not easy for the two who held out on the farm. There was constant worry of losing the land due to lawsuits stacked up against them, and legal fees. When the Depression came, Caroline wrote of milk strikes, food shortages, the drought, and the closure of banks in the local communities. She said it was a good thing they didn't have any money so they didn't have to worry about being robbed.

During the brothers' incarceration, the family remained extremely close and Caroline wrote letters as often as allowed. Leslie and Frank wrote back faithfully and somehow managed to save their mother's letters. Through Caroline's continued faith she stayed focused on bringing her sons home from prison, waiting for the day when they might all be together again. Frank and Leslie often struggled with their states of mind, as anyone would, after so many years of imprisonment.

Caroline Krueger hired several lawyers during the years that her sons were in prison. John W. Reynolds, Sr. and partner T. P. Silverwood, of Green Bay, represented her and the boys initially and lost the case for Leslie and Frank. Caroline felt Reynolds was excessive in his charges and filled herself with bitterness for the man who she referred to in her letters as "R," "Ren," or "Rey." In November of 1926, Reynolds, at the height of his career, was elected as Wisconsin Attorney General and held onto that office for three terms.

In later years, Mrs. Krueger hired Attorney Paul H. Raihle from Chippewa Falls, who stood by the family for several years with very little compensation and celebrated with them when the brothers were at last set free. Attorney Raihle had the guts to initiate a lawsuit against Reynolds for his excessive fees. He took flack for doing so, and was even accused in the press of having Ku Klux Klan affiliations. Raihle later became a writer of Wisconsin history.

After conditional pardons by Governor La Follette, Frank and Leslie Krueger spent nearly two additional years of their lives in insane asylums. Although conditions at the asylums may have been better than in prison, these were still very trying times for the family. It was uncertain if they would ever actually be released back into society, as the pardon allowed their exit only if they were declared "sane." Several German societies from Milwaukee formed a "Krueger Committee," which especially aided in getting Frank and Leslie released. They finally came home together to Longwood in 1934.

Caroline enjoyed a seven-year reunion with her sons until her death in 1941, at the age of seventy-nine, at Longwood. Frank and Leslie, along with brother Louis, went about their lives farming and eking out a living as best they could. Dark shadows loomed over their shoulders and life was never the same for them as it was before September 14, 1918.

The Krueger Family of Longwood, Clark County, Wisconsin, circa 1904. (Top L to R) Louis, Robert, Frank, Leslie; (Bottom L to R) Caroline, Ennis, Ludwig (known as Louis) (author photograph).

Krueger homestead taken before the barn was destroyed on September 16, 1918. (Photo postcard, author's collection)

1 SOLD ... TO THE HIGHEST BIDDER

On a sunny day in the summer of 1963, a large crowd gathered at an estate auction on the Krueger farm south of Withee, in the town of Longwood, Clark County, Wisconsin. Cars lined the highway and side roads nearby. Neighbors from the Longwood area and curiosity seekers from a great distance pushed their way into the yard and studied the hay wagons loaded with tools, antiques, and farm equipment, hoping to buy a souvenir from the Krueger family.

This was not the first time a large crowd gathered at the Krueger farm; it was reminiscent of an outright "mob" that showed up at this same farm back on September 14, 1918, during the First World War. No doubt those in attendance at the auction had grandparents, uncles, or fathers armed with guns here on that fateful day in 1918. Most likely some of those auction goers had relatives who looted the Krueger home and outbuildings, and gossiped about the family's dire situation long after the shootout.

The estate auction was precipitated by the fact that the last Krueger family member, Louis Krueger, had recently died as the result of a local traffic accident. Efforts were underway to locate next of kin, as relatives hadn't been in close touch with the family for several years. It was necessary to sell everything in order to settle the estate and divide the worth. After the sale of all the Krueger property, and an extensive search for heirs, thirteen cousins divided up the estate. They each received about $600.00 after payment of administrative expenses and the funeral bill.

A Clark County historian was busy with her camera, taking several shots of the crowd during the auction. Florence Garbush was both a schoolteacher and a freelance newspaper reporter, and held a fascination with the Krueger story most of her adult life. She observed men trying to dig out spent bullets from the walls of the Krueger house while at the auction. Others pulled screwdrivers from their pockets, removing doorknobs as souvenirs. A mob mentality was still looming in the shadows of the Krueger farm.

Krueger Estate Auction, summer of 1963
(Florence Garbush photos)

2 **PRISON CORRESPONDENCE** Shortly after Louis Krueger's death became public knowledge, Ms. Garbush contacted the probate judge of Clark County. Her wish was to search through the Krueger home for any letters or papers of historical nature dealing with the family's legal troubles following the 1918 shootout. She received permission in writing to enter the home with the administrator of Louis' estate, Police Officer David Bertz. She and Bertz found a large box of letters from the Krueger home exchanged between Mrs. Caroline Krueger and her two sons, Frank and Leslie, inmates of both the state prison and later the prison hospital or insane asylum at Waupun, Wisconsin. The letters spanned the years from 1918 until their release in 1934.

It was clear the historian/schoolteacher wanted desperately to investigate the case and write a lengthy piece about it from the many notes she left behind. The Krueger story appeared to be her lifelong passion, nearly an obsession. She had even attempted to obtain a fellowship and a yearlong leave of absence from her teaching position to do research on the subject and write a book. A small account was kept of her expenses that included purchases of several pairs of shoes and new outfits for her travels to do research on the case, a new camera, and film.

Those boxes of letters, somewhat tattered and musty, remained in the teacher's home until her death in 1995, packed away among many other possessions of her lifetime. You could say she was a hoarder, but thank goodness for hoarders who preserve "meaningful stuff" along with their trivial possessions.

At the death of the spinster schoolteacher, survived by just one brother in a distant state, the contents of her overfilled home were in turn sold to settle her estate. The Krueger letters, discovered in the household accumulations of Ms. Garbush's estate, were again spared by the purchasers Bill and Virginia Elmhorst. The historical significance of the letters was recognized and they were safely tucked away until passed on to me in January of 2012.

Much has already been written about the Krueger affair, but their letters, a few still tied in bundles with strings, appeared to be waiting for someone to open and read them once again.

And so began my endeavor, nearly a hundred years after the assault on the Krueger home at Longwood, to summarize the letters and share the Krueger story. I want to convey the family's thoughts and emotions from the letters they wrote to one another in their never ending battle for freedom. Their letters reflect a journey of true-life happenings on their farm, in their community, and in the prison system throughout the 1920s and early 1930s in the Midwest.

I have pondered on how Caroline Krueger, the matriarch of the Krueger clan, would feel about the publicizing of her family letters. I think she would want to be portrayed most as a mother with unending strength, faith, and patience in her very lengthy fight for justice for her sons.

When reading through hundreds of letters covering a span of nearly two decades, I began to understand the personalities of the family members. Caroline Krueger was a strong country woman. She was not afraid to dirty her hands and work in the fields, with the livestock, and in the garden. From her own sheep, Caroline spun wool and knitted sweaters, mittens, and socks. She loved to pick wild berries in season, and sold fruit and garden produce for needed spending money. It was always her goal to put up enough canned goods and meats, and to have extra food on hand for the day her boys came home from prison. She wanted to be ready for them, to be able to provide for them. She never wasted a spare moment, just like so many rural women of her era.

When possible, Caroline took trains and later buses to visit her sons in prison. Often, time allowed for visiting was just one hour. Frank, a keeper of notes and details, wrote on the back of an envelope all the dates his mother came to see him. The visits began with her first trip to the Wisconsin State Prison at Waupun, on July 7, 1920. In 1921, she visited three times. In later years she came from one to four times a year to see her boys. A tally of her visits came to twenty-seven, from July 1920 to October 1932. Sometimes the frequency of her trips depended on other business she had to attend to in Madison or Green Bay with her lawyers or appearances before the governor when pardon hearings took place. Whenever she could, she combined business trips with visits to the prison.

Caroline sent Frank and Leslie apples and plums from the trees they had planted on their farm. She managed to send homemade cookies, a little money, books and newspapers when allowed, and even mailed a cooked chicken now and then. Frank penned to his mother in September of 1928: "Many thanks for the apples. They are good and the taste is the same as it was before, makes me long to be where they grow. Never thot I would eat home grown fruit in this place. To have it sent from home in here. Well so be it, if it must. I ate 4 of them in succession and my stomach knew right away he had received some of that same kind before. Knew them at once!"

Although Caroline's grammar and spelling were not the best, her feistiness and determination came through clearly in her letters to her sons. She often told of her aches and pains and many times expressed bitterness toward society and neighbors who were not supportive.

Letter to Caroline from an Angry Man in Milwaukee, June 14, 1921

Mrs. Louise [sic] Krueger, To the mother of slackers: The Journal of Milwaukee publishes an item regarding your dead slacker sons property which is held by the U.S. Government, do you suppose you have the sympathy of the man, who served. You criticize the government for his death, now do you think you cared any more for your boys, or had any deeper Mother Love than my own Mother, who offered two of us, all she had, for the good old Flag still proudly waving. With tears in her eyes, she

said, do your duty as my dad, and your father did in 1861-1864.
Your dead son got all he deserved. If I had a word in it, the three
would have been tried by a court martial, lined up and shot, and I
would have liked to been a member of the firing squad also. Your
name is German, still you are supposed to be an American. You
might say, they should not fight the father land, yet my grandfa-
ther took up arms against the south when his son espoused the
cause of the confederacy.

Your a way off, Arthur F. Wright, Gen. Del. Milwaukee, Wis

Despite hard knocks from some, Caroline kept her faith and still also found time to help others, to comfort neighbors in times of sickness and death; these actions were often mentioned in her letters. She received words of support as well.

Letter to Caroline from Mrs. O. J. Little, April 17, 1922

Dear Mrs. Krueger, I have been hoping to hear something of
the boys case but so far, not a word. I am enclosing a copy of the
letter I wrote to Gov. Blaine. ...

I am told that the case of Frank and Leslie Kruger, formerly
of Withee Wisc. is to come before you on March 1st for pardon.

These boys are now serving life sentences at Waupun for the
supposed killing by them of a man where a large mob attacked
their house while they were resisting the draft.

You will see by the review of the case that there never was
any way of being sure who did the fatal shooting as the public
highway, the Krueger premises, outbuildings etc., was one mass
of excited men firing in every direction.

And now that the war hysteria has passed many who were
most bitter in persecuting the boys, have had time to remember
the sterling qualities of their character and to regret their own
part in this tragedy. These boys were left as mere lads to assume
debts and burdens at their Fathers death, that would have
disheartened most adults. But by unremitting toil, frugality and
self-sacrifice they had met all obligations and won a place of high
esteem in the neighborhood. We lived between Withee and Owen
for several years and I knew the Kruegers intimately. Never in

all those years did we see one indication of criminal tendencies
in any of them, or hear one word of disparagement concerning
them. Rather were they mentioned as examples of what quiet,
strong, earnest endeavor can accomplish. It is because they are
not criminally inclined that we believe they should not be incarcerated with those who are.

It is because of their worth as producers, as model farmers,
as examples of thrift and frugality and Christian integrity that
we believe the best interest of the state will be served when they
return to their home.

May we not hope that you can in justice, give these young
men their liberty and permit them to return to their farm, there
to again become the industrious, law-abiding citizens they were
previous to the war?

Thanking you most earnestly, I am, Sincerely yours,
Mrs. O. J. Little, Stone Lake, Wisconsin

Although Caroline lived in Longwood Township, her postal address was
Withee, Wisconsin, the nearest post office. When Caroline wrote to her sons
as inmates in the state prison at Waupun she addressed their letters to "Box
C." When they were patients of the insane asylum at Waupun she addressed
the letters to "Box B." She said she did not want the post office or neighbors
to see the words "insane asylum" or "hospital" on the letters, nor could she
bare to write those words, and hoped that the address of "Box B" would be
sufficient. It was.

Louis, Caroline's middle son, who spent roughly fourteen years home
alone on the farm with his mother, was silent for the most part with pen or
pencil. He rarely wrote letters to his brothers; he told his mother to tell them
he would talk to them when they came home. Louis was a hard worker; he
repaired as much as he could on the outbuildings and the farmhouse. There
was an overwhelming amount of damage from the shootout, the barn fire,
and thefts that took place afterward. Funds were short so fixing was limited.
Louis faithfully did the farm chores, planted crops, cut hay, sawed firewood,
and kept the farmhouse warm for his mother in the wintertime. Occasionally Louis would hire a neighbor to help with jobs his mother was not able to
do, more often as the years went by.

It was hard for Louis to get away from the farm. He did get to make a few trips to Minnesota and Chicago—short trips. Riding his horse to town was probably an important outing for Louis when supplies had to be purchased. He occasionally attended auctions when there was something he thought he might be able to bid on cheaply for the farm. Louis did not have a good hand at penning letters, his grammar was a bit astray.

I could notice the improvement in Leslie's handwriting through the years although he was always a bit simple with his words. At times he appeared restless and low on patience; at other times he seemed deeply religious, quoting bible scriptures and mentioning church sermon topics that he had listened to in prison. The legal red tape that the family had to sort through became overwhelming for Leslie, as it would have for anyone in his situation. He often suggested that his mother hire a different lawyer, or try writing to the federal government for help in getting his and Frank's release.

Leslie was always grateful for the fruit or other food his mother sent him. He worked for several years in the prison binder twine factory and was very generous with the money he made, often sending it home to Caroline. A few of Leslie's prison pastimes were learning shorthand, reading the bible, and studying the German language. In later years Leslie preferred to buy candy if he could, rather than fruit, from the prison system. He had a ravenous appetite and gained a tremendous amount of weight after his transfer to the prison's insane asylum. There he did light work in the carpentry shop and the dining room versus hard labor while in prison.

Perfect penmanship and well-sketched diagrams were often a part of Frank's letters. A 1904 college graduate of Northern Academy in Ashland, Wisconsin, his letters clearly reflected his intelligence. Oldest brother Frank had no trouble reading and writing German, but felt the use of it would cause more trouble than what it was worth. Often he was very serious and somber, and suffered from depression. When in a better state of mind, his letters were quite lengthy; they were brief or non-existent for weeks when he felt the opposite. Frank was certainly a deep thinker and that got him into trouble both physically and emotionally. His depression sometimes caused him to give up on any hope for freedom.

Frank was a reader who taught himself Morse Code and shorthand. In his early prison years he was obsessed with law and studied all he could about it. He copied down notes from the reference materials he gathered, cramming notes written in pencil onto scraps of paper in the tiniest script imaginable. His minute, cursive handwriting was completely legible and almost a work of art in itself.

A sample of Frank's notes using the tiniest script imaginable (author's photo)

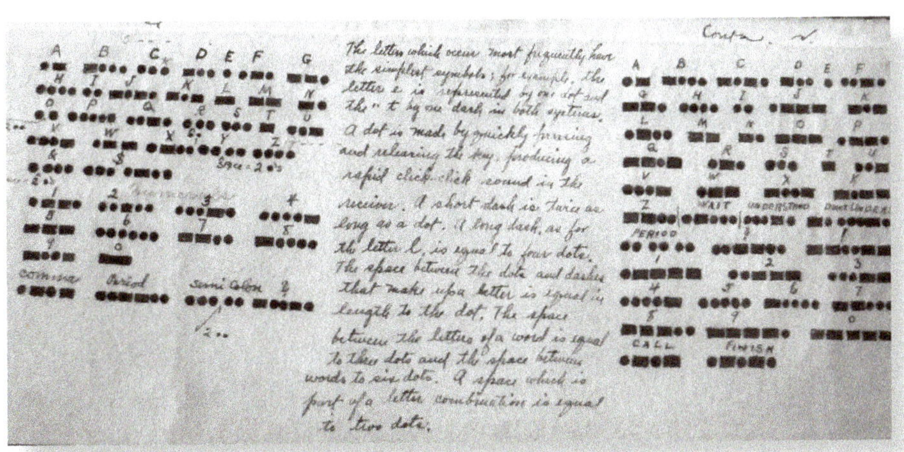

Frank's "cheat sheet" for Morse Code (author's photo)

Frank mentioned that he wanted, and then purchased, a modern dictionary for study.

Frank to Mother, July 5, 1920

I have been thinking of buying me one of those Webster's dictionaries if I could raise the money some way, of course they are quite expensive, costing somewheres near $25. I suppose, but it is a regular library in itself; and would give me an opportunity to keep my mind "brushed up" on all the latest words and give me an opportunity to learn the meaning of quite a few which may come handy some day.

Reading recipes, health advice, home repair tips from magazines and books, and sharing the information with his mother, were some of Frank's pastimes. He responded best in letters home when questioned about a problem that needed fixing in the house or on the farm. Frank gave well-thought advice for brother Louis and his mother.

Frank's letters were also often full of sadness and hopelessness. In later years it appeared he lost his faith. His mother had placed a religious stamp or sticker on the back of one letter. Frank told her in his next letter if she had any of those stickers left it would be better to throw them in the wood stove.

Most of the mail was stamped with a censor or inspection mark, on both the envelopes and the letters themselves. Sometimes there were lines or areas cut out of the letters. There were strict rules on when letters could be written and how many could be sent per month. At times Frank and Leslie could only write letters home on Sundays or holidays (Leslie called them "hollow days"), or sometimes twice monthly. There was also mention that there could only be handwriting on one side of the paper at times. The boys told their mother not to write too extensively about their case since others would read the letters and know what their plans or thoughts were. Some letters had words erased from the writing and often when they referred to particular persons (lawyers, neighbors, victims of the shootout, etc.) only a first initial would be given. In all of Caroline's letters, "L" stood for Louis, her son at home.

How the Letters Were Saved

In April of 1933, Caroline received a box filled with the letters mailed to Frank while in prison and the insane asylum. The letters were sent to her from

Waupun with a note stating that they were in need of space and didn't want to store them any longer. Frank had the foresight to save every letter received, although he had thought of taking notes from the most important ones and destroying them all. Leslie saved his letters as well, as did Caroline, and they all found their way together in a box at the family home in Longwood. They are reproduced here with their incorrect grammar and spelling, although punctuation has been periodically added and corrected for readability.

"MY ONLY WISH WOULD BE THAT THIS LETTER WOULD BE THE LAST I HAVE TO ADDRESS THERE TO WAUPUN." —CAROLINE KRUEGER TO HER SON FRANK, MAY 19, 1920

KRUEG
IS CO

RUMOR
THE GOV
SEIZ

Some Believe
borhood;

3 **CHAOS BEGINS**   Neillsville, the county seat of Clark County, Wisconsin, had two newspapers in print at the time of the Krueger shootout. A clearly one-sided and inaccurate account of the affair was written in the Neillsville Times. It makes one wonder how the family could have been given a fair trial when jurors were later chosen from this area.

ONE KILLED, OTHERS WOUNDED IN FIGHT WITH SLACKERS

Notorious Krueger Family Shoot to Kill in Resisting Arrest

Draft Evaders Barricade Themselves in Their Home Near Withee and Kill One Man. Mother and One Son Under Arrest But Other Boy Escapes.

Battle Held Saturday Night

On Saturday afternoon Clark county reverted to Kentucky methods of resisting arrest, when Frank and Ennis Krueger shot and killed an officer of the law. The shooting had been more or less anticipated for several months, for it was known to the authorities that the Krueger boys were in an ugly mood and were bent on making trouble. In fact, Mrs. Louis Krueger had recently made the remark that if the Krueger family were drafted or molested someone would be killed. However, the insane manner in which the Kruegers resisted arrest came as a surprise and shock to the entire county.

On Thursday Frank and Ennis Krueger, oldest and youngest sons of Mrs. Louis Krueger, failed to register, and on Saturday afternoon Deputy United State Marshals Jos. Gantz and Cyril Marks of Madison drove out to the Krueger farm just south of Withee and Earle Kidd and Peter Rasmussen of Owen, for the purpose of arresting the two slackers. The four men drove up to the Krueger farm in the Kidd car and found both the Kruegers at work in the corn field near the road. The marshals called to the Kruegers and told them that they had come to arrest them, at which both the Kruegers drew revolvers from their pockets and opened fire on the officers. This happened about three o'clock in the afternoon, and the four men immediately drove back to Owen, swore in a number of deputies at Owen and Withee and started out to make another effort to make the arrest. In the meantime the Krueger boys, together with their mother, had barricaded themselves in their house and awaited the return of the officers. The posse arrived very soon after but stopped their cars at the Vater home north of the Krueger house and about 40 rods away.

The return of the officers with deputies was the signal for a general battle and as soon as the posse had gotten out of their cars, the Kruegers opened fire on them. The first round claimed a victim in the person of Harry Jensen, station agent at Withee, who was shot in the chest just below the throat. He was immediately put into an auto and carried to Owen, but died soon after. He leaves a wife and three small children.

The deliberate murder of Jensen was the act which incensed the posse to sterner methods and the battle began now in deep earnest. Additional aid was sent for and the house was surrounded as closely as possible. Emil Laino and Matt Mattson went to the east of the house to stand guard and in crossing a hay field about 50 rods back of the barn, both men came under the guns of the now desperate Kruegers. Laino was shot in the leg and as he lay bleeding on the grass, four more bullets were shot into his prostrate form. Mattson fared better, for as he lay in the grass he was shot through the ankle, but had narrow escapes from death when a bullet struck just in front of his head while another passed over his back so close to his body that it cut his suspenders and trousers. As both Laino and Mattson were within range of the Krueger guns, the two had to lay there until dark, when they were rescued. Laino was rushed to the hospital at Marshfield and is in a very serious condition, but seems to be in a fair way to recovery.

Earlier in the afternoon, however, the posse was successful in wounding Frank Krueger, the oldest son. The two boys went from the house to the barn all the time during the battle, first shooting from the barn at the guarding party in the rear, and then making it hot for the party in front. It was on one of these trips from the barn to the house, that Frank Krueger was wounded. He was shot through the leg and on his way to the house was shot through the other leg. He bled profusely and when the house was finally taken, the lower floor looked like a shambles. So much blood indicates in the minds of some that one of the other boys was also wounded, but this is not definitely known.

Shortly after, Mrs. Krueger appeared in front of the house waving a white flag. She was finally induced to come down the road out of direct range of the Krueger guns, where she was taken to the Vater home, later she and Mr. Vater, the neighbor, went to the Krueger house and determined that the defenders, with the exception of Frank, had slipped away or hidden. Frank Krueger was then taken from the house and he and his mother taken to Owen where they were placed in jail after Frank's wounds had been cared for. They are now prisoners of the United States.

As darkness came on and there came a lull in the battle, Ennis and possibly Leslie Krueger, slipped from the house some time during the night and made their escape through the thin line of guards and are now at liberty. Either this or they are hidden away in a previously prepared hiding place. Whether or not Leslie was at home is not known, but neighbors state that they thought they had seen another man at the Krueger house for several days, but had only seen him at a distance. Leslie and Louis Krueger evaded the draft some months ago, both disappearing from the country and not having been found. Certain it was that the oldest and youngest boys were there with their mother and all are now guilty of murder and have life imprisonment ahead of them.

The Neillsville Home Guards were sent to the scene of battle, leaving here Saturday evening about 7 o'clock and arriving at the scene in automobiles about nine o'clock. They stood guard all night and gave battle also to the remaining Krueger. The beautiful farm home was literally shot full of holes, for the guard about the house banged away whenever they thought they saw a Krueger. The house itself is one of the finest homes in the county, modern in every way, and cost about $12,000. When the house was finally evacuated by the Kruegers, the guards took possession Sunday morning at day light and found the home in a terrible state of blood and confusion. When it was definitely known that the defenders had made their escape, a search was made but no trace could be found, and it is evident that the Krueger boy made his escape during the night. The country is being combed for him and he no doubt will soon be arrested and pay the penalty for his crime. The Home Guards are still on duty there and will no doubt remain to assist the United States Marshal Frank O'Connor and Sheriff Hewett until the other Krueger is taken.

About two months ago, readers of the Times will recall that a considerable amount of ammunition and firearms was taken at the Withee express office by Sheriff Hewett, District Attorney Rush and court Commissioner Kountz which had been consigned to the Krueger boys. It was shown at that time that the Krueger family was preparing for war, and when Mrs. Krueger and sons were brought to Neillsville they were defiant and Mrs. Krueger made the remark that if attempts to arrest the boys were made, bloodshed would follow. Her prophecy came true in the killing of one man and the wounding of several others. It seemed from Mrs. Krueger's attitude that they felt that the government had no right to interfere with them, that they would not enter the army for they were opposed to killing their fellow men, and Mrs. Krueger had the idea that the government would draft her four sons and then confiscate her property. Mrs. Krueger, who is a widow, and her four sons owned the fine 160 acre farm near Withee and also considerable other property and were worth about $60,000. All this was made in Clark county and none of the Krueger family will now live to enjoy the fruits of their labor and toil for they all face life imprisonment as the result of their insane and misguided attitude.

Later Developments

On Monday afternoon cans of formaldehyde were placed in the Krueger barn as there was a suspicion in the minds of the officers that one or more of the Kruegers was hidden in the building. The formaldehyde fumes "gassed" the barn thoroughly but did not result in the desired effect. Instead, when the barn doors were opened a fierce fire ensued. Just how the fire started is not known. Some say that a formaldehyde tank tipped over and caused the fire. Others say that the heavy gas uniting with the fresh air outside caused a manner of an explosion. At any rate the barn caught fire and in a short time was a smoking heap of ruins, together with all the contents. As soon as the ashes have cooled sufficiently it is expected to search the ruins closely for the remains of any of the Kruegers. One thing did develop and that was the explosion of cartridges in the burning building. A supply of ammunition had evidently been hidden in the barn and this exploded when the flames reached it.

In addition to the killing of Jensen and the severe wounding of Laino, several others received minor wounds. Among them were Frank White, Mat Mattson, and Angus Page.

It seems to have been pretty definitely decided that the Kruegers have effectively made their escape, but it does not seem probable that they have been able to get very far. The most plausible theory is that the boys have escaped toward the east and are now being hidden around the farms in territory with which they are thoroughly familiar. It is understood that an organized search will be made through the town of Green Grove, Longwood and vicinity by the state guards and to this end it is understood that the home guard companies from Marshfield, Wausau, Colby, Stanley, and Eau Claire may be brought down to assist in the search.

When one reads the letters from the soldier boys they are at a complete loss to understand the references to such innumerable number of "cooties." The various rumors, stories and fabrications which have been flying to and from the Krueger battle grounds are certainly as numerous as the famed soldier "cooties."

Several slackers have been rounded up in the county as a result of the search for the Kruegers. Tuesday evening a young man was picked up by members of the Colby Guard south of Greenwood and he was turned over to the United States Marshal. It was thought that this young man might be a Krueger as he had a couple revolvers on his person. Two piano men, who visit Neillsville regularly, were also picked up for failure to fill out questionnaires and are now in jail. It behooves every person to be sure to carry his registration card with him, even when he goes to bed, for he knows not when he will be stopped and made to show his card.

The press mentioned that the Kruegers had purchased a "considerable amount of firearms and ammunition" two months prior to the incident and implied they were ready for a fight. From reading their letters, I don't believe this was the case, but if anyone was willing to fight, it was the youngest brother, Ennis Krueger. The brothers liked to hunt deer and other game and for years were no strangers to guns. Ennis had ordered a revolver and ammo of various kinds. When the parcel came to Withee in July of 1918, the railroad agent saw the word "Ammunition" written on it and for some reason became alarmed and contacted the Clark County sheriff. Rather than delivering the package to the Krueger home, Sheriff Hewett took possession of it.

Krueger family members were called to Neillsville in July of 1918 to talk with R. Kountz, city attorney and draft board member. Frank had this to say about that visit ten years later, in a letter home, "I cannot help but think of that Kountz when he called us there to Neillsville and questioned us, we should never have gone there, and when he asked me if we had guns in the house, we as old settlers there in the county and used to hunt and then ask us such questions. Have often thot what business it was of his. One can see what talk will start from such mess. He was just aching all over for trouble himself. Hope he got enuf too ..."

House and Farm Building.

This is the house near Withee, Wis., in which Frank and Ennes Kruger, aged 27 and 20, respectively, took refuge after firing several shots from revolvers at two deputy United States marshals, the Owen constable and two other Owen residents who came to arrest them on warrants charging failure to register under the 18-45 year draft law, and from which they and two other brothers, Louis and Leslie, aged 26 and 23, respectively, kept up a six-hour battle with possemen and state guards who surrounded the place.

From the windows of this beautiful farm residence, the four boys blazed away with high-powered rifles, killing one man, Harry Jensen, sta-

Frank Kruger, Wounded.

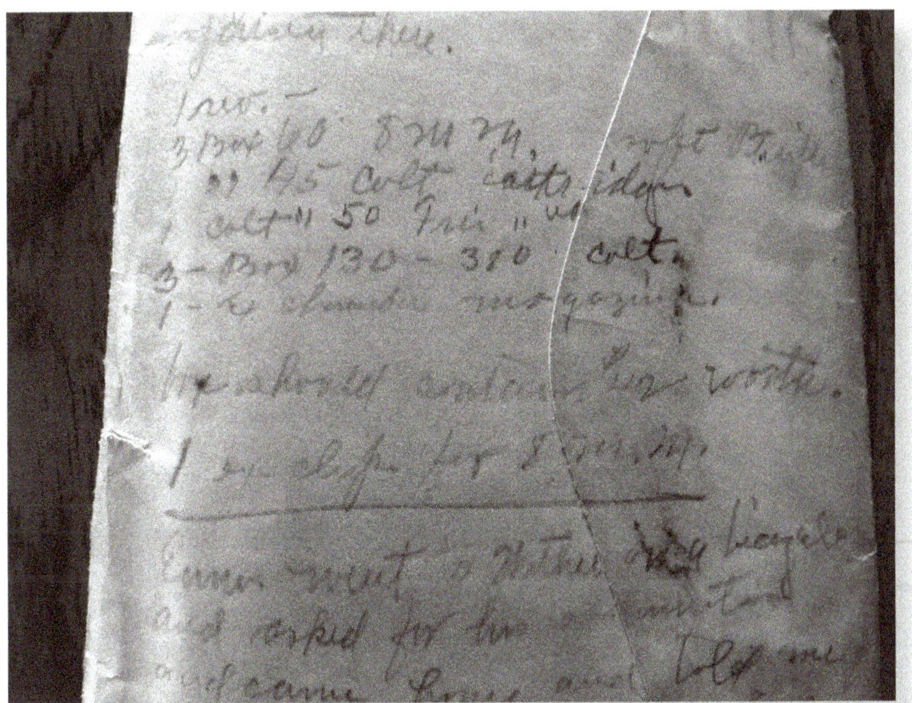

CONTENTS OF AMMO BOX

Frank penciled a list of the contents of the ammo box on the back of an envelope and information about Ennis' visit to pick up the ammo:

"1 revolver; 3 box 60 8MM soft pt. rifle; 1 box 45 colt cartridges; 1 box colt 45 50 cartridges; 3 box 130-380 colt; 1 ex chamber magazine; 1 ex clip for 8 MM; box should contain $42.00 worth.

"Ennis went to Withee on his bicycle and asked for his ammunition and came home and told me that Jensen said Hewett had taken it. I did not ask Jensen for it afterwards.

"Said he would take our land away from us. The Soldiers were promised land and that he was going to take all of us and put us in the army."

Although it is a bit hard to decipher, I don't think this seems to be an exuberant amount of ammunition. There appears to have been only one actual gun in the order.

The very onset of the whole affair remains a major question. When the two U.S. marshals, Gantz and Marks, shouted at Frank and Ennis from the road, who really drew their gun first? The news reporter inferred that both

Frank and Ennis each carried a revolver and each fired at them first. I believe Frank was not armed at the time, only Ennis. Ennis may have shot into the air without realizing the seriousness of what he was doing. When the brothers fled on foot through the cornfield back to their house they were peppered with shots from both U.S. marshals and Rasmussen. Frank received a graze wound to his leg causing him great pain.

Leslie Krueger was home during the time of the shootout. He may have been hiding in the barn at the time the U.S. marshals first appeared at the Krueger farm. Leslie had registered for the draft but failed to appear when called up. He had drifted about all summer and tried to keep out of the public eye. Louis had found employment out of state.

The *Milwaukee Journal* covered the Krueger story quite thoroughly, although the news reported was like other stories in other newspapers, not always accurate. The following article begins with an interview of the nearest neighbor, Mr. Vater, who removed the wounded Frank Krueger from his home.

MILWAUKEE JOURNAL, SEPTEMBER 1918, PAGE 6

KRUEGERS TOOK STAND AGAINST FIGHTING IN FRANCE

Withee, Wis.—"Distinction to go out of the United States and fight on foreign soil is responsible for the action of the Krueger brothers," said Robert W. Vater, nearest neighbor to the Kruegers, upon whose pleading Frank Krueger, oldest of the boys, surrendered Saturday night. "They said that if the war was in this country they would be among the first to volunteer. They declared, however, that it was not right to send American soldiers to France and that they never would go. There does not seem to have been any pro-Germanism about them. Both their father and their mother and all the boys were born on their present homestead. [Not true, but all were born in Wisconsin] They knew nothing of Germany except what they read. Intense self-will also seems to have been responsible for the Kruegers' actions."

Wealthy Farmers

They were prosperous people, owning, it is said, about 400 acres of land in Clark county, the most of which is contiguous [actually 240 acres+] The area under cultivation is fertile and the rest is covered with valuable timber. The Kruegers devoted less of their time to their own farm than to doing work for neighbors, who did not possess the farming machinery they did. They had a threshing machine and also a portable sawmill with which they cut timber for other farmers. They also owned a tractor with which they could pull any kind of farm machinery, thus covering a large farm more quickly than it could be done with horses. All of them were skillful builders. The house in which they lived, one of the finest in Clark county, was built by themselves, the work taking about three years.

Their property appears to have had the effect which it often has on residents of a backward community; that they were a law unto themselves. This tendency was strengthened by the fact that they were apparently of obstinate natures. Those who know them say that they held tenaciously to their opinions. They kept abreast of current events, taking several newspapers and being close readers.

All Well Educated

The actions of the boys are all the less understandable for the reason that they were well educated. Frank, the oldest, attended a local grade school, and finished his education at an academy at Ashland, where he was the coach of a basketball team. Louis, the second brother, graduated from the Withee High school after finishing a local grade school. Leslie, the third brother, does not appear to have been a good student. He finished grade school, and attended the Withee High school for a time, but did not finish. Ennis, the youngest brother, was graduated from a local grade school and from the high school at Owen. Their mother is a great believer in education. She had Leslie take lessons on the piano, but he did not make much progress.

A large American flag was found over the fireplace at the home when it was first entered by the besiegers.

Read Pacifist Books

A large quantity of Pastor Russell's pacifist literature was found in the home. Mrs. Krueger was not prominently identified with any church …

It is interesting that the reporter called the Withee area a "backward community." The Krueger family, with their strong educational values and strong aspirations for betterment, most likely caused some to fear them and have jealousy toward them. A recipe of fear mixed together with jealousy and curiosity helped to create the mob mentality that got so out of hand. Those feelings, along with the "slacker" label attached to the Krueger brothers, made it easy for Kidd and Rasmussen to gather a large number of men who were ready for confrontation on that September day.

The following day, September 15, Caroline Krueger was brought back to her home while the Neillsville Home Guard and others remained at the scene still looking for traces of the brothers, Ennis and Leslie, who had escaped in the night. Caroline recounted in a letter addressed to Washington D.C. shortly after the incident, "The next morning [U.S. marshals] O'Connor and LaMont took me out [from the jail at Owen] and home to get Frank's close [clothes] and also for me to change." Mrs. Krueger got into a scuffle with Sheriff Hewett when she tried to stop them from examining her well in which they thought someone might be hiding. Men ended up firing at least one shot down the well casing after pushing Caroline off the well covering, where she boldly stood. In the fracas Caroline claimed Hewett broke her finger causing her much pain and discomfort in later years. She continued in her letter to Washington, "Then we went back to Owen with Frank's clothes, from there O'Connor took me to Eau Claire, on the way he said now we got you, we'll tend to you, so I went to Eau Claire Jail."

On the 16th of September, the Krueger's massive and modern barn was blown up after being filled with cans of formaldehyde to "stink out" any occupants. The unexpected explosion and fire consumed the entire barn, leaving only the stone walls. The barn was filled with hay and straw. Frank gave a detailed estimate, "Both mows in the barn were full of hay to the roof where Ennis and I got thru but it settled until it was bout even with the purlin plate. The mows were full packed and built over the plates and also crowded into the threshing floor. The north threshing floor was about 3/4 full, only near the doors there were some sacks of threshing screenings and a few saw tables we got from Redville. And the south thresh floor was piled up with straw we threshed when they hauled oats from the other place. There was over 100 ton of hay in the barn besides the straw. It figures out to be that amount."

Caroline Krueger's letter to Washington D.C. continued, "Then on Wednesday he [O'Connor] came to visit me, I said to him they also burnt down the Barn. He said how did you find that out, I told the scoundrel not to say anything to you. Why I said, and who do you mean by that scoundrel. He said Sheriff Gorman. I said no he didn't say anything to me, but I overheard a woman tell others down in the office. Then he said yes it is burnt. I was not there I just had left a little before it burnt. Now this is what Mr. Geo. Ure of the Lynn Insurance Co. said to me as I tell him about our Ins. Mrs. K. you sue us and we will sue the Gov. for it was U.S. Marshal O'Conner that gave the order to destroy it, he sent a man to Neillsville to get a Dr. Frank for he was the only man around here that understood how to use this formaldehyde in the County so Dr. Frank went down and the Barn was set on fire some way. I was not there, none of us, this trouble of shooting was on Saturday toward evening and the Barn was burned on Monday noon." It is not known if Caroline ever sent the letter to Washington D.C., or if she did, to whom. Dr. Frank charged $75.00 for his services at the Krueger farm.

The farm was insured by two insurance companies, but the Krueger family never received any compensation for their losses. The Lynn Mutual Insurance Company claimed the barn was destroyed during a riot, grounds for not having to pay on the claim. The second insurance company, Fidelity Phoenix Fire Insurance Company, stated in a letter to Mrs. Krueger in 1930 that the policy she had with them on her buildings in 1918 was only for tornado protection, so there would be no coverage for the fire.

On the inside of a cut apart legal envelope, Caroline Krueger jotted down an accounting of at least some of the bullets and locations where they entered the Krueger home:

BULLET LIST

16 on the east side
25 on the south side
1 hit on the west side from the south—1 from the north
144 north side
6 in the roof on the south side

2nd story south side
3 front room
2 bathroom
3 middle room
8 in the sleeping porch

1st floor north side
24 kitchen

13 Entrance under stair landing
44 Stair landing
1 kitchen east side

2nd story north side
20 bedroom
7 Front room

1st floor
1 East room east side
3 Middle room south side
3 Front room south side

THE INTERIOR OF THE KRUEGER HOME—BULLET HOLES REMAIN IN
RIGHT AND LEFT GLASS CUPBOARD DOORS

MILWAUKEE JOURNAL, SEPTEMBER 22, 1918

KRUEGERS HAVE MODERN HOME

Elevator and French Glass Show Owners' Odd Taste

Withee, Wis.—While the famous home of the Kruegers, the center of the battle for alleged slackers last week, deserves all that has been said in praise of its modernity, it bears evidence of a peculiar state of mind on the part of its owners. It seems to have been their desire to have a house that was up to the minute in its appointments as far as their means would permit, regardless of whether the improvements installed were needed or not. The most glaring instance of this is the fact that the house has an elevator. It isn't as big as the average elevator in an office building, but it can bear a weight of 500 pounds. The elevator runs from the basement to the second floor. It is counterbalanced by a weight, which makes it possible for a passenger to operate it with a rope.

House Thoroughly Modern

On the second floor is a well-appointed porcelain bathroom. It was in this room Frank was found wounded by Robert W. Vater, a neighbor, who knew the boys well enough to feel sure that they would not fire on him.

The doors and the woodwork in the front of the house are of oak. The windows are of the French plate glass. The floors are of hardwood. The house is wired for electric light, and it is understood that the Kruegers planned to buy a portable electric light plant. The kitchen sink is of porcelain, and in one of the walls is a built-in ice box. The house has a hot water heating system. A chute to the basement enables one to drop soiled clothes from the second floor. As the Kruegers are said never to have worn any other outer clothes other than polka-dotted overalls and shirts, the chute would seem to be somewhat superfluous. Their "Sunday clothes," it is said, consisted of clean polka-dotted overalls and shirts.

The house had a telephone, which was a great convenience to the officials, who had to communicate with men left to guard it. Possibly because a bullet had grazed the wires, good connection was extremely difficult.

Not Badly Damaged

The damage done to the house was not considerable. The steel bullets from the high powered rifles of the posse and the guardsmen cut through the clapboard on the outside walls at such a velocity that they made holes only of the diameter of the bullets. The holes in the plaster on the inside where the bullets emerged are about an inch in diameter. The holes on the outside are invisible at a short distance, and those on the inside could be plugged up and plastered over. Most of the windows were broken, and replacing them could be the biggest item of expense in restoring the house.

The stock is being cared for by Mr. Vater. The cows have "gone dry." As a result of the noise of the battle and the change in their surrounding they have become "wild" and it is difficult for anyone to get near them. The Kruegers' check for milk sent to the creamery at Withee is said to have amounted to $70 every two weeks.

With Caroline in jail awaiting charges, son Frank in an Eau Claire hospital, and Ennis, Leslie, and Louis on the run, things quieted down on the bullet-ridden Krueger farm. Renters came in to live there for a time; they did little to restore the farm to the grand place it once was. The water pipes were allowed to freeze and break in the house, ruining the bathroom floor. It took Louis until 1929 to restore hot and cold water back in the house.

Leslie and Ennis escape[d]
cover of darkness. Authorit[ies]
believed the boys might be [in a]
dairy barn and searched it [but none were]
found. Leslie was captured [and faced]
a charge of first degree mu[rder.]
She was acquitted, but the [verdict was overturned]
by the Wisconsin supreme [court.]
Less than a week afte[r fleeing the be-]
leaguered farm, the youth sl[...]

4 DEAD OR ALIVE?

Ennis Charles Florian Krueger was the baby of the family, born in Longwood in 1897. Ennis' father died of pneumonia when he was just thirteen. His future was undoubtedly shaped by four older brothers, and the death of one of those brothers, Robert, shortly before Ennis' sixteenth birthday. Death was no stranger to Ennis. Perhaps this, along with the fearlessness of youth, made him bolder, scrappier, and more vulnerable than the rest of the Krueger boys.

The press would lead one to believe that Ennis Krueger was shot and killed on September 22, 1918, in a barn where he was hiding out, in southern Taylor County, Wisconsin. Here's how they played out the story.

Defied His Country, Paid the Penalty—Fugitive Shot Down by Secret Service Men, Fearing Attack

Eau Claire, Wis.—Ennis Krueger, who was shot and killed Sunday, is the second victim of United States Secret Service Officer Jones, Montana, who also is responsible for the capture of Frank Krueger, oldest of the Kruegers, who surrendered to the authorities a week ago Saturday after having been shot twice in the foot by Officer Jones. According to reports received here, Ennis Krueger was shot and killed by the officer after he had made a move as if he was trying to pull a hidden gun.

After the fact had been established that the Kruegers were hiding in the vicinity of Polley, Wis., federal officers and members of an armed posse searched the entire neighborhood and discovered Ennis Krueger, hidden in a barn two and a half miles from Polley.

With his revolvers drawn, Secret Service Officer Jones entered the barn. Recognizing the fugitive, the officer commanded him to throw up his hands. Instead of heeding the officer's command, Krueger is alleged to have made a move as if he was trying to pull a revolver from his pocket. A flash from Officer Jones' gun followed and Ennis fell to the ground. The bullet had pierced his neck, causing immediate death.

The notion of a government cover-up can first be initiated by learning that Secret Service Officer Jones of Montana was a fictitious identity given to the news media. The killer of Ennis Krueger was in fact U.S. Marshal Joseph Gantz, who first visited the Krueger farm and approached Ennis and Frank on the day of the shootout in their cornfield. This information was revealed during the Krueger trial in 1919. Mrs. Krueger also stated in a letter to Washington D.C. (it is unknown if the letter was ever sent) that Joseph Gantz had only been working three weeks before the shootout took place at her farm; his occupation prior to becoming a U.S. marshal was that of a bartender. When Gantz testified at the trial he said he held the marshal's job for about a year.

Secondly, the man shot in the neck and killed as Ennis Krueger had no weapons on his body. In another news item, it seems apparent that Joseph Gantz and his driver used unnecessary haste in returning the body of the dead man to Withee. It almost appears as if they were frantic. Was that so necessary?

The scene of the killing of Ennis was a barn two miles south of Polley, Taylor county.

Details of the killing of Ennis received in Owen are that John Downing, barn boy for the Owen Lumber Co., and John Servaty, woodsman for the company, accompanied by secret service agents, were driving in an automobile on the trail of the missing trio. They came to a barn which connected with a farmhouse which was not occupied, the last tenant having moved away some months ago.

This barn is a log structure, such as is frequently seen in this country, with the openings between the logs closed up with clay. It has two floors, access to the second floor being secured through an opening inside the barn. When the manhunters saw the barn they decided to make an examination of it. They noticed that the opening bore evidence of someone having climbed through it recently.

Found Ennis Krueger Asleep

The searchers climbed up, and aroused Ennis from his sleep. There was a commotion in the hay, and the secret service man called upon whoever was there to surrender. The only reply was a still more violent agitation on the hay and the agent fired three shots, one of which killed Ennis. When the hay was turned over no evidence of Louis and Leslie Krueger was found.

The secret service again, making the trip back to Owen by automobile, drove so swiftly that the springs on the automobile were put out of commission. Deputy United States Marshal Joseph Gantz and the head of the secret service bureau here went out to the barn. They brought back the body, and not wishing to have everybody along the way know what they were carrying, they propped the body up between them in the car so that to a casual observer it looked like a living man. They passed through Thorpe and other good sized towns without anyone suspecting that one of the occupants of the automobile was dead.

In addition to Messrs. Downing and Servaty other residents of Owen who rendered valuable assistance to officers were E. W. Kidd, superintendent of the factory of the Owen Box Co, Frank Griffin, druggist, and A. M. Wilson, proprietor of the Owen garage. Messrs. Kidd and Griffin took part in the original battle at the Krueger homestead.

Ennis Buried

Beside the body of his father and his brother, Robert, who neighbors say, if they had lived would have prevented the selective service evasion, Ennis Krueger was buried Tuesday afternoon. Interment took place in the Riverside cemetery, two miles west of Withee.

The Kruegers have a lot there, which Mrs. Krueger frequently visited and carefully tended. The funeral from the undertaking establishment of Griebenow-Weirich Co. was conducted by the Rev. W. H. Sargent, pastor of the Congregational church at Owen, to which the Kruegers belonged. The expense of the funeral will be paid out of the estate, Frank, who is in a hospital at Chippewa Falls, having authorized it. Since the body was brought to Owen Sunday night by Deputy United States Marshal Joseph Gantz, it has been viewed by many residents of Owen and of the vicinity.

Was it really Ennis Krueger who was shot and buried in the Krueger family lot? Perhaps the only sure way to know would be to take DNA samples from the grave. Would Mrs. Krueger have normally been allowed to attend her own son's funeral while an inmate in jail, awaiting trial? If so, she was not allowed. No family member attended the service or witnessed the body. At first Caroline Krueger believed it was her son, but as years passed she began to doubt it, and carried that feeling to her grave, as did the rest of her family.

MILWAUKEE JOURNAL [cont.]—SEPTEMBER 1918

FRIENDLESS TO THE GRAVE

Owen, Wis.—Not a single mourner followed the body of Ennis Krueger to the grave late Tuesday. Deputy United State Marshal Joseph Gantz and several citizens who acted as official observers at the closing of the coffin and the interring of the body, also acted as pall bearers. No relative or friends of the Kruegers attended. The funeral cortege, consisting of the hearses and two automobiles, attracted no attention on its progress to the cemetery.

Those who accompanied the body, in addition to Deputy Marshal Gantz, were Earl W. Kidd, manager of the factory of the Owen Box and Crate Co.; T. J. McCarthy, an insurance agent; M. H. Williams, manager of the Dairy Belt Land Co.; Postmaster Watson; Fred Griebenow, undertaker; Rev. W. H. Sargent, two graves diggers and two strangers from Rock Island, Ill., who attended out of curiosity. Mr. Sargent read a prayer at the grave, and quoted from that passage of the Bible in which Christ, exerting his influence to obey the civil authorities, said: "Render unto Caesar the things that are Caesar's and unto God the things that are God's."

Had a letter from Mrs. Krueger which arrived too late, been received before the funeral, no minister would have officiated. Mrs. Krueger sent the following letter to the undertaker:

"I received the sad news of Ennis' death. I want you to lay his remains south of his grandma. He has a nice suit at home hanging on the bedstead. You put that on him. I think you better get him a new shirt and a coffin just like Rob and Pa. I will pay the funeral expenses. Just lay his remains away quietly. Do not even have Rev. Sargent there as I do not want him there, for I do not know if I am allowed to go there, and about Frank; I do not know if he is able. I think that is all I can say. From your friend, MRS L. KRUEGER."

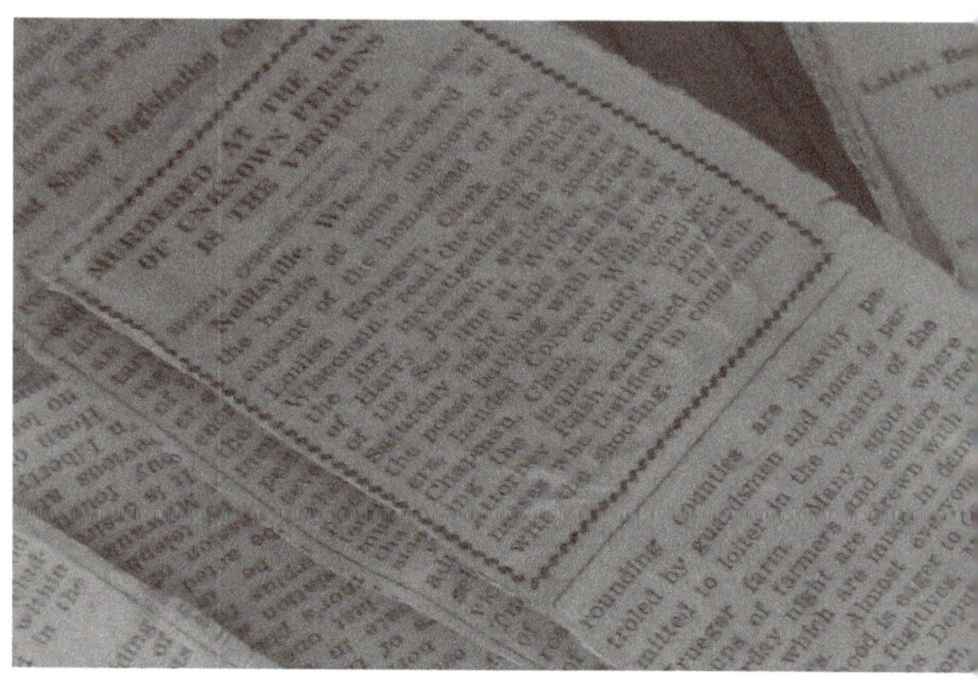

5 CAPTURE

SHEBOYGAN PRESS, SHEBOYGAN, WISCONSIN—OCTOBER 23, 1918

KRUEGER YOUTH UNDER ARREST

BRAINERD, MINN, OCT. 23—Tracing a registration card bearing the name of Phil Shilts, Chippewa county, Sheriff Claus A. Thoerin, Crow Wing county, effected the capture of Leslie Krueger, alleged draft evader from Owen, Wis.

Krueger is wanted by federal officials for military service evasion and has been sought in connection with the killing of Harry Jensen of Owen when at the battle on the Krueger farm on Sept. 14. He was about to be inducted into the Crow Wing county contingent leaving for Camp Cody when arrested.

He was arrested here five days ago. He confessed his identity, declared he filled out his questionnaire and then threw his card away, according to the sheriff. It is said he found the Shilts card in an old house.

Called German Subject

In his alleged confession, Krueger asserted that Danes in the neighborhood classed him as a German subject and that he resented the charge. When he was arrested, he carried an automatic, it is alleged.

"I am willing to go back and I hope I have a fair trial," he asserted. "Mother is not guilty of anything."

He declared that Ennis Krueger was shot while in the barn and that he [Leslie] and Louis were not in the barn. They separated, Leslie running through the woods. He made for Ashland.

Asked to Notify State

Eau Claire, Oct 23—District Attorney Walter J. Rush, Neillsville, Clark county, asked Sheriff Theorin on Tuesday to notify the United States marshal at Madison of the capture of Leslie Krueger. No further action has been taken by Clark county authorities. Louis Krueger is still at large.

Leslie was admitted to the La Crosse County Jail on October 26, 1918. He was taken to Camp Grant, Illinois, prior to January 6, 1919. And lastly he was returned to the Clark County Jail in Neillsville on February 11, 1919, on charges of murder in the first degree of Harry Jensen. Earlier charges of resisting and opposing a U.S. marshal in attempting to serve papers were set aside because the murder charge would ultimately carry the most severe penalty.

Frank's charge of failure to register under the Selective Service Act and Caroline's charge of conspiring to resist service of process were also set aside and replaced with first degree murder charges for each of them.

The courts decided to try all three of the Kruegers together for murder in the first degree of Harry Jensen. It was said this would save the courts money and in no way jeopardize the outcome for any of them individually.

While in jail at Clark County, Caroline Krueger sought the advice of her brother-in-law, Fred Gussert, of Greanleaf, Wisconsin. He had been married to her sister Johanna, who died in 1916. Fred recommended John W. Reynolds of Green Bay as an attorney, so he was hired by the Krueger family. Attorney Reynolds seemed overwhelmed with the case and sought help from Attorney Thomas P. Silverwood. Reynolds convinced the Kruegers to secure a $5,000 mortgage on their property from Fred Gussert. Reynolds wanted to sell the Krueger livestock as it was too much of a burden for him, and he needed cash up front.

Letter to Frank Krueger, Neillsville Jail, from Attorney Reynolds, October 25, 1918

… I am ready to go up to Owen any time and the sheriff can telephone me just as soon as that house is safe to go in. I have written to Eide [neighbor Gunder Eide was the first one to rent the house] yesterday asking him to notify me when the house was clear. I would like to get rid of that stock as I am devoting all of my time to this case and as it is absolutely necessary to do so …

Lawsuits were also pending from the widow of Harry Jensen and others who were wounded at the shootout. Reynolds wanted to ensure there would be enough funds for himself before the entire Krueger estate was wiped out from those lawsuits. Friction between Caroline Krueger and Attorney Reynolds seemed evident from the start.

Attorney John W. Reynolds to Frank Krueger at Neillsville Jail, November 2, 1918

Dear Sir: Your letter of October 30 was duly received. I received a letter from Vater ... and he said that the quarantine would be lifted about the 5th of November, which would be next Tuesday. That is election day and I will try and be at Owen [small village bordering Withee] on Wednesday, but it may be possible that I may not get there until Thursday. As I have things to look up there I can call you when I arrive at Owen and can be investigating while you drive over. I will call Hewett [Clark County sheriff] by telephone and then you can come up. I want to sell the personal property and get some money as this is taking and will take all of my time as there are many things to look up, and of course you realize that the charge is first degree murder and this is punished by life imprisonment if convicted.

... There are a great many things to look up as to the admissibility of testimony, etc. And I am devoting all of my time to this case and my partner is helping me some.

In regard to the change of the place of trial I want to say this: A number of people told at Neillsville that they did not think that you could get a fair trial there on account of the prejudice of the people, and others told me that they thought you could. ... I think that we would get a fair trial in Wood County.

I have gone over all the Wis. Reports in several criminal cases tried before Judge O'Neill and I think he has been a fair judge. ... It would be my duty to say however, that if there really is a prejudice in Clark County against you that we ought to take it away. ... It may seem a long time for you to wait until March or April, but it is a very short time in comparison with what might turn up if you would try it before a jury prejudiced in advance ... there are so many papers in Clark County and they have all

written up the Krueger case in such a way that the people in Clark
County may be prejudiced and if they are, neither you nor I want
to try it there. From the statements that you gave me and that
of your mother I do not believe that a jury would convict your
mother. ... But you have a hard row to hoe and I think you realize
this yourself, but we will do the very best we can, and it is surely
not a case without hope as you did no shooting and the jury may
believe that while you advised the boys to resist the draft that you
did not aid or abet them in committing either the crime of murder
or manslaughter ...

There really wasn't a lot of time to prepare for the trial. The Krueger family was impatient and Reynolds asked the court for a quick resolve. He also asked for a change of venue but Judge O'Neill of Clark County denied it. The trial was set to begin in March of 1919.

Attorney John W. Reynolds to Frank Krueger at Neillsville Jail, February 26, 1919

Dear Sir: I received a letter from your mother this morning in
which she said that the case will be put off forever. ... I am going
over there when Leslie is brought up. I will do my best to have
the case brought on right away as I want it started as well as you
do. Any three officers that told you that I was holding the case
back are liars. They simply want to get you in trouble with your
attorneys as they do in every criminal case as that is one of their
points. ... Before I go into the case I want security for the balance
of my fees. I want a mortgage. I can make $6,000 a year practic-
ing law and you cannot expect me to run a chance on my fees. I
know that I will get them if you people are able to pay, but there
are five different cases against you running up to $25,000 and if
those people get judgments against you they will come ahead of
mine and you cannot pay me ... Yours truly, John W. Reynolds

While awaiting trial in the Clark County Jail at Neillsville, Frank Krueger wrote a list of items stolen or damaged on the farm as requested by Attorney Reynolds. A condensed version of the list follows:

- Canned goods—$50.00; 1 house plant, hydrangea—$20.00;
  Ma's watch and chain; 2 guns; surgical instruments and

tax outfit; buckskin shirt; suitcase; gentleman's traveling outfit; folding umbrella; watch charm; old coins; 1 cream separator—$130.00.
- Barn—$10,000; 100 ton hay; 25 ton straw; bull—$350.00; 4 head sheep; 104 chickens; calf; new planer, planer bolts, knives, wrenches and extras—$300.00; 5 steel stanchions; 2 sets double team harnesses; buggy harnesses; 7 m. of best quality oak and pine lumber; 1 sack of wool, about 100 lbs.; 6 horse collars; 1 old wagon; various barn tools.
- Estimate of $8,000 to repair damage to the house.

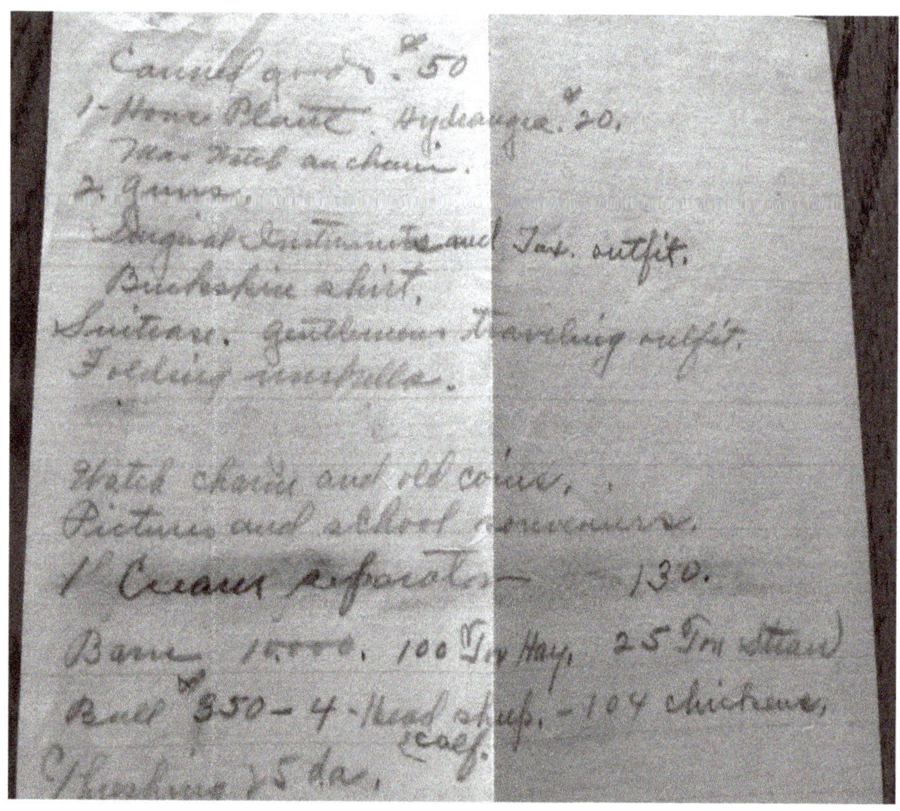

FRANK'S INVENTORY OF ITEMS STOLEN OR DAMAGED ON THE FARM

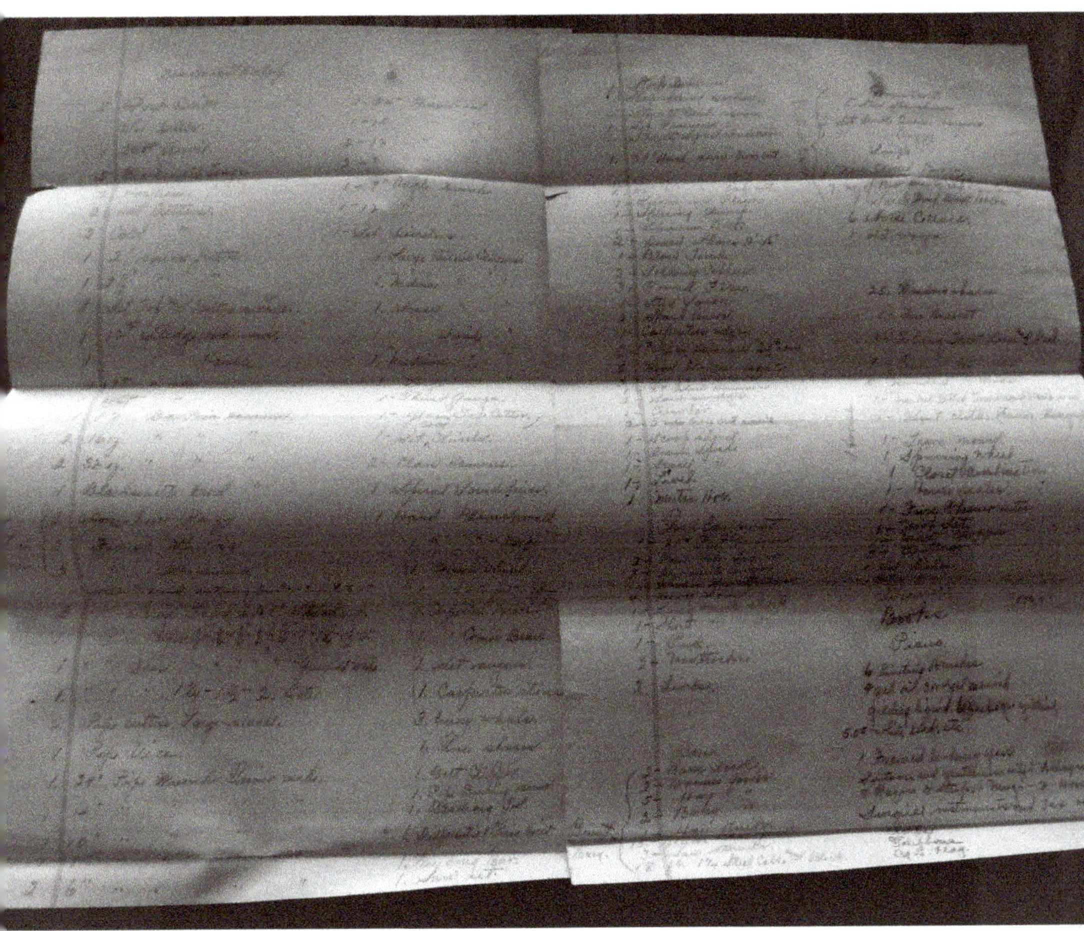

FRANK'S DETAILED LIST OF ITEMS DAMAGED, STOLEN, OR BURNED

6 THE TRIAL

The request for a change of venue wasn't granted. After a lengthy process, jurors were selected from the southern half of Clark County; Longwood was near the northern border. With all the press coverage, it is certain the jurors had heard about the Krueger incident regardless of what part of the county they came from.

The trial began on the 24th day of March, 1919, at the Clark County courthouse in Neillsville with the honorable James O'Neill, Circuit Judge, presiding. Representing the state were Frank Jackson, district attorney, and W. J. Rush. Attorney John W. Reynolds, and his assistant, Attorney Thomas P. Silverwood, represented the Krueger family. The transcript of the trial consists of about six hundred pages. A brief summary of the highlights follows.

The state began with W. J. Rush's opening statements containing the suggestion that the murder of Harry Jensen was both deliberate and intentional. Rush gave the motive as this. "The Krueger family was angry with Jensen, employed as a depot agent at Withee, for turning a box of ammunition Ennis ordered in July of 1918 over to Sheriff Hewett. In their house, the Kruegers kept a long range field glass. This they used to identify Harry Jensen in the crowd and then shot him. Mrs. Krueger and sons, Frank, Ennis, and Leslie were in their house and all acted together causing all to be equally guilty of Mr. Jensen's murder, regardless of who actually fired the fatal shot."

The state also claimed that Frank and Ennis fired the first shots at the officers when they made their initial encounter at the fence.

The defense gave their theory next with Attorney Reynolds making the first presentation. Reynolds characterized the affair as an attack by a mob rather than a posse. Reynolds stated that the U.S. marshals only carried warrants for Frank and Ennis for a misdemeanor. The marshals shot as soon as the brothers refused to come to the fence.

Harry Jensen came onto the scene by himself with a rifle and was shooting at the Krueger house when killed. He might have been shot by some of his own mob that was firing in all directions at that time or by Ennis, who was protecting his mother and home. Reynolds said the Kruegers had to defend themselves or they would have all likely died that day.

C. J. Stockwell, civil engineer from the city of Neillsville, was the first to testify. He presented maps showing locations of buildings, highways, and other landmarks. They were based on measurements and sketches he made at the Krueger premises in October of 1918.

Fred Griebenow testified he first saw Harry Jensen when Harry was brought to his business. Jensen only lived about ten minutes. Griebenow, a store owner and part time undertaker, thought the bullet entered right above Jensen's shirt collar and exited through his shoulder. He saved Jensen's clothes in his store for evidence, but his building burned down on March 8, 1919.

Earle Kidd testified next. He first went to the Krueger farm at about four o'clock with Peter Rasmussen, Joseph Gantz, and Cyril Marks, who was driving his own car. When they drove up to the cornfield where Frank and Ennis were husking corn, Kidd stayed in the car, the other three got out and walked up to the fence. Kidd estimated that the distance between the men and Frank and Ennis was about thirty feet. Kidd said that Ennis started shooting toward them, but he did not hear the bullets. Then Frank shot once. He then said they both shot eight or ten times and the officers began firing at the Krueger brothers as they ran away through the field. He said when Frank made that first shot he fell out of the car and into the ditch. Kidd said Gantz instructed him to drive back to town with Rasmussen and get help. He came back immediately with four armed men (Laino, Paige, White, and Griffin), but he himself was not armed. Kidd parked his car north of the Vater house, got out and ordered the men with him to go through the field and surround the Krueger house. In a sense he "took charge" of the situation. Gantz and La Mont were not back yet themselves. The first shots that came from the Krueger house were about a half hour after the shooting of the men crossing the field.

There was a large picnic in Owen that day, called "The 3–I Picnic." The picnic was put on by a group of settlers who had moved to the area from Illinois, Iowa, and Indiana. They wore ribbons with "I" on them according to Cyril Marks. Kidd admitted that he told everybody he saw at the picnic to get out to the Krueger Farm. He hoped they would bring guns and ammo.

Kidd felt that there was no shooting from the road until after the Kruegers fired their way first from their buildings. At that time there were more than forty or fifty people at the scene, on the roadway, and he did admit that he heard a lot of firing before Jensen was shot.

Frank Griffin was the next witness. He was in the carload brought back out by Kidd. Kidd told him he had been deputized and told the four men with him to go across the field to surround the house so the Kruegers would not escape. Griffin admitted shooting at the barn door and at the house, not knowing his target, but meaning to shoot one of the boys. He had been told they were draft evaders.

Joseph Gantz appeared next, said he lived in La Crosse and was a U.S. deputy marshal for the Western District of Wisconsin. On September 14, he first came to Owen, then drove out with Kidd to the Krueger farm with Mr. Marks, a Department of Justice man, and Mr. Rasmussen, the marshal of the Village of Owen. He said he had a warrant to arrest Frank and Ennis. He had no knowledge of these men so he had to take somebody with him to identify them. He had orders from John La Mont, chief deputy from Eau Claire, to hunt up the marshal at Owen and take him along. Gantz said Earle Kidd volunteered to drive them out in his car. Officer Gantz claimed that the

Kruegers fired first, that they both had small revolvers. He said he eventually fired three shots at the fleeing Kruegers.

Gantz said he was fired upon at least once while on the roadway in front of Vater's. When two automobiles flew by, he shot to stop them; one returned and took him back to Withee where he went to a bank and used a phone to call John La Mont, chief deputy U.S. marshal at Eau Claire, for instructions.

Gantz said there were two carloads of people from Withee who got back to the farm before he did. He said there was quite a bit of firing going on and he could not tell exactly where it was coming from when he got back to the scene.

Gantz was questioned about his background and he told the court that he became a U.S. marshal on August 1, 1917, and was forty-four years of age. Prior to his current position he worked as a U.S. bailiff at La Crosse for one term—about four weeks. Gantz lived in La Crosse for about twenty years and prior to that he lived in Chicago for a short time. He was born in Hartford, Connecticut. His other occupations involved working in the restaurant business and tending bar for many years.

When questioned as to why he didn't go closer to Frank and Ennis at the cornfield, he said the fence kept him from doing so, that wire fences were hard to cross. Gantz admitted that he never gave any instruction to Kidd to send men armed with rifles toward Krueger's house or barn.

Gantz testified that when he called Eau Claire and asked John La Mont for instructions, he was told "shoot to kill," to go after Frank and Ennis, get a posse, and put them under arrest. He told La Mont he was fired on twice; didn't know Leslie was there; was just told to get Frank and Ennis and not hurt Mrs. Krueger. Gantz didn't know any people at the scene other than Kidd, Rasmussen, and Marks. He also said people were firing in the direction of the house and barn, and he didn't really know what they were firing at.

When the Guard came up from Neillsville, the officer in charge asked Gantz what they should do and he told them to surround the house, but to fire no shots. He said he did the best he could to stay in charge. The huge crowd remained along the road until nearly midnight and after that they went away. He thought he stayed at the Krueger farm until Thursday.

Axel Johnson testified that he met Gantz and Marks on the road to Withee and was with them at Berger's hardware store where Gantz asked for rifles and ammo. Gantz gave Axel a rifle and told him, "Use it to go get the Kruegers."

"We all got rifles. All of them [five men] got into the car. I was the last one to get in. The rest of the boys asked me if I was deputized, and they said we want to be deputized and so I turned around to Mr. Gantz and I said the boys want to be deputized. He says you are all deputized, and so we proceeded up to Vater's. There we got out of the car, and I was walking towards a car which I found out to be Mr. Gunder Anderson's car. I stopped to the west of that car, northwest corner of the car. Standing there for a few minutes [north of Vater's house] I heard a gentleman behind me and I turned around to look to see who it was and it was Mr. Jensen. … We had stood there a few minutes when the shooting began from the south. From the sound of the shots it indicated that it came from the Krueger farm. All of a sudden I heard Mr. Jensen say I got hit. I turned to the right. I see Mr. Jensen bleeding in the neck … he went to his knees, dropped his rifle, I picked him up under the arms. There was a scramble for everyone to get away, but there was a man from Unity that told me he would assist me … we took his legs and carried him for half a block [no one close to the scene could get their automobiles started up]; a man named DeLong, we put him in his car with Dr. Williams and this man from Unity and we took him to Greibenow's."

Axel said Jensen had not fired a shot but there were quite a few volleys at that time.

When U.S. Marshal Cyril E. Marks first arrived at Owen on September 14, he went out to dinner and then to a ball game. He testified it was a little after 4:00 when he rode out to the Krueger farm. Marks said he, Gantz, and Rasmussen walked up to the fence and he told Frank he had a warrant for his arrest. Frank told Marks to stay where he was, then Ennis who had continued cutting corn and never stood up, fired a shot with one quick move. Marks said he had no idea where Ennis got his gun from. Then Ennis fired another shot and he didn't know just what happened after that, "things went pretty quick." Marks said he didn't get hit but had a hole in his coat by his shoulder.

After this Marks stated he began shooting, Gantz shot also, and Rasmussen shot and the brothers backed up and ran low down through the cornfield, almost straight up toward their barn. Marks figured he fired three shots, Rasmussen fired all he had in his automatic. Marks said Frank and Ennis were running, dodging, zigzagging once in a while and then would turn and shoot back at them. He figured Frank and Ennis fired about seven or eight shots.

As Marks continued his story he told of how they first went to Vater's house, then back to Withee as neither he nor Gantz had any ammunition left. They went to the bank to call Eau Claire, and came back to the Vater place in ten or fifteen minutes.

When Peter Rasmussen testified, his estimate of the distance between himself and Frank and Ennis differed from that of Earle Kidd. He felt the brothers were about a hundred feet out into their cornfield. He said Ennis started shooting, but upon firm questioning he said he did not see a gun in Frank's hands. Frank only held a corn knife in his hand and pointed at them with the corn knife.

Upon adjournment the first day, a brief conversation took place between the court and the jury as noted in the transcript. "Court is adjourned until nine tomorrow morning. Gentlemen, the Appleton college girls will give a concert at the opera house tonight and you will be permitted to go if you wish, but you must all go if any goes. If you go, the officer will arrange for seats for you, so you will all sit close together. Nobody will talk to you there and do not talk to the audience or anybody except the officer. You may go to the concert if you wish." Jurors: "We thank your honor very much." Court: "We like to keep you as comfortable and happy as we can."

Carl Berger was called up first on the second day of trial. Carl owned a hardware business, Withee Lumber and Fuel Company. Berger testified that several men came into his store on the afternoon of September 14 and asked for ammunition and guns. Harry Jensen was one of the men, along with Joseph Gantz, Axel Johnson, and others, but Harry did not get a gun. "We wrote the names on the tag of the guns and I destroyed them after they brought the guns back." Berger recalled that W. C. Tufts, the banker, took a 38-55. Berger said the guns were loaned.

The testimony of Dr. T. F. Williams, a physician from Owen, followed. Williams said he got down to Krueger's at five o'clock to assist Marshal Gantz in "taking the Kruegers." He rode down there with Joe Fleishman, Sr. Dr. Williams saw Harry Jensen there standing behind the left rear wheel of the car owned by Gunder Anderson. The car was facing south. He was about three feet from Jensen. A series of shots began about three minutes after Williams arrived at the scene. When the shooting started, two shots were fired very close together, within a few seconds of each other. This was the time that Jensen and Paige were hit.

Angus Paige testified that he was shot in the leg just after Jensen. He said he did not know Jensen, but was standing between two or three feet away from him. Jensen was straight back of Anderson's car. Paige was asked if there was anyone back of him when the shooting occurred and he said yes, but didn't know who they were. He said Gunder Anderson walked around just after Axel Johnson reached for Jensen who had fallen immediately after being shot. Paige was taken to Withee for medical care by the two Fleishman brothers.

Gunder Anderson, the man who owned the car Harry Jensen stood behind, was questioned upon re-examination if he saw a Mr. Patrie there with a firearm that day. "Yes, R. Patrie, C. H. Patrie was there." "Did he have a firearm?" "I think he did." Gunder Anderson admitted, "It was just an unorganized crowd."

The court addressed the defense attorneys at the day's end. "We are thinking about some reading matter to send in to the jury for over Sunday. Mr. Calway has brought some *Saturday Evening Posts* of 1916." Reynolds and Silverwood both agreed it would be all right to allow the jurors to read the magazines. The court felt that it would not to be practical for the sheriff to take the jurors to church on Sunday.

The testimony of Herman Bartholemew follows. Bartholemew lived at Withee for eighteen years and was constable of the Village of Withee and also the marshal in 1918. Bartholemew said he rode down to the farm with Harry Hewett on July 25 to talk with Frank, etc. He also went to the Larson place south of Kruegers on September 14. He rode down with Belnap, and they had their guns out in plain sight when they drove past the Krueger residence. Larson's house was located on the same side of the road as Vater's house. "No one in particular was in charge of the crowd," Bartholemew admitted. When asked why he was at the scene he said, "They went down to surround the Krueger property so they wouldn't escape." Bartholemew told how William Tufts bragged about how he put twenty-five shots into the Krueger house and he himself put "quite a few" shots into the house. Bartholemew estimated possibly fifty shots had been fired across from the Larson home, where he situated himself, toward the Krueger house. When questioned if he knew of any boys between the ages of fourteen and fifteen who may have been involved in the shooting, he said he did not but later admitted a boy of about fifteen, Solomon Crum, fired from the Larson home at the Kruegers. He said his bunch fired ten or fifteen shots from the Larson place at the Kruegers when Vater went down to get Mrs. Krueger out of the house. "We all talked about shooting Mrs. Krueger and we had understood that we were not to shoot Mrs. Krueger down there, and there was no one in our party who would take a shot at her because they could have shot her, anyone in the bunch could have shot Mrs. Krueger. There wasn't a one in the bunch that would do it," boasted Bartholemew.

The Neillsville Guard did not arrive on the premises until eight or nine o'clock in the evening and they stayed all night and into the next day. Captain Klopf was in charge of the Neillsville Guard. Mr. Irvine was second in command. Joseph Gantz testified later about Klopf questioning him for instructions when they came on the scene.

The defense made statements to the judge regarding the fate of Caroline Krueger near the trial's end. "Not one single overt act of Mrs. Krueger have they shown, and that surely, Your Honor, is necessary on the part of the state before they can ask that this woman be convicted of murder. She did just the natural thing, she did what any mother would have done with that threatening situation. She did not stay in the house to start with because there was the men with guns around the farm. ... She didn't even counsel her boys to use their arms, not a one word of evidence that she did. And so we submit that in all fairness to Mrs. Krueger she should be at this time discharged, because the court must say the state has failed to produce any evidence. ..."

The state did not want Mrs. Krueger to have any slack. "There was first shooting between some of the Kruegers and the four men who went over in the field. Then there was shooting between them and the people who were up north at Vater's. And there was shooting between the Kruegers and the people down at Larson's. So there are three periods to be considered when there was a veritable battle going on that afternoon. And there is testimony that Mrs. Krueger was seen about the premises walking backward and forward and making motions, and while no witness purports to [have heard] what she said, there is testimony that she was talking to her boys ..."

Robert Vater, the neighbor to the north of the Krueger farm, told what he witnessed starting with the shooting at the fence. He said he heard half a dozen or more shots and hurried outside to see what was happening. "They were still shooting while I was going out and going right across the garden over to the fence toward the car that was standing in the road. I seen the officers shoot into the cornfield, in that direction but I didn't see anybody, that is I mean of the Kruegers until they were in the hayfield ... as they got back through into the field something like ten rods Ennis stopped and fired back, I suppose toward the officers, and of course he stopped shooting again and followed up or kept on going in that direction southeast."

Joseph Gantz came to Vater's house asking for a gun and Vater said adamantly, "I have no gun to shoot a neighbor." Gantz insisted on a gun and Vater reluctantly told his son to find one. The crowd gathered up quickly in Vater's yard. Vater said that Mr. Gantz gave the orders "Everybody get ready to shoot and shoot to kill." The crowd was up around Vater's house, on his porch, and in his yard. He said, "I says don't make my house a shooting barracks, get away from it if you want to shoot." Vater said Gantz told him, "Shut up, you got nothing to say here. If you don't we will take care of you." At that time Vater said there were about twenty people at his place. "The officers and Mr. Oleson would call up to Mrs. Krueger to come down to Vater's and surrender. They shouted to her to bring her boys down there, and she would repeat, 'We can't come down there, you have all got guns, we will get shot, come up here if you want to talk to our boys.'"

Vater told of the standstill between the two groups and how Mrs. Krueger wouldn't or couldn't come down and they wouldn't or couldn't go up and she turned and slowly went back again. Vater said he heard talk among the crowd, "Shoot them, kill them, burn up their house." At that time he thought it would be good for everyone concerned if he could go and talk with Mrs. Krueger himself to try and convince her to surrender. He asked permission from Gantz to do so and was told to go right away but to remember he was doing this on his own risk. Gantz repeated this twice. "Gantz gave orders not to shoot while I was up there … about five o'clock that was." Vater further explained, "Mr. Gantz says you take a cloth, a white cloth, with you and motion it as you go up. So that you will not be hurt, and so I did and I went right along up there, and as I approached Mrs. Krueger near enough so that she could talk to me or I could talk to her, she said now you see what the picnic is for at Owen, to come up here and to kill our boys and to destroy our property." After some conversation Mrs. Krueger walked to nearly 175 feet from Mr. Vater's house, but said she could go no farther. At this time Gantz grabbed her by the shoulder and Mr. Oleson grabbed her by the feet and carried her into Vater's house.

Robert Vater was questioned further by the defense about a man seen there that day who called himself a western man, a big sort of rough looking man with a deep voice. Vater recalled this about the man: "He had a rifle and crept along in the ditch until up to the last elm tree on the left side. … He lay in the ditch and had his gun leveled right over the bank alongside of the tree toward the Krueger premises. He told me he shot Frank. He had supper there and at that time he told me this. He gave me a sort of acorn. He says you will remember me by this acorn. I am the man that shot Frank."

Frank Krueger was the only family member to testify and stated to the defense that he was born in Manitowoc County, Wisconsin, had lived in the area for thirty-six and a half years, and was thirty-seven years of age.

Frank stated that when he was first approached by the men at the fence, Joseph Gantz did the speaking. Three times he asked Frank to come up to the fence so that he could talk with him. Frank kept asking Gantz what he wanted and after the third request Frank said, "If you got anything to say, say it where you are." At this point Gantz raised his hand and began shooting toward Frank—the bullets flew over Frank's head. "I was somewhat shocked and stupefied for a fraction of a few seconds and I got up and I looked to my left and I seen my brother Ennis and heard him say gee whiz, and he grabbed into his pocket and grabbed his revolver and began shooting at the man, toward the fence." He and Ennis then ran toward the barn "while the gentlemen in the road kept firing," Frank exclaimed. "I was shot in the left leg, just above the calf of the leg in the flesh."

Frank said they went into the house and he got his gun from the basement, which was loaded. He went out to the road and fired one shot north to scare the men who'd been shooting at him. Frank said he did not know that Gantz and Marks were government officials, they never said who they were or that they had a warrant for him or Ennis.

Frank said he stood and talked with Ennis and his mother for half an hour on the east side of their house. He then went back into the basement and got more ammo and another gun, then went outside and stood under the windmill, placing himself in a defense mode. When he saw the four men (Paige, Griffin, Elliot, and Laino) coming toward the barn, he hollered at them at the top of his voice, waiving his hand telling them to get off his place. At that time he was shot through both legs. He sat down beside the separator and engine and laid down both of his guns. He removed his handkerchief from his pocket and wrapped it around his wounds to try and stop the bleeding.

Frank discarded both of his guns north of the ice house. He explained further what took place next and no doubt was filled with terror at the recollection. "I crawled into the back porch of the house on my hands and knees and went into the basement. I ordered a basin of hot water from my mother." She gave him water and a rag and he began washing his wounds. The basement floor was so cold Frank couldn't stand it there and crawled to the stairs, took off his shoes, and went back upstairs on his hands and knees. "I was lying on the tile floor with my right leg on top of the bathtub to keep the blood from running out of my wound, to keep my leg high." The volleys continued.

VIEW FROM LIVING ROOM TOWARD DINING AREA

"Well, I could hear [shots] striking the house on the outside and I could see the plaster falling off from the north side of me and the bullets I could hear some go through the room and I could hear them strike the range and I could hear the falling glass on the floor and I could hear the bullets as they struck the china closet which was directly south of me in the room, and I could hear them strike the tinware and I could also hear the falling of plaster upstairs and I also heard some of the bullets when they struck the radiator pipe. I heard it vibrate through the room. Mother stood behind the large chimney on the north side of the kitchen."

Robert Vater came to the aid of the Krueger family about half an hour later. Ennis was in the house at that time and began crying after seeing

Frank's wounds. Although teary-eyed, Ennis also became very angry. When Vater talked Frank into surrendering, he crawled down the front steps but could not walk. It was felt it would be best if Vater returned to his place to get his own rig to haul Frank up to his house.

Frank talked about the field glass, part of the state's theory on the death of Jensen. "There was a hunter that came and hunted with us one fall about twelve years ago and when he left, he left the field glass with us, gave it to us. On the 14th … it was in the northeast room of the house upstairs, in my mother's room, hanging on the dresser. I did not use it that day."

The defense had several people testify that the crowd did the first shooting at the time Harry Jensen was killed. They were Andrew Replogle, James Taylor, and William Buxton. Taylor said that there were over two minutes of shooting before Jensen was shot and he had been standing right across the road from him when it happened.

Dr. Williams said, "There wasn't very many people when we got there [to Vater's] but it wasn't but a very few minutes before there was a mob there. Before the first shots were fired there was quite a bunch there, and the first were fired as near as I could tell to the northeast, then a lull, but after the shooting was started then there was no lull, believe me, unless their guns got hot and they had to drop them. I don't think either side was wasting any cold fingers on it at all."

Frank's cross-examination testimony was noted by the press in the following article. The closing statements were given and the jurors were asked to push aside any sympathy for the family.

NEILLSVILLE TIMES, April 3, 1919

… On cross-examination he [Frank] stuck to his story and was not affected materially by the searching questioning given him by Attorney Rush. He said he did not register "Because I do not believe in war."

In closing statements Attorney Rush told the jury, "The state has not shown you who fired the shot that killed Harry Jensen, but it has shown you that these men shot into the crowd and killed him. We only have to show that one of them shot and we have done this. Then all are equally guilty under the law, even if it was Ennis who fired the shot.

"Here is Mrs. Krueger, a gray-haired woman. If she had reared her boys as she should have done, if she had, as thousands of other mothers did, send their sons to fight for their country, we would today have been paying her homage, but she put murder into the hearts of her sons. What are you going to say to her? Do you not think it is your duty to find her guilty of murder? You have soon to do your duty and you must do this. We do not want to disgrace Clark county and the state of Wisconsin by turning this band of murderers loose. It may be a painful duty, but it is no more painful for you than for us the court."

The Defense Begins: Attorney Thomas P. Silverwood, for the defense, began by referring to the importance of this case. He said Louis Krueger is not being tried. Whether he is a deserter or not is not a question in this case. His name is dragged in by the counsel for the state simply to prejudice the jury.

Your only question in this case is, "Who shot Harry Jensen and whether the shot that killed him was justified." On your decision rests the fate of three human beings.

Put yourself in their place. Dozens of men armed with rifles came and attacked this place. What for? To shoot up the Kruegers. …

The Kruegers made a mistake. They lived here. The country got into war. They opposed war. Many able men in this country opposed war. The Kruegers should have registered. There they made a mistake.

Then the government made a mistake. When Louis did not appear for examination February 24 they should have arrested him, if it took 100 men. That should have been done. Yet it was not done and you nor I ever heard of this case until September 14.

Mrs. Krueger is not liable for harboring her son, under the law. You have a legal right to harbor your own family, even if they have broken the law.

These men should be punished by the United States government for not registering, but that is not in this case. There is no proof here that any of these defendants shot Jensen. If Ennis shot him, it was clearly in self-defense. His home and his mother were being attacked by a mob of armed men. He had a right to defend himself and his family. …

"Mrs. Krueger has made mistakes, but she has paid dearly for them," he concluded. "One son is dead, one a fugitive and two, with her, are charged with the highest crime possible."

JACKSON CONCLUDES ARGUMENTS

District Attorney Frank Jackson closed the state. He made an impressive argument and closed with an excoriation of the Krueger home that was unique in the arguments during the trial. Referring to the description of the Krueger home as "a place which the Kruegers loved better than any place on earth," he exclaimed. "A pretty home indeed. A roost for deserters, a refuge for draft evaders, a harbor for murders and a shield for assassins.

"This was indeed a peaceful home, as the counsel for the defense has described it," Mr. Jackson continued. "It was so peaceful that these farmers on the Krueger place went to their work with pistols strapped to their belt, with a deserter hidden in the barn and two of the others did not register. It was peaceful, indeed."

The district attorney asked for justice, but warned the jury not to be misguided by sympathy. He said Mrs. Krueger was just as guilty as her sons. She gave the signal for the fatal volley, he said.

THE COURT'S INSTRUCTIONS

Judge O'Neill then read his instructions to the jury. As had been forecasted in The Times last week he provided for but one degree of guilt, murder in the first degree, punishment for which is fixed by the Wis. Statutes as imprisonment for life ...

The case went to the jury at six o'clock Thursday evening.

The jurors found both Frank and Leslie Krueger guilty of murder in the first degree, the only degree offered to them by the judge. Caroline Krueger's charge of murder was dismissed.

SENTENCE IS PRONOUNCED

It had not been expected that sentence would be pronounced immediately, but Judge O'Neill decided to do this Saturday morning at ten o'clock, at which time the two convicted men were brought into the courtroom.

Both replied to the judge's query that they had nothing to say why sentence should not be pronounced at that time.

"It's impossible for me to understand your actions," said Judge O'Neill. "You have set yourselves up to defy the laws and offices of your country and even resorted to murder to do this. On the part of Russian anarchists your action might be understood, but for men of your intelligence and education to do this is beyond my comprehension. I wish the evidence had been such that the jury might have found a verdict in your favor. I hope you will make good records in prison and it may be possible that at some future time mercy may be extended to you. The court will keep your case in mind. It is the judgment of this court that you be confined to hard labor in the state prison at Waupun for the period of your natural lives."

Neither Leslie nor Caroline had spoken during the trial.

On Saturday afternoon, Sheriff Weaver, accompanied by four extra men, took Frank and Leslie on the train to Marshfield. From there they rode the Soo Line to Waupun, Wisconsin, with the Krueger brothers handcuffed together.

7 THE BATTLES CONTINUE

*NEILLSVILLE TIMES, **APRIL 10, 1919***

… Immediately after Mrs. Krueger had left the courtroom [fol-lowing the murder trial] Deputy U.S. Marshal Gantz arrested her on the charge of conspiring to resist the draft laws. She was returned to jail and taken to Eau Claire Friday evening. …

Caroline Krueger was allowed out on bond for this further charge, which was paid by her brother-in-law, Fred Gussert, from Greanleaf, Brown County, Wisconsin. Her lawyer, John Reynolds, felt it best that she stay at the Gussert home and not return to the Krueger farm at this time. Fred lived on a farm near his son, George, and George's unhappy wife, Martha.

At Greenleaf, Caroline began writing letters to Frank and Leslie at the state prison at Waupun, a labor of love that would occupy her time for many years to come. She still had many clouds hanging over her head and also worried about what would become of the beloved farm at Withee.

The inevitable lawsuits from the widow of Harry Jensen, and several others wounded in the shootout, loomed over her. The question of whether she would be able to keep her property was always on her mind, that and the worry of what had become of her fugitive son, Louis.

Letter from Caroline to Frank with Inspection Stamp

The Letters Begin

Caroline from Greenleaf, Wisconsin, to Frank at Waupun, April 24, 1919

Dear Frank, I suppose you are longing to hear from me. ... I had to go with Ganze to Eau Claire that day and his lady friend Mrs. Jensen (as he goes with her) then, so Fred and Reynolds was not there. They took me to the jail again where I was before and the next afternoon as Fred came, took me out, got me before a man, bound me over to the fall court, each going my bonds, so got out but that man said to Ganze and also to Fred and Ren—What are they doing up their at Neillsville, them boys could have been set free, how can they convict 2 men and only one shot killed that man, their was no need of making any more expenses that could have been settled right their and his daughter came

to me and talked. I sayd it is hard for life (Oh no she sayed, they
wont be their long as the war is coming to an end, that will be
straightened up to so it will come out all right.) God will be good
to us yet. Well I have been very sick taken with terrible chills
coming down, am not over with it yet but feel much better but
have not been any where yet and the roads are so bad they can
not go with the car. ... I am going through an afful hard time. I
cant think of anything but of you 2 and Louis and the dead ones
of my family day and night. You wrote to fetch apples, do you not
get any or have you no money. I can send you a little. Well I hope
you are better but I was surprised you had the [rheumatism] so
bad, the cheese factory is a bad place for Rhu people as it is very
damp, but they will no doubt put you somewhere else if you cannot stand it. ... Fred and Ren. was up to Withee and they rented
the place to Robinson for a year ... got your close [clothes] all
right but cryed bitterly as I saw them. What have you on now the
prison "garb." I will go to Green Bay perhaps soon and get myself
some clothing and my teeth fixed. O yes some ones of Withee or
Owen sent me a nice bouquet of carnations, on the card it sayd
from friends. ... From your loving mother, Mrs. L. Krueger

Letter from Attorney John Reynolds to Frank Krueger at Waupun, April 5, 1919

Frank Kreuger [sic], Waupun Wis

Dear Sir: Got your mother out on bonds at Eau Claire
yesterday afternoon. She came back with Fred and me. No stone
will be left unturned in your defense. Any books you may want
write me. Came down to office for purpose of writing to you.
Yours truly, John Reynolds.

After the trial and all they had been through, Reynolds still didn't spell
the Krueger name correctly. The case was on appeal with the State Supreme
Court.

Mother from Greenleaf, Wisconsin, to Frank at Waupun, May 1, 1919

Dear Frank, I must write another letter as I want to tell you
some more from Home that Fred sayed and done. ... All of the
14 calves are gone, he sold 7 of them to Gunder [Gunder Eide

was the first renter of the farm] and the chickens and the geese were all gone and Gunder sayed Dollie died but Fred did not see anything of her in the pasture or woods so no doubt they sold her too. Only 3 cows and 4 horses are there yet and Robinson [the second renter of the farm who was given a one year contract] has got to keep them and 15 sheep through the year. Only 5 cords of wood are there the rest is gone, my close that was their—them peticotes and cap and summer hat that was their last fall as we were their is all gone too so we had to pay Gunder and he let it go to the winds ... also the bicycle is gone ... my pillows also, and canned fruit all gone. I told Ren. not to pay him, but he got his pay all right and went his way. Fred let Vater take our feed grinder, he came after the cable and Arno said there were 2 pieces and he let them have them ... now I do not know why he let him have them ... I didn't like to say anything of Fred ... I was mad about it offul. ... Well I hope you are all well and out of pain again. Your loving mother, Mrs. L. Krueger

**_Mother at Greenleaf, Wisconsin, to Frank at Waupun,
June 8, 1919_** [After a visit to the prison]

Dear Frank, Must let you know that we came home all right, started just after we left you and did not stop but to take water and oil. ... I am getting tired of staying here. I am going to ask Fred if he will take me to Bertha Geize [a relative of Caroline], for this one does not even speak to me at all here and if I speak to her she snubs me. I never said a cross word to her but she just seems to be so jelous [Fred's daughter-in-law, Martha]. Well I hope my case will come off next month and then I will know what I am at, I will not be under bonds then any more, either in prison or 300 dollars if I lose, so Ren. said. Well I will send 2 Equity papers this week and I will try to get some Wis. Farmer paper, then you can pick out which you like best and then I will order it for you. ... From your loving Mother, Mrs. Krueger

Caroline Krueger returned home via train for a three-day visit to the farm at Withee with her brother-in-law, Fred Gussert, in September of 1919. She told Frank it was the dearest spot on earth to her.

Caroline had a good chance to look around the home place and observed that the pile of irons in the blacksmith shop were all gone, along with all the tools except the large saws and smaller rusty ones.

She was able to go to Withee and shook hands with many friends while there. They told her they felt it was a little too early to do something for the boys—it would take some time before actions could be taken. This gave her some small comfort, knowing neighbors were supporting her.

Mother at Withee to Frank at Waupun

> ... We went over to the cemetery and what do you suppose we saw, a grave dug between Pa and Rob (suppose Ennis) but their was not one bit of dirt from that grave thrown on Pa or Rob's graves or anywhere else around. All other graves had a big pile of durt laying beside it but their was not one ounce to be seen their nor was the grave settled, all others are by this time. You know I wish I could talk with you about that ...

Caroline wished her brother-in-law, Fred, would take her to visit Frank and Leslie in prison before her trial came up, but she felt he either had no time or did not want to.

Frank and Leslie waited for any action of their appeal and were again represented by Attorney Reynolds. It took several months before the state made its decision.

Mother to Leslie at Waupun, October 28, 1919

> Dear Leslie, I suppose you are waiting and thinking why the trial does not come up, well Ren. telephoned Sunday morning that nothing doing this week ... it will come up some time when God is ready for it. I do not fear it at all so you just wait patiently and everything will come out all right ... don't get discouraged. I have got my share to bear to, I have not even a warm bed to sleep in. Well I will not write much this time, was glad to get your letter. Frank did not write to me this week. Well I hope to see you soon. I remain your mother, Mrs. Krueger

Lawsuits Filed Against the Krueger Family

THE SUNDAY SENTINEL, MILWAUKEE, NOVEMBER 30, 1919

FIGHT VICTIMS SUE
KRUEGER FAMILY

Stevens Point—Eight separate civil actions, demanding judgments aggregating $62,450, have been instituted against the Krueger family, draft resisters of Clark county, as an aftermath of the gun fight precipitated at the Krueger farm in September, 1918, when a United States marshal attempted to serve warrants upon the four Krueger boys of draft age.

A change of venue from Clark county to Portage county has been granted in each of the eight cases and four of the cases have been noticed for trial in the December term of the Circuit for Portage county, which opens here next Monday. The cases are brought by victims of the battle.

All of Kruegers Sued

The cases follow: H. M. Root, as special administrator of the estate of Harry Jensen, deceased, vs. Frank Kruger, Leslie Krueger, Ennis Krueger and Caroline Krueger, Judgment of $10,000 demanded in behalf of widow and three children of Harry Jensen, Soo line operator at Owen, who was killed in the gun battle at the Krueger farm.

H. M. Root as special administrator of the estate of Harry Jensen vs. George E. Crothers, as administrator of the estate of Ennis Krueger, deceased. Judgment of $10,000 demanded for the death of Harry Jensen.

Mads Madson vs. George Crothers as administrator of the estate of Ennis Krueger, deceased. Judgment demanded in the sum of $5,000 damages, $100 for medical attention and care and $300 for loss of time.

Mads Madson vs. Frank, Leslie, Ennis and Caroline Krueger. Judgment demanded in the sum of $5,400.

Angus Page vs. Caroline, Frank, Ennis, Leslie and Louis Krueger. Judgment demanded in the sum of $5,000 damages, $100 for hospitals and $75 for medicines.

Frank White vs. Caroline, Frank, Ennis, Leslie and Louis Krueger. Judgment demanded in the sum of $5,000 damages, $100 for hospitals and $75 for medicines.

C. A. Olson vs. Caroline, Frank, Ennis, Leslie and Louis Krueger. Judgment of $1,000 damages demanded.

Emil Laino vs. Caroline, Frank, Ennis, Leslie and Louis Krueger. Judgment demanded in the sum of $20,000 damages, $150 doctors … [rest missing]

From Caroline at Stevens Point to Frank at Waupun, December 11, 1919

Dear Frank, By the headlines you will see where I am. The trial started Tuesday afternoon and today Thursday evening just before supper it finished and now after supper the jury went to work so will know by tomorrow. … Oh the lying tongues … I will write the particulars in the next letter … it is pretty hard to fight with the world alone but I got through alright … Ren is very good to me, this case is only Laino, the others are postponed again. Well its Friday morning … Ren was here and said you have lost everything, Mrs. K., 6 thousand against you, everything will be sold for auction but the homestead and he wanted to know if I wanted to keep that. I said yes I am going to keep that. He said I would not like to live there anymore. I said I am going to keep it… that is our hard earned money. O my it is hard. … Mother

From Frank at Waupun to Mother at Greenleaf, December 21, 1919

Dear Mother, I received both of your letters and was glad to read that you are well. I didn't care so much for the news as I was anxious about your health as I did not know but what that trial would unnerve you somewhat but am glad it didn't. …You mentioned in the second letter about someone made a statement about you apologizing by publication in the paper. It must be getting on their minds or else they would not have mentioned it. It would not do for us to humiliate ourselves by bowing to such an inquisitive bunch because by so doing would be throwing the guilt on us. Righteousness never swerves to the right or to the left but goes straight forward. You mentioned R. being good to you, by jove I fail to see it, when a man comes to you and tells you, you lost everything and threatens by selling everything at auction because a measly court grants a decision in favor of a certain Mr. Laino. R. asking whether you wish to keep the homestead. Such a question, wonder if he thinks we should give it to him. All lawyers are alike. ... So they had another gun at the testimony at the Point, well. I suppose at the next trial they will have a few cannon and swear that we had them too. ... They are only pulling themselves in farther that's all. Ps. 35:8.

You stated that you would send a Christmas box. If this letter reaches you before you sent it, send me a couple pounds of peanuts, a couple pounds of almond nuts, a package of figs and a package of dates. I don't know if they will allow any other thing in besides fruit and nuts. ... Will write you again on Christmas Day. Am well at present. From Frank

From Leslie at Waupun to Mother at Withee, February 15, 1920

Dear Mother, ... Well next week is another hollow day, it is Washington birthday. I do not think that they will leave us out for there are quiet a few that are sick in hear. I had a awful headache last week, it lasted almost all week but I am alright again ... they do not leave any visitors in hear because there Is to much sickness around. ... Well I ordered from my hollow day order a half dozen apples, three packages of cocoanut and package of seedless raisins and I will celebrate Washington's birthday eating that. ... I am still working at my same old job and I will know how to make twine from now on. ... Well will close this time, Leslie Krueger

From the start of his prison sentence at Waupun, Leslie Krueger worked in the binder twine factory at the prison. He was paid monthly, and received extra if/when he did overtime. The money he earned went into his account and he received statements showing his balance each month. Most of the statements were saved and tied together with a black string. At times he would send money home to his mother when she needed it for something. At the start of his prison sentence in 1919 he was earning about $4.00 per month. He was paid 2 to 2.5 cents per ton, depending on the grade of twine being manufactured and given 10 cents an hour for overtime. Depending on the amount of overtime, at most he cleared about $7.00 for a full month's work.

Wisconsin State Prison Twine Plant

Earnings for the month of......*May*............192*7*

Reg. No. *14653*... Name ...*Krueger L.*

(If register number is not correct advise Supt.)

Amount $ *4⁰⁰*

LESLIE'S STATEMENT SHOWING HIS MONTHLY EARNINGS FROM WORKING IN THE BINDER TWINE FACTORY.

Money earned from working was what Leslie and Frank used to order treats for holidays, usually fruit and nuts, sometimes candy. In the 1920s they were allowed to order up to $1.00 worth of fruit, peanuts, etc., off a list given to each prisoner.

In December of 1924, in celebration of Christmas, the annual holiday order sheet was handed out to prisoners at Waupun by Deputy Warden G. S. Taft. The orders had to be placed no later than noon on Saturday, December 6. Choices with prices for 1924 were: apples, Jonathans, 25cents/dozen; oranges, California, 45 cents/dozen; bananas, 11 cents/lb.; figs (8 oz. pkg.), 10 cents; cocoanut (4 oz. pkg.), 7 cents; dates, 20 cents; peanuts, roasted, 16 cents lb.; peanuts, salted, 20 cents lb. Leslie ordered one dozen apples, one dozen oranges, and 1.5 pounds of salted peanuts.

SAMPLE HOLIDAY ORDER SHEET

HOLIDAY ORDERS

Decoration Day

1929

Inmates cannot order more than $1.00 worth of fruit, peanuts, etc.

The following prices will be charged, make your order accordingly.

Turn in your order for Decoration Day by Thursday noon, May 9.

Apples, Winesap	35c doz.
Oranges, California	42c doz.
Bananas, average 3 to a lb.	10c lb.
Figs, good grade, 8 oz. pkg.	10c pkg.
Cocoanut, 4 oz. pkg.	07c pkg.
Dates, Dromedary	20c pkg.
Peanuts, roasted	15c lb.
Peanuts, salted	17c lb.

G. S. Taft,

Deputy Warden

Frank Krueger worked in one of the cell houses, cleaning up cells, dusting, etc. when he first went to prison. He said the cells were similar to the ones at the Neillsville jail and it was his job to keep them clean. He later worked in a cheese factory, but the damp conditions caused him to have aches and pains he called rheumatism. Frank was not as stout as Leslie, and mentally less stable at times. Because of his seriousness, his deep thinking, he suffered bouts of depression. The job he was given did not pay as much money as Leslie's binder twine factory work did.

From Frank at Waupun to Mother at Greenleaf, February 22, 1920

Dear Mother, As I have a chance to write to you again before you get to write me, I thought I would drop you another line or two. It being a holiday today and having time that you would be glad to hear from me between. I sent this letter to Greenleaf as I do not know when you will be back there or not.

You asked in one of your last letters how my leg is getting along. I forgot to tell you the last time so will do so now. It hurts some in my instep when I walk altho not enough to bother me. I don't know why that should be why it should hurt there when I was wounded further up. The rheumatism has not altogether left me, there is a small pain in the right knee, perhaps it comes from the wound and I feel it most when I step down from a stair or other object such as a chair or box. Altho I am not complaining it might have been worse, but it is a fine thing to get in such a high civilization as we have at the present time under the pretense of liberty. ... From Frank

Caroline questioned Frank if he would like to study music while in prison. He told her that he didn't care to study it unless he was a free man. "I am like the Israelites when they were taken captive. Their captors wanted them to play the harps and sing while resting in camps but they hung their harps on the willow trees and said: How can we sing the Lord's song in a strange land."—Frank at Waupun, January 18, 1920

Judgment on the Laino Lawsuit

THE MILWAUKEE SENTINEL, FEBRUARY 23, 1920 (front page)

KRUEGER VERDICT IS FULLY UPHELD

STEVENS POINT, Wis.—The verdict of the jury in the Krueger case, tried in Circuit court for Portage county last December was approved in its entirety by Judge Byron B. Park in a decision handed down on Friday. The court ordered judgment to which the jury found the plaintiff entitled is $6,015.50, of which $5,015.50 represents compensatory damages as a result of injuries sustained by Laino when he was shot while a member of a United States marshal's posse attempting to arrest the Krueger brothers as draft evaders, and punitory damages of $1,000.

Held Responsible

The jury also held that the Krueger brothers, four in number, had conspired forcefully to resist arrest, that they were responsible for the shooting of Laino, and that Mrs. Caroline Krueger, the mother, was a party to the conspiracy.

The action was brought against Mrs. Krueger and Frank, Leslie, Ennis, and Louis Krueger, but was dismissed as to Ennis Krueger, who met death while resisting arrest, and Louis, who is an alleged fugitive from justice.

In analyzing the jury's answer to the question regarding the alleged conspiracy of the Krueger brothers, the court held that the evidence presented is "amply sufficient, if deemed credible, to sustain a finding that Frank, Leslie, Louis and Ennis had a common understanding that Louis and Leslie should evade service, and that they would forcefully resist the arrest of both or either one of them."

Seek $50,000 Damages

The action of Laino against the Kruegers was the first of eight civil actions for damages growing out of the pitched battle at the Krueger farm in September, 1918. The total amount of damages sought is in excess of $50,000. It is probably that, unless settlement is reached, some of these cases, at least, will be combined and tried in Circuit court here at the May term.

Laino, as the first to get a judgment against the Kruegers, will make the first levy against the property of the Kruegers. Others who may get judgment will share in what is left. The total value of the Krueger property has been estimated at $30,000 or more.

Caroline at Greenleaf to Frank at Waupun, March 17, 1920

... Well am sorry to hear that your leg bothers you so, is
it from the wound or is it from rhum [rheumatism]. It was the
auctioneer that shot you, he talks quite smart now, at least did
in the Point [Stevens Point, Wisconsin—the damage suit for Laino
had recently taken place there, so the auctioneer must have been
there talking or bragging about shooting Frank.]

Frank at Waupun to Mother at Greenleaf, March 21, 1920

Dear Mother, I received your letter and was very glad to
hear from you, in fact I was worried a little thinking perhaps
you were not well or something had happened to you. ... My
foot seems to be in better shape than it ever was. I thought the
rheumatism would return again this spring but it seems to be
getting better right along ... I would never have thought that the
man you mentioned would have shot me. I suppose he was mad
after having such a close call when down the road during the first
trouble and perhaps he wanted to avenge that poor car of his, and
to think that he did not even want to be mentioned in the case. ...
I have thought some on the matter and wondered whether it did
any good by shooting me that way, whether by making me suffer
for if it has opened the eyes of many people, if it did, then I am
glad to have suffered for it. ... I have been doing alot of thinking
since I have been in prison. I sometimes think I would like to write
a paper on the causes of this great warfare that has just passed
within the last 6 years, even the last 50 years. The causes that
lead to it. Who is to blame and what the outcome will be, and also
state the remedy to prevent more wars in the future if it would
help and confine myself entirely to the Bible. The Bible certainly
covers it well if one studies it and reveals itself nicely.

... I can't help thinking of some of the things Louis said
about this time of trouble. He knew what he was talking about
and he is well able to take care of himself. I am not ashamed of
any of my brothers and also my mother. I have every assurance
God will take care of them all. I am positive he can do more for
them than any earthly father ... I am well at present. From Frank

Caroline Krueger Returns Home

On a short visit to her farm at Longwood in February, Caroline Krueger wrote to Frank and updated him on the neighbors that had moved away from the area. There had been many changes in the year that she was gone.

Caroline wrote Frank that there were 105 bullet holes in the east side of the entrance door up to the roof, and that wasn't counting the bullets that went through the windows. She said there were seven holes in the dining room door in the wood and the glass was all out of it. The cook stove had two bullet holes shot through the warming oven and through the stovepipe. These holes were nearly an inch long and they made baking a bit difficult. Caroline told Frank she also counted over 230 bullet holes inside of the house.

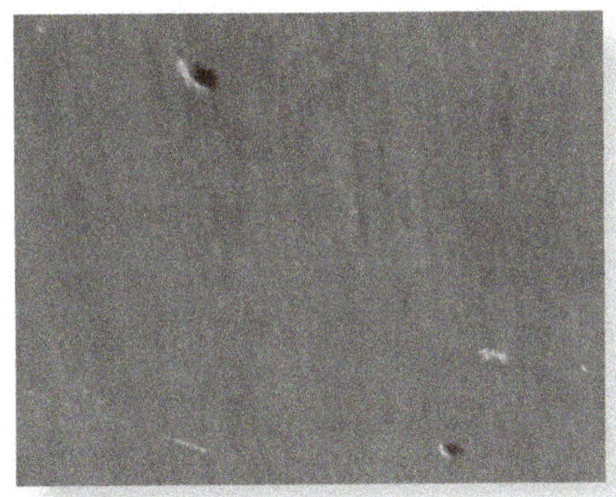

Frank at Waupun to Mother at Greenleaf, April 4, 1920

Dear Mother, ... Yes Pa is dead now 10 years, it does not seem long and still it is quite a while at that, we never had much trouble before but when it began it seems as tho one came after another. When one thinks of all the events that have taken place there, it amounts to quite a lot. Threshing, sawmilling, logging, the western trip and Robs death and Pas and lastly this trouble which is now on and isn't over yet, but when it takes a turn again it may be over for a time and things will go well for a time again, whatever is Gods will will be done. From Frank

Near the end of April, Caroline came back home to stay. She could no longer tolerate living at Greenleaf. Spring had arrived and the contract was up for Mr. Robinson who had rented the farm for one year. Robinson had sold the lambs born of the sixteen sheep left on the farm before Caroline returned. She wrote to her sons right away to let them know she was back home, alone, but ready for the day they would soon be together there again.

Mother at Withee to Frank at Waupun, April 22, 1920

Dear Frank, I must let you know that I am in my home and Oh how good it seems to be back. Mr. was at the Station with the team and nearly the first thing he said was he heard Leslie was coming home too, perhaps with me, so they know more than I did. One of the sheep died and left 2 lambs, one found a mother, the other I will have to bottle, it is 3 days old. ... Will write more next week if you are still their yet. It's raining so hard today that I can't go out and look around.

Mother at Withee to Frank at Waupun, April 28, 1920

Dear Frank, I suppose you are expecting to hear from me, well I am alright and well hope you are the same. ... Well how do you clean that pipe from the kitchen sink, where do you open it in the basement—where that wooden plug is in? The water don't go thru very well. I pumped out the water in the cellar today and done my washing—their is nothing left of the bed close but my 4 fetherbeds and they are emptied out too and 1 mattress and 1 strawtick so I bought 5 yd to make one bed sheat and 2 pillows are left. Martha gave me some flour sacks along so I use them for pillowslip—no quilts left either so I will tell you how my bed is—a mattress then a fetherbed then that new bedsheat and pillow and over me another fetherbed, so far it is all right until it gets warm. The wool carters are gone, also the quilt frame, spinning wheel lays outside, all the chairs are broken but 2 and the dining room table is here yet and my sewing machine they bent one piece but Bessie's husband fixed that for me so I am at least using it for the rough sewing. 3 pieces of the cream seperator is gone too so I went to Owen yesterday and they are going to send for them then I will make butter from them 2 cows. ... It is getting dark now and I don't light no lamp—have none to light of my own, a borrowed one so will finish in the morning then send it out. ... I have lots more to write but will close for this time hoping you are well and soon released from that false accusation that the enemy brought against us. I remain your mother. ... My hardest work is carrying the wood up from the mill.

Louis, the Fugitive, Comes Home for a Short Visit

Mother at Withee to Frank at Waupun, May 3, 1920

Dear Frank, No doubt you have heard the shooting hear again. Louis came home Friday evening and well I'll not mention who saw him so at 11:30 Friday night a car came in and the men out with their guns around the house, one almost knocked the door down trying to get in but Louis jumped out the den window and run east and of all the shooting after him—there were 5 men but they found no blood so he must have been protected of God otherwise I don't know, so Saturday the Officers from Neillsville were down after dinner (now in the mean time these Owen men got a blood hound and they also came) a little ahead of the Neillsville District Atorny Jackson and Deputy Sheriff so they were down at the woods so Jackson called them back and told them that the State or Co. hadn't anything against Louis—how they had that right to do what they did—their is lots more to it but will not write it. Anyway they went home at 2 o clock looking pretty cheep. ... Sunday an officer was here from Madison—he seen what was what—he was sorry they did not leave Louis alone, he could have been on the farm with me now, he thought I was in a pitable shape and I had to have some help and the land must not lay idle. I sayed give me my children I'll work it, for I want to live in my own house.

Mother at Withee to Frank at Waupun, May 10, 1920

Dear Frank, I must write again as I feel kind of lonesome—it is raining so can not stay much outside. Before it rained I was planting my Gladiolias and Dalia roots that a woman gave me, she also gave me 2 1/2 bus. potatoes, some pickles, rutabaga's, carrots, beets, and parsnips—wasn't she good. Then I howed around the rest of my flowers, carried manure on them and fixed them all up nice so they look good now and I raked up all around the house and well it looks better now although their is lots to pick up yet. As I was doing this work I thought of what that German paper said in Neillsville, do you remember, it said

as Kruegers lived their everything was so clean and neat around
there but after the guards left it looked as if Indians had camped
their, well it did look frightful now—their was manure a foot deep
around the well. Then I pumped the water out of the cellar that
was nearly up to the stairway, it was hard work but got it out at
last. Built up the fences all but one place. Well the renter had to
haul hay in the barn so after he was done with hauling I told him
to let me have the horses so he said I could until noon, so I got
up 3 loads of wood but when I go to feed the little lamb I always
bring a few sticks along. I will have to find someone to shear
our sheep too and to tend to our lambs. Nellie had her colt but
she is so poor she had no milk and it died. ... The elevater dont
work as it should so I don't use it at all, and the overflow tank
in the bathroom leaks so I can only pump about one pail full in
it. It must have been shot through—if I pump more in it, it leeks
down on the book case east of the fireplace. Tomorrow is Leslie's
birthday poor boy. I thought you would have that case decided,
but push it out always a little longer now—2 weeks more from
tomorrow—if you could have gotten out we could have some
plowed up and put in barley but it will be too late. I am home all
alone but I am contented and will wait until it's god's time that he
will let you both free.

Mother at Withee to Frank at Waupun, May 19, 1920

Dear Frank, I received your letter today, am always glad
when two weeks are around. Yes Louis is or was then alive, any
how poor boy had to go again—wish they could let him go and he
would have been with me. He looks well, yes we each were glad
to see each other but we know up here who reported it. I have to
go to town once in a while tho so got to leave the house ... and
besides I can't sit in the house all the time, you must know I am
alone. ... It took me nearly one day to clean the refrigerator, it was
not cleaned I think since I cleaned it last. I put on Kerosene and
then I'd let it soak then wash that off and then put on Ker again,
I even used a knife to cut the dirt loose but now it is just as white
and clean like new. ... From your Mother

Dear Frank, ... Well I am quite well as can be expected after such a nerve breaking sene but I hope it will never happen here again with such an outfit. Well I sent for my trunk and Fred wrote that he will send it like today, suppose it will be here tomorrow with the 11 oclock. I was in need of my summer close and I have my winter underware on yet. I don't know hardly what to write. Les said that if I write certain things they cut them out. I think I will draw a wire across the driveway that them curiosity seekers won't have a chance to run in so easy with their cars all at once. I hear "Oh see the bullet holes"—their they stand with their car. If I tell them to get out they go but what they say you have no idea. I feel like taking a club to them. ... I wish I knew where Louis was driven to—I would get him. Their was quite a story about him in them old lying papers too, it seems just so long and then they must bring up something about us. The garden I made is all up nice. Well I washed and churned and fixed a little dandelion wine, just a little, sugar is so high priced I can't hardly reach 30 cents and upward today. Well as the papers say you both will have to stay their. O but that is hard to bear but you know it won't be long—those that studies the words knows better. Well I would like to say something to cheer you up but can't. ... From your mother ... here now 2 cars again. Pripanow from Curtis—she wanted to look at the house because they want to build one like it. I said no.

Frank wanted his mother to support herself, he did not want her taking handouts from neighbors. She wrote to let him know she would certainly try to take care of herself. She told Frank that she planted four rows of potatoes "all the way from the plainer to the woods," and thought that would be sufficient along with her other garden produce. During mid-July, Caroline told him she was living on bread and berries and a small piece of meat once in a while.

Caroline found someone to cut her hay on shares and felt she would have enough that way to feed what little stock she had. She bought a grass scythe to mow around the house and toward the barn so her clothes would not get so wet in the mornings or when it rained.

She also purchased a single buggy harness for $42 from her shoemaker friend. She did not have enough money to pay for it all, but the shoemaker told her "not to hurry herself." Their old harnesses had burned up in the barn fire.

Caroline Shoos off More Sightseers

Mother at Withee to Frank at Waupun, June 23, 1920

As I was hoeing in the garden this afternoon I thought a car stopped so I came up and sure enough a little girl taking pictures with a little camera and a bigger girl with a larger camera and 2 young men (they were on the road at the mail box). They got off and marched right in along the drive-way, by that time I was at the well—they passed me, never said a word, walked right toward the barn, I said "where are you going"—to see the barn, "who gave you that right to go there"—no one, "then out on the road with you, the boldness of you comming in on other peoples premises that way." He sayd thank you, I said shame on you, they did feel cheep as they got out on the road and he told the little girl to get in the car. That is what I got to put up with. I should think their was a law to stop that.

Withee Wis Sel. 7 1920

Dear Leslie

What is the matter that you dont write I did not get eny letter from you since the 15 of Aug. I feel worried it is hard enough to bare with out not hearing from you I send you each a box with appels & plums did you get them. Well news I dont know but only that they are going to sell the land the 18th then I suppose it will mean for me to get out as they have the home-stead in on that sale to so no doubt some rich one will buy it then it mean out I did not write this to Frank but you can

... Yesterday a car stopped out on the road and 2 men got off with each a little camara, took the house and barn, their must have been as much as a thousand pictures taken of this place this summer if not more ...

CAROLINE KRUEGER'S HOME CIRCA 1921 (AUTHOR'S PHOTO)

The appeal of the murder conviction was denied in the spring of 1920 by the state and Attorney Reynolds was not able to get a new trial. The thought of Frank and Leslie serving life sentences actually began to sink in, although hope for an early release kept Caroline Krueger from losing her mind. What little she could do to manage her homestead filled her thoughts and time. Her faithful letters to her sons attempted to keep them uplifted in spirit, only as a mother could. Caroline worried about the loss of her home due to the impending lawsuits and the Laino suit already decided.

Mother at Withee to Frank at Waupun, August 10, 1920

Dear Frank, I received your last weeks letter and I sent you one and told you in it to answer right off but I suppose they did not let you write. Well this letter is not going to be good news in it for I heard from S. [Supreme] Court in Madison they decided in the Neillsville jury's favor so you will have to stay there, but it

will not be as long as they say, for you know the time is at hand
of Jesus coming so don't feel bad about it as they are telling me
you will be out soon. ... the Kidd sent word over to tell me when
the patition is made up for you boys to be pardoned he wanted
to sign it, be sure to let him sign it he said, and all over thier they
said that they never thought that it would come to that of selling
the land and they feel bad about it now (or rather sorry) at that
time they thought they done something great, not now no more
thou. ... I got my share of the hay put up if I can keep the cattle,
unless they will sell that to they said—it said in the paper cattle,
machinery and everything. but it dont say that on the paper that
is tacked on the stump out here ...

Mother at Withee to Frank at Waupun, August 18, 1920

Dear Frank, ... They are going to sell Lanio's share on
the 18th—that is posted up out here on the stump. I do not go
anywhere but only to town and cemetery—it looks so nice their
that it makes any one feel it must be nice to rest their too. But
no doubt God has something for me to do in this world so will
be contented as it is. It is very lonesome at times though. ... You
say about me to manage alone—why I do the chorse morning
and even, and the rest of the day I do what else is to be done and
what I can do I don't hurry. I suppose the winter wood I will have
to get after it myself soon now but I am expecting you both or all
for that matter home before the winter is set in. ... Mother

Mother at Withee to Frank at Waupun, September 2, 1920

I sold my lambs and Oh it hurt me so to see my little lammie
go—he looked out of the box and said baa as they went away with
him. If I was in the pasture he was right with me until at the end
of the lane, then he would go back to the sheep again ... But I got
his picture taken.

I have that anyway to remember him by.

Mother at Withee to Frank at Waupun, September 14, 1920

Dear Frank, It is just two years ago today that this happened. You asked how the potatoes was, they are good and how I will get them dug—well if they will drive me out now, I will sell them. And if I had enough to keep lot more than enough. About my wood for the winter, well I perhaps will not need any. If the partie that buys this will make me go out right away, I do not know what I will do or go. Martha left George [Fred Gussert's son] so their is trouble their and I do not want to go their anyway—no their is no feeling for one another no more. ... It seems cruel to keep the prisoners in so long, it is such nice weather yet. Well I feel offul to think our long hard work is going into some rich mans hands for nothing, me working for 40 years. ... I am all through with my work and it is only 10 minutes after 6 so I will write letters, then I sit in the dark and watch the autos go by until bed time. Oh it is lonesome then. O why does God allow that to be done in such a way, it is almost unbearable when I think over that I am not even allowed any one of my children to be with me and be driven out of my home besides—it seems there is no heart any more. Well I know you know all of that yourself so will not write any more about it. It is offul hot today, looks like rain. Well must come to a close for this time, hope you are well. I remain your Mother Mrs. Krueger

Frank at Waupun to Mother at Withee, September 19, 1920

Dear Mother, Received your letter and was anxious to hear from you. I notice you are quite wrought up on account of them waiting to dispose of our property. Of course you know how I feel in regard to that. ...

Our government has been wrong since the pilgrims first landed at Plymouth rock so why should one be opposed if he fights against it.

After nearly all the natural resources have been cut off, that is the timber, they feel like taking a small wood lot that my father kept for his heirs and selling that I suppose.

Now if that lawyer, by getting a judgment for Laino, can make me believe that wrong is right he is badly mistaken, it may possibly be able to sell the land but it will be wrongfully and illegally. ...

Well I don't know of more to write so will close, am well at present hoping this finds you the same. Well stay on the place, don't let anyone chase you off. From Frank

In the end, the inevitable happened—the land was auctioned off and Caroline Krueger was left with just forty acres of her original property where the home and outbuildings were situated. At times she was able to use farmland nearby in the years ahead.

Mother at Withee to Frank at Waupun, September 19, 1920

Dear Frank, I thought I would write today for you no doubt are anxious to know about yesterday's sale. Well I and my north neighbor and wife and daughter and the one that lived but sold out just 1 mile west from here where the creek runs thru his land, went together. And our south neighbor wife and son and G. Ammenthorp wife and daughter were their—thats all. Well Crosby bought the north 40 and the 80 over to Langs, and Larsons the 80 here back of him. The Homestead has no right to be sold, that is mine so I will always have my home now. I will tell you how it was sold. The Sheriff came out and read of what was to be sold, then he said only Caroline, Frank and Leslie's interest or claim in that land is to be sold (that ment their share) but now listen, but not

Ennis or Louis share or interest—them two are out their share is going to stay in it. That's what the Sheriff said so Ennis must be raised from the dead soon, or he never was dead and Louis must be all right too yet. Well they sold it in all for 5,850 dollars. Laino did not get all he was supposed to. ... It was to be cash, Larson went up paid for it and I did not even see that he got a receipt for it. O they scared him after they asked him what he has got to show for his money. Well he asked the lawyer if he could cut the timber, the answer was no. That he had not even the right (well I just had to order 2 cars off the place, one went north the other south) to walk on it—that it was ours just as if it wasn't sold at all for we had 15 months time to redeem it in. They laughed—said it was a rotten business. Well then I had a talk with Schoengarth, he said he would have bought that land right off but it is in such a mess that he dont want anything to do with it. ... Hoping you are well, I remain your Mother

On Saturday, Sheriff Weaver sold five forties of the Krueger farm at Withee under a sheriff's sale of execution, to meet the judgment given to Emil Laino awarded in his suit for damages for injuries received during the battle at the Krueger farm. E. W. Crosby bought three forties and Jorgen Larson bought two, the five forties selling for $5,850. Mrs. Krueger was here to attend the sale.

A Letter to Frank on the
Loss of Their Collie Dog

Mother to Frank at Waupun, October 20, 1920

Dear Frank, ... I wrote to you in the last letter the people wont stand for it much longer for the people know it wasn't you boys that done that deed. They speak right out now and besides they dont want me here alone, and I can not help myself any longer as the winter is before the door and I can not cut any wood—it hurts my back so. They are getting sore and I dont blame them. ... Leslie asked for Collie—he is dead last year in

Sept as Fred and I was here. He was so poor and so hungry that
he could hardly walk. He looked at me so pittyfully as if to give
me something to eat. O I feel sorry for him now yet when I think
of him how he looked at me. I told the renter to shoot him and
he did. No I never pittied enything so much in my life as I did him
and could not help him. ...

Caroline Prepares for Her First Winter Alone

Caroline had much to do to prepare herself for her first winter alone at the farm. She picked her apples from the yard and sold four bushels of them for $2.00 each. Apple trees from the orchard on the farm were of the Duchess and Wealthy variety. Four apple trees had been cut down by someone before Caroline returned home to stay. She was quite upset by this, as they had just started to produce. Who would do such a cruel deed, it could only have been prompted by spite or jealousy.

Caroline canned plums and crab apples. She dug up her rutabagas and carrots from the garden and tried canning pumpkins, a new venture for her.

Digging up the potatoes was a challenge. When she could get her old horse, Nellie, to come up to water, she would hitch her up to a jumper. Then Caroline would load up the potatoes in the field onto the jumper and have Nellie haul them to the cellar door.

Caroline worried about how to run the furnace, having no knowledge of its use.

She spoke of building a ladder to climb up into the garret and remove a mouse she heard gnawing up there.

Spinning wool from her sheep was a chore that Caroline enjoyed before the shootout. Her spinning wheel had been destroyed and left lying outside so she had to send in the wool from her sheep to have it spun. The Chippewa Falls Woolen Mills charged her 60 cents per pound. She then knitted stockings and mitts for herself for the colder weather and later a sweater.

When the first snowfalls arrived, Caroline banked up the outside of the whole house with the new snow; she also banked up the basement windows. She removed a small heater from the chicken house and put it in the cellar where she sawed up her firewood.

Dear Mother, ... You asked whether there are other means to fill the range boiler except by windmill. No, there are not, that system is all tied together so one depends on the other to make it work well. I am going to give you some advice as best I can to arrange things so as to get along for the winter. You do not need any water in the boiler behind the cook stove. That won't hurt if there is none in it. Where the pipe comes thru the wall there used to be a small faucet, we used to open it and let the water out of the pipe, this ought to be there. The pipe there goes upward and along the ceiling, fasten the pipe at the ceiling some way near the wall. Then cut the pipe about 4 feet up from the faucet, unscrew this piece and have a thread cut on it, a coupling put on and a plug put in the coupling. This will disconnect it so when the pump is going you can get some water from the faucet and let it up on the elevator. That is when you pump water to the barn.

I would paper up all the windows on the outside that are in the basement except one next to the furnace for light. It will make the basement warmer.

Better fix up the Kitchen to live and sleep in by getting a small cot to use at night and in the daytime push it in the dining room or front hall, as it is out of the way, have the east door papered up outside, something to hang over the dining room door to keep out the cold. Make everything tight. Another good thing is to put a tee in the stove pipe and set up a small air tight heater along side of the cook stove that will keep you warm at night. ... It surely does not make me feel very pleasant to see my work all go to smash that way, you know how well it worked before and how you have to get along with it now ... From your son, Frank

Caroline Keeps Hope
Alive for Ennis' Return

Mother to Frank at Waupun, December 15, 1920

Dear Frank, Well tomorrow is the 16th—Ennis birthday—oh dear it hurts to think of the young lad as he was, such a busy body always to work at something. I heard of good authority

that they got the story started again in the community that it
was not Ennis that was killed and others say it was him and they
were after Greib [Greibenow, the undertaker] and he won't say
anything, he wont let out, that is the way they talk but they say
Mrs. Krueger will find out now pretty soon, you see, so dont know
leave it to H—yes they preach to do this and that then ruin it so
anyone can not live in comfort in their own house and home. ...

During this time, there were many men of all ages traveling about the country looking for jobs, anything to get by—lost souls you might say. Some, too, were evading the draft like the Krueger brothers. A young Polish immigrant by the name of Narkofski/Narkowski was said to have disappeared from the Polley area at the time of the shooting. If the man shot at Polley was not Ennis, perhaps Ennis was killed at another date at a different location, and that incident was not revealed. The desire to capture or kill the Krueger brothers was so strong, especially in the minds of the U.S. marshals who were at the scene of the September 14th shootout. They wanted to be heroes.

In a late December letter Caroline Krueger wished for a Happy New Year that would set all of her children free, including Ennis. She hoped to hear from him, too.

Mother to Frank at Waupun, January 26, 1921

Dear Frank, ... Well Monday I got a letter from a boy that
was in Illinois 1 year and as I pulled out the letter thier was a post
card with Ennis picture on it. This boy wrote that that picture
went with him where-ever he went and he would not give it up to
anyone but to me. He said he heard that I had no picture of him
so he would give me the one he had but he did not like to give it
up or rather not like to part with it. O but it did hurt me as I see
it I cryed nearly all day—he looks as if he wanted to talk with me,
if he is dead how cruely he was murdered, no chance for life was
given him at all. I would not like to have that man's conscience to
carry around.

8 CAPTURED, HOME AGAIN

Mother to Frank at Waupun, December 1, 1920

Dear Frank, ... Well they had it in the paper that they got Louis in Chippawa Fall [County Jail at Chippewa Falls, Wisconsin] but he did not write to me yet. They had the review of the whole thing in Owen paper again, what does that person think of himself! Their were parties here last fall said why don't they put in the paper what they done, I say so too. Well in Gods own time they will have to own up what they done and everyone will see it to as the scripture proves. ... Wonder what they will do with Louis if they have got him. Wish they would let him come home—war prisoners are supposed to be all let free 6 months after the arms are laid down, but it is over 2 years and no show yet so far, shame on them, well must close and don't worry about me as God has helped me so far and will further on. ... Mother

Caroline received her first letter from Louis, from the jail, on January 25. He said he felt fairly well and had read in the newspaper about himself being found guilty by a Grand Jury, of what he didn't know. He also read in the papers that his mother was still home alone on the farm at Withee. Louis had no idea when his trial would be coming up. He thought it was being held up because there were over a hundred liquor cases to be tried ahead of him. He also talked with the U.S. marshal that had been at the farm after others had shot at him when he escaped through the window in early May of the year passed. He was now labeled by the press as a "War Objector."

Men Want to Buy Machinery from Mrs. Krueger

Mother to Frank at Waupun, March 9, 1921

Dear Frank, ... Well I did not hear from Louis either and I feel lonesome if I don't get a letter once in every few days. Well last week a man from Loyal was here wanted to buy an Engine and sawmill. I told him the factory's were turning them out every day, yes he said and laught but they are too high priced, just as if they would get one given to them from here. Another from Neillsville was here last Sunday wanted an Edger. I told him the same thing and Hansen from Thorpe was here too on Sunday, he wanted the sawmill—I told him I didn't have any, that what there is left of it the boys would soon want to use their selves, he said as well as Vater can use it and wear it out without paying, you can sell it just as well and have the money. ... He came to the entrance door—never rapped—walked right in and then he could not get up them steps into the kitchen. I was mad at him thou, I could have kicked him out, the old dane. ... Hoping your well. I remain your Mother C. K.

THE KRUEGER BROTHER'S TRACTOR THAT THEY REFERRED TO AS "THE ENGINE," CIRCA 1920 (AUTHOR'S PHOTO)

LOUIS KRUEGER MAY BE GIVEN BAIL

LA CROSSE, WIS.—Louis Krueger, one of four brothers who evaded the draft law, and whose opposition to conscription resulted in a battle with federal officials in which one man was killed near their farm home at Withee, Wis., is to be arraigned in court here before United States Commissioner Alfred Harrison and given a chance to obtain his freedom pending trail, on bond.

Krueger, who evaded arrest for nearly two years, has been in jail here since December, when he was apprehended in northern Wisconsin.

Two brothers, Frank and Leslie, are serving terms at Waupun, while a third brother, Ennis, was killed trying to escape arrest.

Louis Chats with
U.S. Marshal Joseph Gantz

Mother to Leslie at Waupun, April 27, 1921

Dear Leslie, ... Louis also wrote that Gantz went with him to the courthouse and on the way he told Louis what he should do when he got home—that bar tender [Gantz] swore on the stand that he done nothing else all his life but tended bar and now he wants to tell L. what to do when he gets home, a boy that was born and raised on the farm? And Gantz also swore that he did not know how to get over the fence as our Lawyer asked him why he did not go up to the boys and serve the warrant, then dictate to Louis what he shall do when he comes home. ...

Louis at La Crosse County Jail to Mother, May 25, 1921

"Judge not that ye shall be judged."

Dear Mother, Well did you recieve the bond and did you sign or return it. You write to Alfred Harrison, U.S. Commissioner La Crosse. I think your letter will get there alright.

You better write to La Follette office at Madison and see who would be a good attorney to see. I will have to have an attorney if there is going to be a trial. The way I heard a hearing is set for June 7.

You see if there is crooket work, I want to know I shall surely fight it.

I have not heard a thing from the Governor.

I read one time in a paper that the federal court will be held in Eau Claire in June.

Let me know what you think we shall do.

There is a good attorney in Eau Claire I forgot his name.

I am getting tired of laying here.

From L. E. Krueger La Crosse Wis.

I am not feeling good. I have to order a doctor if it does not change. I am thinking about being transfered to some other place closer home if I have to stay much longer, that is if I can, like to be out side, I will be some day.

Leslie at Waupun to Mother, June 5, 1921

Dear Mother, ... Did you get L out yet, answer that next week. I hope that you did, that would make me feel alot better. I do not like to see you alone their, it does not make so much difference to me but I would like to get out to. ... I am not working noons any more they changed making different grades of twine so I quit at 12 oclock at noon and at 5 at night, do not work at Saturday afternoon—they have a ball game here every afternoon and we changed suits, we have a heavy suit in winter and a light one in summer. I guess that I will go to church today then the day wont be so long—have to stay in my cell all day on Sunday, they do not have moving pictures any more when they leave us out on Saturday. It seems to stay cold yet we did not have any rain hear decoration day, they were playing ball in the forenoon hear. Well I can not write for two weeks now. ... Hope that I will not have to write many letters from here any more. Leslie Krueger, Withee Wis

RELEASE ALLEDGED EVADER OF DRAFT

La Crosse—Louis Krueger, one of the Clark county brothers charged with evading the draft during the war was released from jail here today on a bond after being detained seven months awaiting trial in United States court. The bail bond of $3,000 was signed by residents of Withee, Wis., near which village the Krueger farm is located.

On June 8, Caroline wrote to Frank to let him know that Louis was home. "He looks good but he is soft, but he done and fixed up so many things for me that it seems that I have nothing to do now ..." His first job was to fix the pump in the cellar and then replace or repair the broken rod on the windmill. The sheep needed shearing as well. And the curbing was caving in around the top of the well. This too would need to be repaired soon.

Caroline took a quick train trip to Waupun to visit Frank and Leslie, asking them to jot down their questions ahead because their visits were so short. She sent a postcard to let them know of her safe return back home.

In late June, Caroline went to Madison to see Attorney Reynolds. He had placed a judgment on the farm machinery, lathes, lumber and shingles, everything that was left. All the Krueger family members also received papers regarding the probate of Ennis' estate. They had not initiated this and wanted no part of it. They felt it was a ploy for those involved in the suits against them to obtain more of their property including the homestead itself.

In July, Caroline shared with Frank the amounts that persons involved in the lawsuits would agree to settle at with them: The widow of Harry Jensen, $1200; Mads Madsen, $800; Page, $500; White, $500; Olsen, $250; and Laino, $6313.32. Lawyers representing the above were the ones who wished to have Ennis' supposed quarter of the estate probated. Later it was decided that Ennis did not own any shares of the farm, so there was nothing to probate.

But turmoil never strayed far away from the Kruegers. It found a way to infiltrate every nook and cranny of their lives.

16 Years
OF LETTERS FROM PRISON

9 ENNIS' WATCH   And so began the long stretch of years with Caroline and Louis alone, yet together, on the farm at Longwood. There was much to be done and little resources to work with. At times there was little to eat and no money to buy food. Legal issues kept turning up. Many times they chose to ignore letters and refused to sign documents, stalling out whenever they could and hanging tight to the farm. The ultimate goal was always to get Frank and Leslie back home again. The thought that Ennis might be a fugitive or locked away was often in the back of their minds. Caroline was torn apart whenever she thought of Ennis.

An idea came to Caroline in 1921 to ask Clark County for the return of any items that may have been recovered from Ennis' body, if indeed he had been killed. She was referred to the U.S. marshal's office and O'Conner at Madison became quite angry with her demands. He admitted he wasn't sure where Ennis' personal effects were located, but Marshal John F. LaMont told O'Conner he had to oblige Mrs. Krueger's request.

Frank wrote and told his mother that when he last saw Ennis at the house the night of the shootout, he had given his youngest brother a buckskin bag with money, a knife, a whetstone, and a pocket watch.

Two weeks after her request, on June 24, 1921, Caroline received a letter from John LaMont of Madison, U.S. marshal's office, stating that he had succeeded in locating Ennis' watch and $8.40 that belonged to him. He mailed the watch to her along with a money order for $8.40. Caroline asked Frank again how much money he had given Ennis. "When Ennis and I parted I gave him everything I had, a buckskin bag with about $90 in it. You know we just got back from doing a little threshing. I gave him Rob's 'Hamilton' railway watch with either 18 or 28 jewel movement, which I had been carrying, also a knife and a small whetstone."

In July, Caroline wrote to Frank, "All I got from Ennis things is the watch and $8.40 and the undertaker told me who took that, but as I asked him he denighed it, so another wrote to me that he found it on another place (that is funny)."

On August 26, Caroline received a letter from John LaMont regarding a letter she wrote to him two days prior. There was mention of $40.00 cash taken from her home following the shootout. The money was in a box marked "Sunday School Money" and was turned over to Sheriff Garman of Eau Claire County. Mr. Garman had turned this over to Sheriff Hewett of Clark County at the time Caroline was transferred to the Neillsville jail. LaMont said he knew nothing about that $40.00, but he said this about Ennis' possessions: "The money and the watch which I sent you were all that were taken from Ennis' body at the time he was killed, at least that is all that was turned over to us by those who had charge of his body. If you desire to take this matter up with Mr. O'Conner direct, you may address him at Madison, Wisconsin."

The question comes to mind as to whether the watch returned to Mrs. Krueger matched the watch that had belonged to Robert Krueger, the oldest brother who died in 1913. If it was indeed Robert's watch, one would think they had really killed Ennis. The only other explanation would be that they killed him at another time or held him in custody somewhere, and for some reason were covering it all up.

10 STRUGGLES ON THE FARM

Mrs. Krueger on the Haystack—
So Many Callers

Mother to Frank at Waupun, July 20, 1921

Dear Frank, Your letters not received yet this week but will have to write just the same. Well we are getting along fairly well with the haying. ... Well did you read that in the Sunday paper about us, well as soon as that is over next month no doubt we will get through with the mess if it is true. ...Yesterday as I was on the hay stack I just take the hay away as Louis throws it up as the stack gets high then he gets on and spreads it apart. So all at once a car came along and one woman in her fine voice said oh that will make a nice picture—out came her camera but Mrs. Krueger thru herself down behind a bundle of hay just as quick as I heard that (L. said what is the matter, he did not hear that) and one of the women said Ha Ha she is gone ...

Frank at Waupun to Mother, July 17, 1921

I suppose you miss the barn more now during haying. Its hard to stack hay. I remember how we used to do it—before we had the barn. If some of those men that had a hand in burning down our barn had to pitch and stack hay they wouldn't be so ready to burn down barns. ... Well I wish I was there to help make hay ... From F.

Mother to Frank at Waupun, September 29, 1921

Dear Frank, ... I had callers from Ohio, Humbert [Humbird] Greenwood and Wausa a week ago last Sunday, they all come here and then go away more determent to do the right and uphold it after seeing how God can protect his own. I tell you those that can see and do see it in that light gets a great help of this and then another car came and they was going to run all over in the buildings. I went out and told them not to go any further. One said, what have you to say here, this is Goverment property. I said I have so much to say that you had better get out on the road as quick as you can and Louis heard that in the house—he came out so quick, he said to them what is this about Gov. Property but you ought to seen them go. Well I could tell you lots of them cases but will talk them over when we are together again. ... I remain your Mother Mrs. Krueger

Insurance Money on the Krueger Barn

Caroline was hoping to finally get some much-needed money from the Lynn Mutual Insurance Company that had insured the barn. She was told that the U.S. marshals orchestrated the formaldehyde fiasco. The marshals gave the order to purchase the formaldehyde from Dr. Frank of Neillsville and told their officers to spread it out on the barn's thrashing floor. Since the federal government was responsible for the fire she would have to sue the insurance company, who would in turn sue the government for damages.

Leslie at Waupun to Mother, December 4, 1921

Dear Mother, ... Well I will send you $14 this month. I think that they changed the time to send money out this month. I think on the tenth they payed me five dollars and eighteen cents for last month pay, they pay for the amount of twine I handle. I handled pretty near a hundred ton since July 1, they run through between 1750 and 1800 pds a day, pretty near a ton a day. They are going to put in two new spinners, yet it don't work me too hard, they [hands] are in good shape. When is our case coming up before the governor, did he say what date, has Silverwood been up there yet. ... I hope that we will have good success and God see fit to set us free. ... So will close for this time. L. Krueger

I did not order anything for christmas, they were too high priced. We have to put our order in a month before the hollow day.

Caroline's Late Christmas Letter to Frank, December 28, 1921

Dear Frank, Your letter recievd today—it was short, but no doubt you dont feel as if you want to say much, was you and Leslie together at Christmas and have you no money to order anything for Xmas? No I do not know much to write. Got a letter from another Lawyer that he would take the case of the Lynn Ins. Co. up for an offul offul percentage, he says its a good case, well as I have 6 years to sue in I think or L. and I thought perhaps someone else would come along some day a little cheaper. Was to church last Sunday, they had an Evangelist in Owen a different denomination entirely so thought I would go but it certainly was good. I enjoyed it very much, now they have 7 different Deno., their 1200 Inhabitance. He said as he goes thru the communities he finds that the Spirit has withdrawn entirely from some cities and villages, they are dead, they have stept over the deadline and they are gone, gone forever and Owen is next to it. ... Well we fixed up a little xmas tree and hung it up. L. said if I only can see it even if their isn't much on it, it shows more like christmas and their is more rememberance of the past to, so it hangs their in the corner of the book case. Well Page White and Olsen cases was thrown out in St. Point by the Judge that they had against me, only me, did you read it, the reason was that they had been on the calander so long and never tried—now I hope they are sadisfied for coming here that time, and specialy Olson. ... Well this is my last letter in the year 1921. ... Both of us wishing you a Happy New Year and at home God willing with us again ... I remain your Mother Mrs. Krueger

11 THE FIRST PARDON ATTEMPTS

A governor's pardon was Frank and Leslie's only hope at gaining freedom now. In January of 1921, Caroline received a reply to a letter she wrote to Senator Robert La Follette. La Follette told her that he wanted her to make an application for a pardon to Governor Blaine and to the Pardon Board. She expressed in a letter to Frank that she did not know how to make out an application nor had the money to pay an attorney to go ahead with it. The pardon procedure was a learning experience for the Krueger family, but one they would pursue many times in the next decade.

By March of 1921, Leslie was more than ready for Caroline to attempt a pardon and hire a lawyer to do it. She waited to hear from Frank on his approval; he was cautious and thought it possible to do the paperwork without the aid and cost of a lawyer.

Fred Gussert, Caroline's brother-in-law from Greenleaf, visited Attorney T. P. Silverwood in Green Bay in April to discuss preparing the pardon applications for both Frank and Leslie. Silverwood told Fred and Caroline that the application had to be accompanied with an affidavit showing service on the judge and district attorney from Clark County, followed with publication in the press. It was also recommended that a certificate from the warden at Waupun be obtained showing both brothers with good conduct, and a peaceful and obedient nature in their time spent there. Attorney Silverwood also recommended petitions be circulated and signed throughout Clark County asking that the pardons be granted. For his services, including a trip to the governor to hand deliver the paperwork, Silverwood requested $250. He also asked that Attorney John Reynolds assist him, with Reynolds charging an additional $100.

In mid-October, Mrs. Krueger went to see Silverwood and hired him to proceed with the pardon applications. She had saved up money from her summer sale of lambs and had a little sent to her from Leslie from his wages in the twine factory. She questioned the court system at Neillsville regarding reimbursement for the pardon fees and was told they would not pay unless it went in the Krueger's favor.

Louis took on the challenge of going door to door and had good success at getting signatures for the petition, upon Silverwood's suggestion, to accompany the pardon applications. He told his mother he had some hard knocks along the way. Louis used his bicycle to travel as far as he could manage and the early November weather was not kind to him. A group from Owen stopped by one Sunday and wanted to know why the petition hadn't reached up their way.

From T. P. Silverwood at Green Bay to Mrs. Krueger at Withee, November 8, 1921

> Dear Mrs. Krueger
>
> ... I am very glad the petitions are being well signed. You tell me that you have about 250 names so far. Of course if possible I would like many more than that number. ... If you think advisable, I will go down some time next week and have the boys sign the application. I don't want to set the hearing too early on account of getting these petitions well signed.
>
> Yours truly, T. P. Silverwood

Frank made a handwritten copy of his pardon application for his personal records. His writing does not bear a date.

Frank on Getting a Pardon

> On my part I have had considerable patience in this matter. It leaves me in a position such as I never was before to tell the truth. I cannot concentrate myself as I could before the event at our home took place. I have it on my mind nearly all the time. Just because I did not put my name down for war on registration day, men come to my house and destroy it and myself too and those dependent upon me, and when I defend myself one of them gets the worst of it—I have to go to prison for it.
>
> The law seems to be rather queer in falsely sentencing me

and then offering no chance for a second trial. The state puts itself rather in 'beyond good and evil.'

Better take it to the Governor anyway. We ought to have a pardon or a new trial.—F.K.

Late in 1921, Frank's letters home became shorter and less frequent. This was not a good sign; he was becoming more anxious and depressed as time passed. He had been incarcerated for more than three years and hopes for a pardon were all he had to go on. Attorney Silverwood informed Caroline that her sons' cases would be up before the governor on March 1st, 1922. Louis decided that there was no need to continue writing letters to his brothers for they would soon be home again and told his mother to tell them so. All members of the Krueger family had such high hopes for those first pardon applications.

March came and it was such a disappointing time. The first pardon applications failed and were tried again with a new lawyer in January of 1924. These too were ignored.

Through the years the pardon applications submitted to governors in office had to be changed to suit Frank Krueger, or he would not sign them. He did not want to admit guilt nor infer that he wanted forgiveness for a crime he did not commit.

FEBRUARY 6, 1922 LETTER FROM LESLIE TO MOTHER

12 FRANK IS HOSPITALIZED

Caroline's Trip Home
from a Visit to Waupun

Mother to Leslie at Waupun, March 20, 1922

Dear Leslie, Thought I would write today to let you know that I came home safely the next morning, the man that unlocks the doors from the sidewalk said that I could get out on the St. Paul road at 7 o'clock that evening to Oshkosh than have me take a buss to the Soo depot. It would cost a quarter and I did do that way, the train left their at 11 oclock out, so got to Owen in the morning and got home here at 5 oclock, but it was an offul road to walk home, so icy the snow did not all thaw away yet, and it froze on that and it made it so slippery that I thought I'd never get home, but we had sleet Sat, but Sunday morning the wind had turned to the north and that saved our trees. ... Now that I am home again and think over what was said and done their, I know you wont stay their long any more, but seeing Frank look so bad I don't know, I forgot everything what I did want to say. I am told that every one of certain class blames me for everything you done. I keep you boys from going to war by teaching you the Word of God—if I would have not done that everything would have been different. But that dont bother me. God hears every word they say. They don't think that God planned every individual's course before the foundation of the world was laid. ...

Well I sowed my tomato seed to. But we have so many left yet of last year but they might all be gone before the others get ripe. I had quite a lot of beef left, the 2 hind quarters of our beef that we killed so I put it up into fruit cans—they do that down there below so thought I'd try it to. ... Well I read in the Wis. Farmer paper that you had quite a nice time on Washington's Birthday. Mr. Coles must be a good man to take so much pains to do that for the Prisoners, well they are all human being's and God will reward him for doing the best for them. Must close we are well. From your Mother Mrs. Krueger

In March of 1922, Frank Krueger was taken to the prison hospital at Waupun. He had trouble in the past with rheumatism and this condition returned to him again. It may have been due to the dampness of his cell, or the conditions of the daily work he was required to do. From the prison hospital he was transferred directly to the Northern Hospital at Winnebago, an insane asylum, for his severe depression. It can be assumed that the failure of the first pardon attempt brought on his condition or exacerbated it. By June he stopped writing letters home and Caroline became frantic.

Mother to Leslie at Waupun, April 7, 1922

Dear Leslie, Your letter received, am always glad that you are well. Well I had a bad spell yesterday, didn't have such a spell since I had the xray taken, but feel pretty good again this morning. But I feel kind of worried about Frank, him being in the hospital again, but I did expect that the last time I saw him hope he will soon be alright again. I wrote to him if their is a caraprac-tor in town their and he was allowed to have him to get him for they certainly are good for Rhumatisim. ... Your Mother Mrs. K

Frank at Northern Hospital, Winnebago, to Mother, April 16, 1922

Dear Mother, Received both your letters and notice you have not been well either as you wrote you had one of those bad spells again. I hope you are entirely well now. I am in the hospital yet. It does not seem to get better very fast. I feel better today tho than any day I have been here. My right hand is swollen. That is the reason I cannot write better. ... I wish we had never hired Mr. R. All he does is spend our money and seems to do no good. If we had not hired him perhaps we would not be here today. All he wants is money money money. Well I must close for this time, hope the next time I write I will be better in health. From F.

Frank at Northern Hospital, Winnebago, to Mother, May 5,1922

Dear Mother, ... You asked me to write about myself and how I got here. Well I will write as I think best. On morning of the 16th of March, the day you visited both L. and I at the prison I was taken sick with the rheumatism, on the 20th doctor took me to the prison hospital. I was there until the morning of the 24 of April when the guard came and told me to be dressed by 7 oclock as they were going to take me out. I did not ask any questions, but they ordered me to the tailor shop where I was given a different suit of clothes and brought here by one of the prison guards, arriving here about 11 oclock in the forenoon. No I did not see Leslie before I left as I did not get a chance to, altho I wish I had seen him before I was taken out. Am sorry he has to be there alone. I am getting better slowly altho it hangs on to beat everything. My right hand is not well yet, it is hard to straighten the two middle fingers altho I can write with it as you see. Yes, I can write any time it is not the same here as it is in the prison. ... Write me again soon, once a week same as you did before is well enough. ... From Frank

Caroline received a letter in late June from Aden Sherman, superintendent of the Northern Hospital for the Insane at Winnebago regarding Frank's condition. "He is somewhat depressed, and does not speak or associate with others. His mental attitude is such that he takes no interest in writing. His physical health is satisfactory. He will be told to write to you."

In July, Caroline wrote to Leslie, "Well for one thing Frank is feeling much better, not at all like 2 months ago—he wrote last week for which we can feel thankful for to God."

A Stranger Gives Caroline an Organ

A glimmer of hope, a little ray of sunshine, came to Caroline by way of a kind-hearted stranger who knocked on her door in June. The stranger was wishing to sell her an instrument and she told him there was no money for such things. He expressed to her that his music rooms were so full and wished to share an organ with her, at no cost. The organ was delivered shortly before the Fourth of July, 1922. Caroline said it was a beautiful color, like the piano they had before that was destroyed in the shootout. She spent Sundays playing the new organ, a much needed therapy for her broken soul.

Caroline also was given a hydrangea to replace the one that was dug up and removed from her flower garden by some rotten scoundrel when she was in jail. She told Leslie her new plant was very beautiful and had twenty-one blossoms on it.

Leslie at Waupun to Mother, August 2, 1922

Dear Mother, Your letter received Friday—glad to hear that you are well, am well same as usual. Was out in the yard yesterday afternoon, got wet. ... It was awful hot the first of the week—did it hurt the garden much. They cut off the leaves of the tomatoes here, only about half are left on, they ripen faster that way. Well Blain [the governor] went through the prison last week here and at two oclock he made a speech up town. I hope that he gets in again. The warden has a sign up that friends and relatives can not send any more nuts with hard shell on, they wont leave them in, only peanut in shells. If you send me any fruit dont send any plums, they smash up too much. Apples are alright. We had corn to eat here, they are canning it here, also had tomatoes last week. Well the chaplin has a sign up that his topic to speak on is the greatest short story, so I must go and hear what he has to say. They have a different music teacher here, the other one quit. It is dark today, looks like rain, it rained last night. Well hope that both of us will soon be home. ... L. K. The topic the preacher preached about was the prodical son like it says in Luke 15 and 11 verse, he called it the greatest short story, it was good too

More Gawkers at the Farm

Mother to Leslie, August 4, 1922

... A week ago last S. there were 18 people here and last Sunday 13, some of them a week ago. I just cut down one, then a man came here and said who is living here I want to know. I said why what do you want to know that for. Because this is

Government's property. Well what of it I said, he said to the others, lets go over in the barn and other buildings. I said no sir this is private property but I will tell you where Gov. property is—out on the road. So they looked at the north side of the house yet and then they went, if anyone comes like that again I will take a piece of firewood to him. I never done such a thing before but if they will drive me to it, I will, I just simply will not take them sneers from such blue belly Yankeys. All the rest was good ones.

Frank at Northern State Hospital to Mother, October 1, 1922

Dear Mother, Thought I would write you another letter today because it is the First of October. I am writing this letter in the afternoon and it has been a fine day up to this time. Like a day in June.

… While reading one of the [news]papers I happened to see a recipe for making tomatoe catsup as I copied it, am going to send It to you In the letter. You can use It perhaps, try it out anyway.

What you asked in the latter part of your letter. I will say No, I am not bothered any more. Am getting along fine at present. Must close for this time. From Frank

Frank's Recipe for Tomato Catsup

1 peck ripe tomatoes; 4 onions; 1/2 cup sugar; 1 pint vinegar; 2 Tablespoon salt; 1 Tablespoon each: black whole pepper, whole allspice, and cloves (no heads) tied in bag.

1 teaspoon of mace and papricka; 1/2 teaspoon (scant) of cayenne pepper; ginger or ground mustard; Use any or all according to taste.

Boil tomatoes and onions and a few sprigs of parsley, if desired, for 1/2 hour or until soft in a porcelain lined kettle: then press thru a sieve to remove seeds and skins. Return liquid to kettle, add spices in bag and other spices and ingredients. Stir thoroughly. Now boil again for several hours until thick or reduced about one half. Remove spice bag add one more cup vinegar and boil ten minutes longer. Bottle and seal while hot.

I found the tomato catsup recipe in the center of Frank's folded letter. I felt it was a touching expression, with all that Frank was going through, that he would take the time to jot that little recipe down and share it with his mom. It, to me, helps humanize Frank, and humanizes his story a bit more. I think of how times have changed so much, how hard it may have been for Caroline to get to a library, to get good cookbooks. We have everything we want thrown in our faces today via the Internet and take so much for granted. To me the recipe was like a small gift from Frank to his mother, all he could give, the best he could do at that time.

If Frank was feeling better physically, he must have been clearly struggling mentally, as he remained at the Winnebago Hospital for a long period of time.

Caroline wrote to Leslie that she had found a huge flat bullet in one of the kitchen cupboards while cleaning house. It had entered the cupboard through a hinge in the door.

On February 8, 1923, there was a hearing at the Clark County courthouse in Neillsville to appoint R. F. Kountz as Guardian Ad Litem for Frank Krueger. On page two of a legal document from the courts it was stated that Frank Krueger was an insane person, totally incapable of conducting his defense regarding the pending lawsuits, and stated the fact that he was confined to the Northern Hospital for the Insane at Winnebago. The document was signed by Emery W. Crosby, Judge of Clark County, notarized and dated January 30, 1923.

Caroline Hires a New Lawyer

Caroline wrote to Frank in February and told him she had hired a new lawyer that was recommended to her by "one of the high officials." The lawyer told her to tell Frank to "hang tight to that letter that [erased] sent to you, don't let that get away from you." Caroline said the letter she received from the Board of Control did not say that Frank was ever "insane." The new lawyer also told Caroline, "I will not have them boys stay in their much longer, I am going to get them out the way it stands now ..." A new lawyer gave a new ray of hope ... for a little while.

While Frank was a month away from being released from Winnebago and returned to prison at Waupun, Leslie got into a tangle and became argumentative about not receiving the pay he thought he had coming from his twine factory job. As a result of his outburst, he was placed in the Insane Asylum at Waupun Prison for a short time. Caroline sent him a letter with a hair comb in it. She was relieved to hear back from Leslie that he felt fine, and was allowed to go outside every day, thinking that would help his mental state. Frank and Leslie were both showing signs of breakdowns, inevitable after over four years of incarceration.

Leslie at Waupun to Mother, March 18, 1923

Dear Mother, Your letter received. ... Well they tell me that they are going to bring F back in here again. Why is it that the Governor can not do justice. I do not want to go out on parole, I want to be free from these charges. Who told you that they were going to straiten up our case or is it nothing but talk. Who is that Lawyer you got now, what is he going to charge you—did he make a price or have you got any witness to that so that he can not go and say that you have not payed him enough like R did. Make him give you a paper that he is going to defend you for so much. Them mistakes that the judge made aught not to make any difference to the governor, he can let us go with out them being straitened up. No dought it is because they do not want to do anything, it will be four years the 4 of April that we have been here and there is nothing done yet about letting us out that I see. ... Next time I write will be Easter and I don't know much more to write so I guess will close. L K

Mother to Frank at Waupun, March 28, 1923

Dear Frank, received your letter yesterday—see that you were taken back, well I did expect that, seems strange that that pardon can not be acted on, now the Gov. had to sign up that power to have you taken out, and no doubt he signed it again to have you brought back their, but it will show them Neillsville ones that you wasn't quite so insane as they made you to be. ... Last week I finished up my spinning or at least I had to stop so I can do other things, yet knit some, yet got to make some shirts for L and dresses for me and make some bed sheets for the first ones I got as I came up here are going to pieces. The hens are laying good [she had 41] and so I will be able to get me a few things, sold my Onions all of them this week, got 3 cents a pound, now I

have to pick over the beans yet about a bushel and sell them yet,
so I will have enough to do until planting time, my tomoatoes are
up nicely too. ... I wrote to the Lawyer about my tax and he said
that he will look that up when he comes up here, but it does or
will take him a time to look it all up for it is a big job, and by the
way he said he is going to make a good and satisfactory one of
it. Well I see you all 3 last night—you, Leslie and Ennis he came
running up to me smiling, holding out his hand to me, but he
looked so thin and worn, poor boy. Well it was 13 years last Friday
that Pa left us ... From your Mother Mrs. Krueger

Frank at Waupun to Mother, May 30, 1923

Dear Mother, Must write you another letter so you hear from
me again. I was outside and visited with Leslie this forenoon. It
is the first time I have talked to him for over a year. ... How is
the fence Ennis and I put up on the west side? The one we put up
shortly before haying the same year we were taken away. I have
often wanted to ask you in one of the letters I wrote to you, but
I did not know whether any of you ever went there to look at the
fence so did not write you about it. It was a high woven wire fence
and in the short time we had and being short on help we put the
posts quite far apart, so I have often thought about how it was
standing up. I notice you have not as much wood as last year. Well
I have written quite a letter this time so must close. From Frank

When Frank returned to the prison at Waupun he was given a new job
that he kept for several years. He helped do odd jobs in the hospital and the
work was much lighter than what he had done before. It was also warmer
and not as hard on his rheumatism. He did not get paid for his work and was
not able to send money home like Leslie, nor have extra funds to buy fruit,
nuts, or treats on holidays. Caroline questioned the State Board of Control
on Frank's pay and was told, "Frank is not capable as his brother, Leslie,
who is at work in the twine plant and receives the compensation provided
for such work. Your son Frank is being dealt with fairly, and in accord with
the rules. All life prisoners are allotted 3 cents a working day for the first
year of confinement, and one cent a day thereafter. This amount is credited
to his account at the close of the fiscal year. Very truly yours, State Board of
Control John J. Hannan Secretary"

The Auctioneer that Shot Frank

Mother to Frank, August 29, 1923

A man was here a few weeks ago and he was on an auction where the auctioneer was the one that shot you and an old rusty gun came out for sale—all hollered give it to O, that he can go up to Krueger's and shoot them with it, and they kept it up all day. He turned all colors in his face he was so angry, this party said they had a great old time thier, that was good for him.

Leslie to Mother, August 5, 1923

Dear Mother, your letters from the last three weeks received. There is a different board of control in now, the old ones are out of office, that is making these changes. I hear that the president Harding died last week in California so we will have a different president again. Well was that Lawyer of yours up there last week, what did he do when he was up there. Well he can not get us out too soon for me, I hope that I will be home to thresh. When is our case coming up, before the Gov. is going to be in office, the fifth right after labor day. They say that they are going to have a hollow day when they bury the president so we will have a day off. Well I don't know any more to write so I guess will close, am well. L K

Many Deaths in the Community

Mother to Leslie, October 17, 1923

Dear Leslie, Well no doubt you think what in the world is the matter with her that she dont write, well I had to go away and did not come back for 3 days, so I thought I would write like today. I went to get the vases home from the cemetery and their were 9 new graves. Dr. Williams died 2 weeks ago today—he was in the insane asylum then he got better, they got him home and shortly died after that—doped him up and sent him home. ... I don't know what to do about going to see you. I would like to but to make 2 trips, I don't like to do that either, costs to much money, 3 1/2 cents a mile, but O I would like to tell you some things that would make you feel good and happy. ... I remain your Mother Mrs. Krueger

Governor Denies Second Pardon Attempt

Mother to Leslie, January 8, 1924

Dear Leslie, Your letter received today. I see you feel bad about that case but it did come before the Gov. This is what the Lw. wrote, Well the case came up before the Gov. Jan 2nd and I will copy some of the letter of the lawyers that he wrote to me as he was their, he did wish that I would have been their.

"According to schedule I appeared before Gov. Blaine Wed. Jan. 2nd, I urged upon him the pardon of your sons F. and L. The Gov. seemed to be very sympathetic with you of your attitude toward the war. He seemed also to agree with us concerning the actions of the Federal Officers and the bad judgment they exercised at the time of the attempted service of the warrant. It appears however that some of his personal friends in Clark Co. had written him opposing the pardon at this time saying that the boys had not served a sufficient length of time before making thier applic. for Pardon. I was unable to get him to commit himself and therefore can not tell what he is going to do. If he does as he talked however, he will give the boys some consideration. How much I am unable to even guess. I fired the statements signed by the 4 jurors and the special letter written by Mr. ----, one of the jury men, I argued to him that if 4 members of the jury would now say that they favor Executive Clemency their surely must be sentiment in the community for their receiving consideration, this argument seemed to take hold on him, I told him that the jury knew better than anyone else whether or not the boys should continue to serve a life sentence or whether they should now have their time limited. We have done everything that could be done to present the case fairly and completely to the Gov. and if he does not give us favorable consideration it will be because of the letters which were written to him, so you see the same bunch wrote letters and papers to him and if you don't get consideration you know whom he favors, these same ones did not vote for him the last time but this time only from Clark Co."

O them wicked Politics, well it will be the last time for the wicked ones but he might do something yet as he has 22 to

decide on. The Lawyer wrote lets be hopeful. ... How long must
you stay their for to get a pardon or parole? It said in the paper a
woman was in only 1 year and got a pardon, its only them fellows
here and of course Blaine ought not to listen to them the Lawyer
wrote.

Caroline, in her desperation, wrote a letter to Senator Robert La Follette
in 1924 asking for advice and guidance. She wrote herself a copy of the letter
as follows:

Mr. L. F. Dear Sir: Thought I would write to you and see if
you could do something to get F. and L. out of the pen, as they
are not guilty of killing that man and their is no evidence to this
very day on record that they did kill him. An answer to a letter
that I wrote to you once was, that all I need to do was to make
out an app. of Pardon and send it to Gov. Blaine which I did the
first time 2 years ago last March 1922, the second one was 2 of
Jan 1924 but the Gov does not give them boys any consideration,
does not pay any attention to it at all—the last time the Pardon
came up to him my Lawy said he was so crankey that he couldn't
do anything with him. Now the party that killed that man he can
go free, they know who it was no doubt, Gov knows who it was
too. Now I want to ask you if you could or would do or speak for
us to whoever is in office that can do something for them boys,
for them boys are not guilty and they are needed very much
on this place. The last 3 years part of our crops went to waste,
no money, no help (and starvation is looking the people in the
face already). I will send one of the letters of Mr. R. the Law[yer]
that time, he knows the true facts and says they are political
pr[isoners] so why not let them out, its only prejudice that put
them their.

13 FRED GUSSERT DIES

Caroline hired Attorney R. E. Smith of Merrill, Wisconsin, who helped orchestrate the second pardon attempt before the governor. She also wanted him to help straighten out her mortgage on the homestead and get his thoughts and perhaps actions on Attorney Reynolds' overcharge of the family. Here is a copy of the letter she sent to Mr. Smith.

Caroline to Attorney R. E. Smith at Merrill, February 25, 1924

Mr. R. E. Smith, Your letter received today, am very glad that the Bonds have been taken off of us. Now under a separate package I will send some of the letters and other papers which I think you will need, now I have also a few letters which I got from Reynolds and if you think you will need them I will send them to you to. Now as to this money that Fred Gussert paid to Reynolds, you will find in his letters which I am sending to you what he wrote to me, but I will copy the amount and also the amount he had in Green Bay. I would have copied it their but as Mr. Davis sayed that he was willing to give you any information you desired and I also have the same amount in his letters here, I thought I would have you write to him as he is a very good friend to you he said, and he also said Reynolds would have been very well paid with $2,400 that R. went too far and that he Davis would see to it that we would get our Deed back which Louis and I signed on the homestead for to streighten up with Rey. and to get rid of him, that was $2,700. And I think I told you about the morgage as I was their how Rey wanted us to take up a morgage on the land in order to keep that much if they would take away all the rest,

and afterward Rey. said to Fred that it was made in <u>trust</u> for him,
and that way Frank let him have the amount in his letter which I
sent you once now. Besides that he sold our cattle for $1450. and
$250 cash. The cattle was worth that time $3,000 and the sheep
he sold for $10 each and they sold on the market for $25. a head,
that time we were behind the bars and could not help ourselves. I
paid Fred $400 the 12 of Sep 1923, now their is no such word as
<u>trust</u> in that morgage Fred wrote to me, and Rey. said he sold the
cattle for $1250 and it was $1450, you can find that on record
in Neillsville, and in the fall of 1919 (you will find that in Fred's
letter that Rey. addressed to him) that I told him to stop working
for us and I had no money to pay him but he went right on, after
that I told him to take it to the S. [Supreme] Court, now them are
the only 2 cases he was asked to work for us, in the others he
went right on without any permission, now I do not know if I have
explained it right so you can understand it or not, this is what I
wanted to explain to you as I was their but you did not seem to
give me time, but if I must come up their that you do not understand it I will go to see you again let me know by return mail.

 Yours Truly Mrs. C. Krueger Withee, Wis.

 $2,000 is enough for what Reynolds done for us and he also
told me that he would not make an open show of it, as we talked
about it once, if I thought it was too much. I read in the paper of
the new Parole System by the Board of Control to parol all those
that are eligible for Parole that are in good health, how long must
the Boys stay there before they will be eligible, how many years, I
found them well and in good health.

Fred Gussert, Caroline's brother-in-law, died unexpectedly in 1924. His
name was still on the Krueger farm mortgage, which caused the settlement
of his estate to be held up. Fred's son, George, who Caroline had stayed with
after her jail time, had no compassion or patience in getting this matter settled.

Caroline's Generosity

Caroline attended the Lutheran church at Withee in the spring of 1924 and
someone from the congregation came to her door asking for donations one
day in May. The money was to go to poor starving children in Germany who

were "asking for bread, when there was none." She gave them what she could and told Leslie that if they came back, she would donate again.

Frank's letters home were very brief and infrequent again. Caroline became more worried when an old friend stopped to see her who had recently visited both Leslie and Frank at Waupun. He told her that Frank was not well at all and gave her "quite a lingo" about him. Caroline asked Leslie to give her a report on how Frank really was.

Letter from Neillsville Regarding Judgment and Suit of Laino
To Mrs. Krueger from Victor H. Nehs, Neillsville, October 7, 1924

Dear Madam: I wish to call your attention to the partition suit which I started a long time ago for the purpose of having the Krueger Estate sold and divided amongst those who have an interest in it. After starting this action we were in no particular hurry in bringing the matter to a conclusion and now Mr. F. Gussert who owns the mortgage is dead and the attorney for his estate is insisting that this partition action be wound up so that the Gussert Estate can be closed. If this is not done he will of course resort to foreclosure of the mortgage, so in either case there will be developments which will not be favorable to your interests.

Now all that we are interested in in this matter is to collect the Laino judgment and to get for Mr. Jorge Larson what he has stuck in the land [it didn't say how much] and it has occurred to me that perhaps you would now be in a position to pay up these matters, in which event we would drop the partition action. I think we would be willing to even throw off $1000.00 from the judgment if you could see fit to settle it.

Now Mrs. Krueger I believe that you yourself would like to see this matter straightened up so you and the children would know where you are at, and so if you are inclined to something along these lines I will be very glad to co-operate with you and help you to adjust matters to the satisfaction of every one. Of course if you are not willing to do anything there is no other course for us than to take our partition judgment and sell the premises under the order of the Court. Kindly let me hear from you and oblige.

Very truly yours, Victor H. Nehs, Neillsville, Wis.

The Klan at Withee Burns Crosses

Mother to Leslie, March 26, 1925

Dear Leslie … Must write so you hear from us as I did not write last week. Well was to Ben Krom's Auction this afternoon on the Brock place on the Owen road, cows went for from $40 to 45 a head, everything is going down so no doubt the Farmer will end too. One of our cows was to come in the 9th but no show so far and Ben said he would give me $30 for her, if he had payed me cash I would have bought one today. Well we got so far from 14 sheep 24 lambs but 2 were dead so got 22 left, pretty good isn't it? The snow is all gone, but you ought to seen the autos stuck right out here, as it got soft one night a man came in and rapped at the door at 2 in the morning—wanted L to help him out with the team. I did not like that tho, but we could see his car he was from Greenwood where he was of so late and full of strong drink. L had to take him to Withee to the Garage. L charged him $2. We are sawing our pole wood yesterday and tomorrow I do the firing. The Klan's are burning their crosses all around us, at Owen too, right near the Catholic church. Withee had a meeting Friday evening and the people outside never heard such nice music before they said. Madsen built a big brick building right north of Jallings and upstairs is a hall and their is where they are in, they organized last fall in Withee also Maplehurst … well I must close for this time, hoping this will find you well as it leave us. From your Mother

Leslie Asks for Another
Job at the Prison

Leslie to Mother, November 15, 1925

… I was down and unloaded four carload of potatoes, they had them shipped in from outside. I am still working in the twine plant but I go all over sometimes in the warehouse, sometimes switching cars or unloading cars. I told the foreman I wanted a change of jobs and he gave me this work whenever a man is sick or leaves his place I go and take his place—have been so long in that plant that I can do almost any work. ... I guess I will not write thanksgiving day, will write to a paper publisher to stop sending me a paper, its no good anyway, have no more to write. L K, am well

Frank Worries about His Mother's Health

Frank to Mother, January 17, 1926

Dear Mother, Must write another letter so you hear from me. Am glad you are getting along better and hope that trouble leaves you soon. The trouble that has been heaped upon you during these last years has a lot to do with your health. Has a lot to do with your nerves and of course that leads to other troubles. Has Withee a Dr. now? Has it still a drug store? What he told you about those germs I would take with a grain of salt, nothing but a lot of trash ... must close for this time. Am well at present. Frank

Frank to Mother, February 7, 1926

Dear Mother ... I had a talk with the doctor here about your trouble, he said it is acid on the stomach and intestines. He gave me the names of the two makes of Pills that you can get at any drug store. One is No. 156 "Antacid" No. 4. put up by Chicago Pharmacal Co. Take one or two tablets in a little water after meals and as often as necessary.

The name of the other is Calcax. Made by G. D. Searle and Co. Chicago. The directions are the same as the one above. In fact both these are made of the same kind of ingredient's only by different companies and each Company has a different name for it's goods. So if you can get one of those you have both. The doctor said if you would take two (2) grains Calomel once a month and then a dose of Castor oil to take out the Calomel it would help you. You see the stomach has different acids in it and sometimes one gets too much of one kind and therefore it does not digest the food well. Better not eat much after you take physic if you should take the calomel. Well I must close for this time, am getting along well at present. It is snowing here this afternoon. From Frank

In January of 1926, Caroline was given back the important papers that were removed from her house on the day after the shootout by the U.S. marshal, in particular the deed and abstract to her Longwood property. Leslie wondered if they would ever get back the field glass taken as evidence and their guns and other items removed from their home.

Representative Sympathizes

J. D. Beck, representative for the 7th District of Wisconsin, wrote a letter to the Krueger family, probably to Louis or "L. E.," as he often signed his name, in sympathy of their situation but stating his helplessness to solve any of their troubles. Beck said he often thought of the irreparable wrongs and injustice done to the family. He felt that nothing could be done at that time because Congress was still being controlled by the same interests which controlled it during the war. Beck tried to introduce to Congress a resolution to remedy the injustice inflicted upon good citizens during the war but saw no action by the committee to which it was referred.

Caroline Attends Decoration Day Service at Riverside Cemetery

Mother to Leslie, June 1, 1926

Dear Leslie Must write so you hear from us. I was up to your Uncle but did not stay long, came home Friday evening and as I went away I had 19 little chicks as big as a fist and as I came back I had 7 left and L. had them in the house. The Windows were open in the chicken coop and the rats got in and killed them, O I felt blue, I do not have any luck with my chicks this year, they always leave their nests, they just seem as if they don't want to sit any longer. And we got a new milk cow yesterday and one lamb yet, that makes us 39 I think. ... Well I got a letter from F. today but not from you. L. [Louis] had 6 teeth pulled last week, he had so much toothache he will have to get them all pulled on the top, they are all in a bad shape. Did you get them Withee papers I took down there and the fruit. Was on the cemetery Monday, they had a nice program, Owen School band played 2 pieces and the other children sang 2 and one girl spoke a piece and the Minister from Withee made a speech—said that Isaiah Prophesied on 2-4 that war will be no more and we are now first in that transition period but he had only the war from 61-65, he hardly mentioned this war. I wish I could write the whole of it, it was good. But their are O so many new graves again on the west side down that hill already and on the east the same clear down. Hope you are well as we are, Your Mother

Louis' Frustration
on the Farm

Mother to Leslie, November 16, 1926

L. is fixing up the old barn and nothing to fix with, it makes him so mad he would like to leave at times, if they would only left the Barn alone he says, even if they did steel everything, and he is right this old thing isn't to be made warm. But I hope something in our favor will turn up our way.

THE BARN WITH A NEW ROOF SET ON THE OLD STONE WALLS (AUTHOR'S PHOTO)

14 NEW HOPES

Although his name is not given, Caroline first mentions her new lawyer, Attorney Paul H. Raihle, from Chippewa Falls, Wisconsin, in a letter to Leslie dated September 16, 1926.

"Well Blaine [governor] got in at the primary but, perhaps he will do something for you before he goes out. I guess he knows by now that it wasn't the Neillsville fellows that helped vote him in for they didn't, but he done for them what they asked of him, not to let you Boys out yet because they thought that you 2 wasn't long enough for the deed you done—just think, you didn't do the deed at all. A party was here last Mon. and he said why do they keep them boys their, it was one of their own number that shot that man, so is the way they talk. No do not believe what they tell you their that we must make up another or every year a pardon, ours is their and until the Gov. acts on it, it is good. When he acts on it he will either pardon you or refuse it, then first we will have to make up another pardon but we will not have to do that any more. I have a Lawyer so you need not write to any. I will be down their after thrashing is done and tell you all about it ... Are you together on Sat. yet. Am well. From Your Mother

Frank Becomes Obsessed
with his Weight

In July of 1926, it appears Frank developed an obsession with his weight gains and losses. He kept a monthly list of his weight from that point on until 1932. In addition to his weight, he noted a few of his ailments. His weight at the start of his personal record keeping was 173 pounds on July 1, 1926. Frank's lowest weight was 142 during a couple of months in 1926 and again in April of 1931, at which time he noted that he was sick and had missed taking his weight the previous three months. On the last recorded date of November 3, 1932, he weighed 163 at the prison hospital. Perhaps his record keeping was more of a diversion than an obsession for someone who enjoyed keeping stats and calculating percentages, etc.

Frank to Mother, December 5, 1926

Dear Mother, Got your letter yesterday. Am glad you are getting along as well as you are under the circumstances. It would be helpful if you had the insurance, but expect it will be hard to get. They are probably busted and cant pay. It would be hard perhaps to even make them believe it was burnt. It does not even pay to consider putting up another one on account of security the way matters stand now. Barns cost too much money and hard work to be used as targets.

Well I gained some in weight. On Sep 30, I weighed 157 and on Nov 4, 142, so lost 17 pounds between those dates. But on Dec 2 I weigh 152 so gained 10 pounds between Nov 4 and Dec 2. So between the first dates I lost 8 ounces or 1/2 pound per day and on the next I gained 6 ounces a day. Well I feel better about it anyway. My bones are heavy enuf to carry some flesh on them. I don't care about walking around like a skeleton. Oh I'll get along as long as I can get plenty of salts and J. D. Rockefellers Oil. Don't see how I ever got along without that when I was home. Wonderful.

Do visitors go thru the house yet? Tell them you got two Boys in States Prison for trying to defend it. Private property is not defended. Such places as the one you and myself were in in Neillsville and the one they put up east of Owen are "fully" protected. The persons in charge can even call on anyone to help protect them, and if he refused can be fined of it. No such luck for us. Property we put up can be used as targets and be burned down.

Well you can't send any more Withee newspapers for us to read. They put the ban on it here. Won't let them in. We all got

notice to that effect that we were to notify the senders. Don't sell all the good beef, keep some for yourself. I had it in mind several times to ask you when you first came to Withee and you told me before but I only give it half attention. Long time. Seems quite a change. Well I eased my mind enuf so will stop now. Will close.
From Frank

Caroline felt optimistic with a new governor coming onto the scene in 1927, and her new lawyer. She was again worried about Frank and questioned Leslie, "... and how is F. coming, is he getting doped up again—two times he gets doped up and then down again, a great way. ..."

Governor Blaine Denies Pardon Again

Leslie read in the newspaper about the denial of his and Frank's third pardon application before Caroline was aware of it. Governor J. J. Blaine wrote a letter to both Frank and Leslie at Waupun, dated December 16, 1926, stating his reasons on the denial.

"This case arose during the war, and grew out of the failure of the Krueger boys to submit to the draft. The record clearly discloses that the mother of these two boys and the boys held to a certain religious sect that advocated resistance to the draft, and I am convinced that it was their religious fanaticism that led to the unfortunate act.

"They held literally to the commandment, "Thou shalt not kill," which, of course, precluded actual participation in war. The mother still insists that they did not kill anyone, and therefore have observed the commandment. It is unnecessary to comment upon the merits of the case, inasmuch as they were convicted by a jury and the conviction was sustained by the Supreme Court.

"However, there is this consideration, that notwithstanding such conviction, there appears to be no repentance.

"The unfortunate situation in this case is that all of this trouble might have been avoided but religious fanaticism, mixed with the war urge, has for its toll two lives and the incarceration of these two men in prison.

"While there are elements in this case that would have justified a conviction of murder in the second degree, the petition is denied, without intending to prejudice the action of future Governors who may find that the conduct of these men in prison would justify a review of the case from the other standpoint.

"Therefore denied. J. J. B."

Mother to Frank, January 5, 1927

I was so glad to know that you are fairly well. Well I suppose you felt blue for what Blaine done but yet he didn't do so bad, he left it open for the next Gov. The way it said in the papers is not all of it, only the worst part was put in. Now I will tell you how I found it out—a party, O I might have seen them 1/2 dz times in my life, lives far away from here, wrote to Blaine why he didn't let you out and B. sent him a copy of the memorandum and that party sent it direct to me, you have a better show now. It also said that their are elements in this case that would have justified a conviction of murder in the second degree but I wont say any more what the rest is. ...

Frank to Mother, January 16, 1927

I did not see anything in the papers that B. had put in. And it is just as well that I didn't. He might as well have kept still after waiting so long. I don't see how he makes out that 2nd degree stuff, whether it is that or 50 or 100 prove anything. I did not expect anything anyway and in a way do not blame him. We should have got a better deal in Neillsville, that is the place where matters should have been proven. Wonder where he gets that sect stuff from. Strange ideas. Repentence. Well we will have to be contented I suppose.

You wrote something about the constitution. Wonder how often that is violated. If you have one, read Article 4. and see where it was violated in our case. ...

Mother to Frank, February 24, 1927

See you are fairly well which I hope they will stop feeding you with D. & R. Oil. I will have to take medicine for some time yet Dr. says. ... Well their isn't a family but what has its trouble with this or that sickness, oh my, not a home. Dr.'s wife told me they are getting a law passed that will prevent sickness, everyone has to come and get an examination every so often a year, so if there is anything they can stop it right off. ... Was you allowed to see Leslie the 22nd, you wrote about 3 more months then you will be outside again. I guess before that you know I am always busy, I wont give up until you are free. ... This summons is going to start up something they thought was dead long ago but something dont stay dead, truth will rise sooner or later—is bound to. Well must close for this time, have been spinning quite a little bit this winter, will soon finish up then make some quilts yet. From your Mother

Leslie Has Trouble
with His Teeth

Frank to Mother, March 6, 1927

Dear Mother, Must write again. Both your letters have quite a bit of news. Hope you are getting over the cold you have. Better be careful now as it is so near spring. Keep your throat clean by gargling and that will do a lot toward keeping the cold away. Remember how Pa used to like thick milk you used to serve at meals? Get you some of that, that is make it, and eat it. It will do you good perhaps. ...Yes I see Leslie on the 22 of last month. He is having trouble with one of his teeth of which the dentist is to blame. L. had a tooth pulled. The dentist told him to have a bridge put where the tooth was, to keep the other teeth from spreading. So L. told him to go ahead. In putting in the bridge, it was necessary to anchor it to the other teeth. This made it necessary to drill them to fasten the bridge. In doing this he drilled too deep in one and instead of treating the sore, went on and finished the work. Later it began to bother, but fastening from the inside. Now he has another dentist and he has been doctoring the tooth since before Christmas and perhaps will for some time. More botch work. Makes L. pain and a lot of trouble. ...Well I gained some last month. I bought 5 1/2 pounds of peanuts for Feb. 22 and ate them and gained 7 pounds. I have a book here in the cell that shows the "Composition of a peanut." thot I would draw it and send it to you just for curiosity. Will close for this time. From Frank Peanuts have 2560 calories per pound. [A pie chart diagram drawn by Frank was enclosed showing the composition of a peanut.]

Dear Leslie ... I finished spinning yesterday and today I am going to wash the yarn so I am thru with that. O I have lots of work to do—clean house, all of the summer sewing, knitting yet, and we didn't even eat a forequarter of our beef so now I will have to can as much as I have empty cans and make mincemeat so when you come home I will feed you on canned food. F wrote about the trouble you have with that tooth, too bad such botch work—jerk them out and get a set rather, L. will have to do that before long to. Well must stop. ... Mother

Frank Expresses Rare Grit

Frank to Mother, July 3, 1927

Dear Mother, I got your letter last Friday the 1st of July and when I saw it on the bed I made a grab for it, anxious to know what move is going to be made next, but it was just as I thot they would do. They have about lawed till they have come to the point to where they can do nothing, except one thing and that is stall the whole matter. If it has come to a thought of taking $300 less than the mortgage states, they can come to a conclusion of taking a whole lot less than that, in fact we are not to pay one cent on it [presumably referring to selling land to pay off the lawsuits].

One does not know what to think at times. A piece of property like we had before it was all damaged and attempt made to pickle it up was certainly an eyesore to many. When one stops to think of it. Anyone with some authority has a mouthful to say and is here today and somewhere else tomorrow. Anything but the owners. Well I won't write no more about it. The general conclusion and that is for us to keep our mouth shut, but I have the last say of it anyway. I have so much determination in me yet even where I am now. From Frank

Frank to Mother, September 4, 1927

Dear Mother, Must write a few lines again. Have a holiday tomorrow here so guess I will not write even if given the privilege, as I think it not necessary. ...

I read a book that I wish you could read also. I am sure it

would interest you and you would get quite a lot of satisfaction from it. The name of it is, "The House We Live In" by this he means the body. It is written by William Elliot Griffin, and printed by Funk and Wagnall's Company, New York City, New York. If you write to them and request the price they will send it to you and you can order it direct. Should not be over $1.00 at the most. Perhaps you can get it from some Library. Perhaps from the Library in Madison could borrow it.

Am getting along well at present. From Frank

Caroline Mentions Ennis but won't Say Much

In 1927, Caroline and Louis had the grave exhumed where Ennis was said to be buried at the Riverside Cemetery near Withee. The body had been placed between the remains of Louis Krueger Sr. and Ennis' brother Robert. Both Caroline and Louis denied that the body was Ennis' after viewing the remains. I have found no mention of the body exhumation in the letters. The following letter appeared to discuss the subject without discussing it!

Mother to Frank, July 10, 1927

… I was over to the cemetery last Sat, toward evening and we had something done there that stirred up an offul hornets nest a while ago, but will not say anything further about it, nor dont write anything about it, as we were in need of that on this case, I will tell you all about it when I see you, no doubt the 8th of Sep as I can not go to see you any sooner then the ----- will come up [probably referring to another pardon effort]. …

Caroline tells both Frank and Leslie she will "tell them more" when she goes to visit them in prison soon. It seems she wants to prove the point that Ennis is still alive in their hearts and minds, as well as hers, and perhaps in the minds of any unknown readers of her letters sent to the prison.

Mother to Frank, September 12, 1927

... Well I will ask Mrs. D. Tufts, she is Librarian in Withee, if she has that book, she told me once any book I would want I should tell her and she would get it for me, she wants me to get books to read in the Winter but I never did, but this one I will try. She is always so good to me, also Dan. and her Mother, but D. was here and shot too, he has been paralized several times already ... yes tomorrow it will be 9 years, O I daren't think of that, it always hurts so, poor Ennis—but where did he have to wander around all these years, well I will tell you more about it when I see you in little more than 3 weeks. ... Am glad to hear you feel good and well I feel pretty good to now again. From Your Mother

Mother to Leslie, September 12, 1927

Well Wednesday it will be 9 years that this happened and poor Ennis, where did he have to wander all this time, but will tell you more when I see you ...

Mother to Leslie, Octber 4, 1927

Dear Leslie, Your letter also F. received today, am always glad to get them as it is such a comfort to hear from you both. I wish E. would write too poor soul, but we musn't talk ...Yes I thought I would go to see you, but got a letter from the Lawyer, he said that it was going to be brought up this month but he is a man that will not say anything, only what you press out of him by force, and I do not like to do that as L. and I was there. He said I am going to get them boys out, one that knows said that man had worked hard on that case this whole year, and when he wrote last Sat. he said only be patient a little longer. I was so mad but he said better keep still, you don't know what he is up to, so I don't know what to do, let him off and get another or wait a few weeks yet for this one to act, see what he will do. O I feel so discouraged, well will see him and if not it wont take me long to get the one you have there. Well we got a new milk cow yesterday so now we have 7 to milk. L. is digging the rest of the taters now, it stoped raining a little. Their was a big Funeral went north today, don't know who it was, also the Hurse went by Sun. and came right back for the 1 o clock train—wasn't gone long. Now I have to take up my Onions yet, it is getting time for them too. We have nice cabbage too this year and carrots, them are in too yet but we will leave some of them outside and cover them up for the spring. Well must close for this time, we are well, hope the same of you. From Your Mother

I believe the issue of opening Ennis' supposed grave was not one they wanted to converse about in letters that were censored, but probably was discussed only on visits to the jail. Both Louis and Leslie in later years pondered over the whereabouts of their missing brother Ennis. Both felt he was still out there somewhere, but afraid to come home. Frank wasn't sure at first, but later doubted his death as well.

Fellow Wanted a Bullet

Mother to Frank, September 27, 1927

... A week ago Sunday a fellow from New Richmond came in and wanted a bullet for a souvenir, just think I would not given any to him if I'd had a car load. L. said sell him one for $25.00. I said no.

Attorney Reynolds' Justification to Raihle
of His Contested Charges

Caroline's lawyer, Attorney Raihle, forwarded a copy of the following letter to her in early October regarding her wish to sue John W. Reynolds for overcharging her.

Mr. Raihle told Caroline that if she did not give Reynolds the authority to sell her cattle or appropriate her money that she might have a chance to recover some of her money back from him. He requested $50 from her in advance if she wanted him to go ahead with the attempt. Raihle was willing to take on the case but warned Mrs. Krueger that it would be difficult, doubtful, and hotly contested.

Mr. Reynolds had recently been elected as attorney general. A suit against him would be hard fought, with much at stake against his growing career and popularity.

Dear Sir:

The $1450 mentioned in your letter of September 28th was received for the cattle of Mrs. Caroline Krueger.

They were sold by her authority and her request and the money given to me to apply on fees for not only defending her sons but herself also for first degree murder. It is true that she did not receive any of this money as she gave me full and complete authority to apply it towards our fees (I was in partnership at the time. The firm name was Kaftan & Reynolds). Mrs. Krueger was notified at the time of sale of the amount received and was apparently perfectly satisfied. Before I received another cent, except the $1450., I had prepared and tried the murder case in Circuit Court where Mrs. Krueger was acquitted and the two boys convicted. I had paid out the expenses from this sum close to $500.

We represented them also in five different civil cases where herself and sons were charged with shooting different parties.

We represented her also in the United States court in a case for aiding her sons in evading the draft. We went to Superior with her ready for trial. The case was put off, however, and never brought to trial.

Our total charges for the work we did for her amounted to the sum of $6793.93. We paid out in expenses (an itemized statement of which we sent her) the sum of $1918.61. Up to July 30th, 1920 she had paid us the sum of $3303.85 towards our fees and expenses mentioned in this paragraph, making a total of $5222.46.

After being unsuccessful in getting our money, we were compelled to sue for the balance of our fees. Personal service of the complaint was made on her and her two sons on the 30th day of July, 1920. We put in proof before the Circuit Court of Clark County and the presiding judge made his findings on the 3rd day of September, 1920, in which he found that our charges were reasonable and gave us judgment for the balance which with costs amounted to $3581.59. We sent the execution to the sheriff of Clark County but before proceeding to sale, Mr. Gussert, her brother in law, now deceased, at her request paid us the sum of $2700 and we made an assignment of the judgment to him. We paid Mr. Silverwood out of the $2700 the sum of $300 (at my suggestion and with Mrs. Krueger's consent Silverwood was retained to assist me in the trial of the murder case only). So we received, for all the work we did, the sum of $5703.85 which any attorney in the state, knowing the work we did, even yourself, would say was reasonable.

It has cost Mrs. Krueger, with what she paid us and the expense, $7918.46. We used our best endeavors together to settle those civil matters before the expenses or attorney fees were near as high, but were not successful.

Although this matter is res adjuciata long ago, and although she has taken this matter up with several attorneys who wrote to me at Green Bay, I deemed it courteous to you to reply in full, although Mrs. Krueger is fully conversant with all the facts.

Yours very truly, John W. Reynolds, Attorney General

It would take a year and a half before a decision was made, but Caroline did hire Attorney Raihle to sue John Reynolds for excessive fees.

Caroline's Christmas Letter to Leslie, 1927

Mother to Leslie, December 18, 1927

Dear Leslie, It is very lonesome here today, not a person on the road no cars running today, the snow plow came up from the South last Sunday night and the cars were on the go again, then the S. Plow came back the night before this last storm and it filled up the road again, we have quite a little snow. You two are to write to us today, I have been thinking of you all day long today, well I will not see you this week as I wrote to the Gov. if this case is coming up the 20th as the Lawyer had it in the paper and I got the letter or answer yesterday from him saying, "The Governor directs me to reply to your letter of Dec. 12th in which you ask when F. and L. K. Pardon Appl. will be heard, the record in this case is not complete at this time (the 20). However, we think it will be complete before the next Pardon hearing, which will be

January 4 – 1928, write us again at a later date, and we may give you a definite answer..." So you see I do not have to go this week so will not see you, dont know what I will send to you, if I come down their I could buy it their then, but will see we was offul disappointed but what is to be done about it. I was so in hopes we would eat xmas dinner together here, I was busy canning chickens this week—they were them late roosters, got a few left for xmas and N. Year, done some sewing this week made me a new dress and L. a woolen shirt but this week am going to make a quilt of wool for another bed as it gets cold toward morning. Wishing you a M. Xmas and H. N. Year, I remain your Mother—am all over with my cold.

December 19 letter from Frank to Mother (author's photo)

Mother to Leslie, December 26, 1927

...We got a Christmas tree and we will let it hang until I come back from Madison—the Lawyer wrote I should be their on the morning of the 4th next week Wed. Well I have lots more to

1928—Another Pardon Application Denied

Caroline appeared before the governor at Madison with her lawyer, Frank E. Bachhuber, law partner of Brayton E. Smith of Wausau, whom she hired to submit the pardon applications this time. After the Madison visit, she took a train to Waupun to visit her sons, and continued home that same day. She was again hopeful but only for a short time. Governor Fred R. Zimmerman denied the Krueger brothers pardon. Charges by Smith and Bachhuber to Caroline for drawing up the paperwork and making two trips to Madison were $100.00. Although faced with another denial, this was another step closer to the pardon that would finally give Frank and Leslie their freedom.

Attorney Paul Raihle was hard at work setting up a trial with Judge Grass of Green Bay regarding whether or not Mrs. Krueger had a right to sue John W. Reynolds for fraud. Raihle was of the opinion that fraud had been committed. Raihle also expressed his great hopes that Frank and Leslie would be given a new trial. He wanted to secure another attorney with great experience, and study all the evidence carefully. He hoped that with a new governor coming in the following year it would increase their chance of getting a new trial. Attorney Raihle also told Caroline he felt very strongly that the brothers should and would eventually be pardoned. He agreed not to charge any fees until he accomplished something for her.

15 THE INSANE ASYLUM

By the end of January 1928, Leslie wrote to let his mother know he had been taken to the Central State Hospital for Criminally Insane at Waupun. He apparently became angry and felt cheated about the money in his prison account, money he earned from working in the twine factory and other odd jobs, and lost his temper. He had a few strikes against him from years past, although they were not of a serious nature. Perhaps they added up enough to put him over the line and to be labeled "insane." When Leslie was admitted to the hospital, he had $86.62 transferred to his account from the prison, money he had earned from prison work.

Although somewhat embarrassed when having to tell others where they were being held, Caroline felt a sort of relief when her sons were patients in the asylums. Frank had been in hospitals on two separate occasions prior to this. Hospital patients had more freedom, were not forced to work at hard labor, spent more time outside, and had fewer restrictions on receiving and sending mail. Leslie's condition was deemed serious enough that it kept him in the hospital or insane asylum for the remainder of his incarceration—over four years.

Caroline received a letter from Warden Oscar Lee at Waupun State Prison in early February of 1928. He told her that Leslie was not sent to the hospital on their order. Warden Lee said that Leslie was examined by a committee of alienists (someone specializing in the legal aspects of psychiatry), was found to be insane, and ordered to be transferred to the hospital by the State Board of Control. Caroline wrote to Frank that Leslie's letters were just as usual from the hospital, perhaps even better. She felt there was nothing to his insanity charge, that it was only politics.

Mother to Leslie at Waupun redirected to Central State Hospital, February 9, 1928

Dear Leslie, Got your letter day before yesterday, was offul glad you wrote Well keep up good courage, it wont be long any more before the Gov. will act and he can not pardon you because you did not do the deed, he has just got to give orders to let you both go, for thier is no evidence you 2 killed that man but only lies, just as you wrote in your letter, and I suppose that they can not do anything any more they that put you there. I should think them officials had enough counts against themselves without more. How can they put you in such a place without an Exam— why it is impossible and to get away with it, as I was in the Gov. Office we had a long talk and by that I know what is comming but it takes time as I said to you. ... L. says Satan is trying his last and the night is the darkest just before the dawn, help is not far away. ... Be strong and brave and study your Bible. God will soon help you out. Don't write to no lawyer. From Your Mother

Mother to Leslie at Central State Hospital, February 28, 1928

Dear Leslie, did not write last week so must write a little earlier this week. Well how do you feel now that you are more outside, I suppose lots better. It isn't really nessesary to write every week but I do like to hear from you. Well I am glad you got your money if that was the trouble with you and them in prison, you ought not to have let them keep it so long, but did you get all that was due you? Well it is no more than right for them to inspect every thing that goes in their. They make such a talk if they hear that you are in the Hosp. that we hate to address your letters thier so will put on B., only they want to know everything. Well got a letter today from Mrs. Van H. from Owen saying that Granpa passed away Sun. Evening at 10:45 and will be buried Wed. 2 p.m. be sure and both of you come, so I will go as far as Owen. L. can not go, that is Mr. Van's Father he is old. ... Well I wish that we would soon hear that you are set free but 7 lawyers said to me that is an offul big mess to clean up and it has got to be cleaned up to the deepest detail, every bit has to be looked up and righted so you see it takes time to do that all, but it will come out all right. Well last Frid in all that cold a little lamb arrived but L. was just out in the barn and so he took it and run into the chicken coop with it and now it is doing fine, but don't expect any more just now, he got loose once. Well last Sat. I milked for once and where Hewitt [Sheriff Hewett of Clark County] knocked me down that time, that finger hurt me so I could hardly use it, we are going to have 9 cows this summer so you must come home and do the milking I guess. Well I have some more to write but will close for this time—are well. From Your Mother Mrs. Krueger

How Frank Celebrates Mother's Day in Prison

Mother's Day was treated as a "holiday" in prison so the inmates were allowed to write an extra letter home on that day. Frank took advantage of that on Mother's Day in 1928. He told his mother how they celebrated the day with the handing out of paper carnations. Some prisoners wore them on their coats. Those who had mothers living received a red carnation and those whose mothers had passed on were given white ones. As Frank looked around at the colors of all the carnations of those who surrounded him, he was thankful to be wearing a red one. He reflected on how close he came to losing his mother on account of the acts of man on that fateful day in September 1918. He longed to be home so he could repair the well, a pressing issue at this time.

Caroline's Decoration Day 1928

Mother to Leslie at Central State Hospital

Dear Leslie, Your letter received Tus. But I did not write last week either. Well was on the cemetary yesterday, their were cars from Brants corner North and South and nearly to the river west on both sides of the road and I was the only one their with a horse and buggie—tied her at the barn east of the Cem. on the hill and then I had to wait until all them cars left. O their are a lots of new graves again this year. Well Orin Miller's oldest daughter died with the flu and pneumonia, left a 1 year old girl and her husband. ... Well must close. From your Mother Mrs. Krueger

Frank's Reflections on Attorneys, Berries, and Airplanes

Frank's mental health was improving—his letters were becoming lengthier and contained more content. He was allowed to spend much more time outside and only had to work half days on Saturdays, so that may have been the reason. He wrote home in August that his group was allowed to go outside for one hour every day, week days and Sundays. The work day had also been shortened by a new ruling.

He asked his mother if it was a good berry year and longed to be home to help pick and eat them. Caroline loved picking berries and in season she picked blueberries, blackberries, and raspberries. If she had extra, she would sell them. Blackberries were her most profitable wild fruit and she picked them along their nearby woodlot and took them to town.

Frank wished he had never hired an attorney and felt he would have been better off without Reynolds, whom he called an old paper hanger. He had the opinion that Reynolds aided in the loss of their property, the mix-up with the Gussert estate, and thought he might be out of prison if he had taken charge of their legal matters himself. He also faulted the judge at Neillsville and the mob for making advances on the family, who was only defending their own property. Expressing himself and venting were probably good therapy for Frank. When he wrote longer letters he seemed in better health, and there was little else for him to do.

Frank had a message for Louis in August of 1928. He told Louis not to go near any airplanes, to stay away from them. Caroline also had an aversion to airplanes. She felt they would be the most dangerous weapons in the next World War, so wanted nothing to do with them.

A Stranger Returns Pa's Razor

Mother to Leslie at Central State Hospital, August 29, 1928

Dear Leslie ... Well a couple of weeks ago a man came up the back steps, he said how do you do Mrs. Krueger. I answered him and he said, I came to make Restitution. I said all right (not knowing what he ment) so I let him in. He said as you had this trouble here I like all the rest helped myself to things here, and

now I want to return them, the sweater he said I wore out and
I want to have you set a price, dont care how much you charge
and these (their was Pa's razor and another one and a muffler)
he gave back. He said that time I was not converted but now I am
and you don't know how my consciense has condemmed me, O it
was bitter and I could not bring myself to return them, but I had
no rest day or night so here they are and you have no idea how
hard that was to come here. O he said it was bitter bitter hard to
come in here from the road and he was as pale I felt kind of afraid
of him fainting. Well I talked good to him and told him I thank
God, for this razor as that was Pa's. He bought that as he was
15 years old for 50 cents and he never had any other one, then
he shook hands with me and said now I am glad I rejoice in my
heart that this is off my consciense and he was so glad, so I got
2 pieces back anyway, the one of Pa I was glad we got that. Well
perhaps I will see you next month if nothing turns up in the mean
time, your Mother

Leslie's Horizons Broaden at the Asylum

As Leslie was no longer at the prison or working in the twine factory, he learned a few new trades while at the insane asylum hospital. In the spring of 1928, Leslie started weaving baskets. Frank wrote home about it: "Quite a trade. Wonder if he ever dreamed of such a thing. That's what one may call going back to the indians. Perhaps he can use it to good advantage some day and make a little at it." Caroline told Leslie she could use a large basket for egg gathering. He wrote home about making two chairs of marsh grass in April and he thought they looked fine. He also began working daily in the carpentry shop.

With a more sedentary lifestyle, Leslie began to put on weight. He had a ravenous appetite, and started craving candy more than fruits.

He also took a greater interest in reading and wanted his mother to help him purchase some books on shorthand so he could master it. Frank suggested "The Gregg Shorthand Manual." He said it could be ordered from The Gregg Publishing Co. in Chicago, Illinois, for $1.50. Leslie did secure a copy of the manual and practiced shorthand a bit.

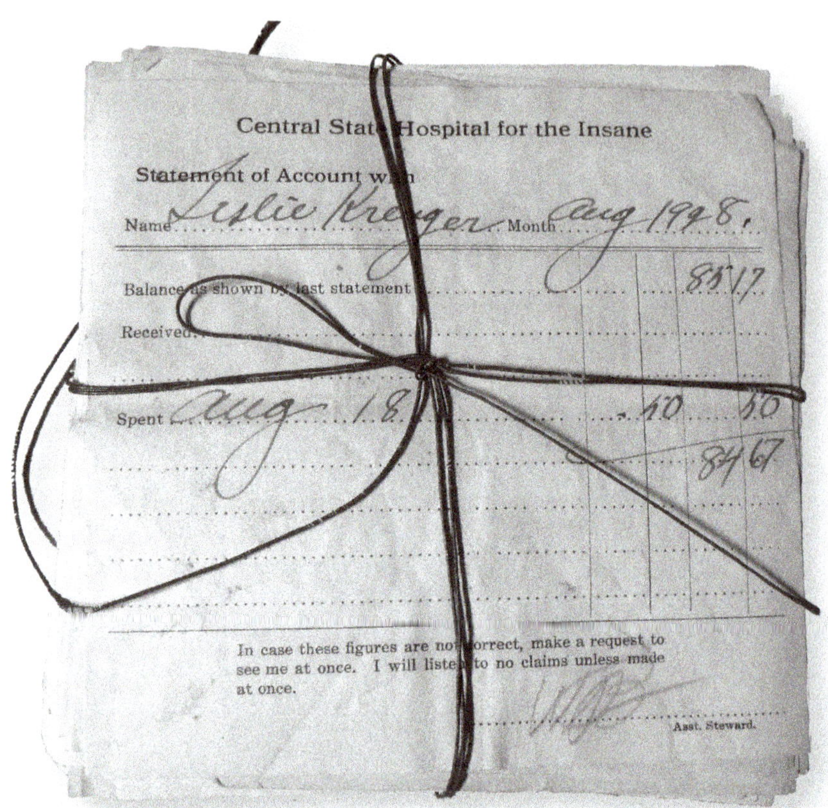

LESLIE'S STATEMENT OF ACCOUNT WITH THE CENTRAL STATE
HOSPITAL FOR THE INSANE, AUGUST 1928 (AUTHOR'S PHOTO)

Mother to Leslie at Central State Hospital, December 13, 1928

Dear Leslie... [in regard to the whitetail deer season just
passed] Deer—only 5 passed here, it is very dangerous to go
hunting now days—9 lives were taken in 1 day, just think, is the
deer or pleasure worth it. ... You wrote of snow, we have no snow
here at all cattle and sheep are out in the pastures—the young
stock L. gives them some straw in the morning and nothing in
the evening and they are full. I am glad of it to as our hay isn't
so plentiful this year. ... Well I got a letter from the Law [Attorney
Raihle] and he is well again, now he had quite a time with the flu,
had to have a light operation too, but he writes that he hoped
nothing would interfere with going ahead with this case, now he

asked the judge for another date perhaps next week and then I
will go to see you both. I have been so disgusted with it, O you
dont know, wanted to go to see you so long ago and thier is some
more going to be done for you but will tell you when I see you ...
hope you are well. From your Mother

Christmas Letters—1928

Mother to Leslie at Central State Hospital, December 19, 1928

Dear Leslie, your letter received Tus, also F.—am always
glad to get them and hear that both of you are well. L and I
are well again to from the flu. ... No I never found out what the
number of F. watch is, why, his watch is in the safe their in Prison.
I seen it once. ... Well L. sent you and also F. each a xmas box but
I told him not to buy so much as everything is so high priced now
just before xmas and I will get you something when I get their.
Got a letter for the Lawyer saying this is comming up against
R. on the 3 of Jan. in Green Bay, so if nothing else turns up, will
see you the day after that. ... L. has gone after a load of hay—he
bought about 4 ton for $30. We are afraid we will not have
enough and then in the spring the price will be way up when any
one has got to have it. Where are the Phesants now that were their
thru the summer, do they go inside? ... Can I stay longer than
one hour with you, let me know in your next letter. Wishing you a
merry xmas from your Mother

Caroline always liked an accounting of the fruit she sent to Leslie. She
was always leery of someone stealing it along the way, so Leslie wrote to tell
her he received fifteen apples along with the peanuts, his Christmas present
from Louis. The pheasants were still around at Christmas time in the yard of
the hospital but Leslie did not know where they stayed at night. They liked
to come around for something to nibble on and were a source of diversion
for him. Leslie said Christmas was "the greatest day of the whole year on
which the greatest thing took place." His religious beliefs were childlike and
innocent. His faith no doubt pulled him through the bad times.

Frank wrote his mother a letter on Christmas Day and thanked her also
for the apples she had sent him. He had already eaten them but received two
more at lunch time in the prison. It cost Louis 27 cents to send the apples

to Frank and Leslie. At times it was a struggle to find an appropriate box to mail the fruit in. Louis would often go to Withee in search of a box for their shipment. Along with his letter, Frank enclosed a Christmas card that was given to him at the prison. He noted how the card did not mention anything about a prosperous New Year, attempting to inflict a touch of humor in his writing. He wondered how Leslie was doing with his practice of shorthand. And he gave some extensive details on how to repair the pipe on the furnace at the Krueger home. It had rusted and needed repairs, normal maintenance for a stove pipe in a cellar. Frank also told his mother to make sure that all the spider webs were swept away from the stove pipes and the floor joists in the cellar that surrounded the furnace. He was always thinking of ways to keep the family safe and sound, still the big brother, the man of the house, even though he'd been gone from home for more than ten long years. He also fretted about the repairs to the well.

Drilling a New Well

Mother to Frank, February 7, 1929

Dear Frank, Your letter received, am glad you are as well as you always write, no doubt you will want to know about the new well first of all, they went down 92 feet and all at once the water came up just as they pulled up the last bucket of dirt before supper, and the water came up too, so they came in and ate and then they went home to Greenwood and L went out to measure it, and it was 21 feet from the top in sand rock, so it's quite a bill he put in all new pipes 72 feet but our cylinder and the bill was $200.00 but we have water now, but as L filled up the can's and pails for the last time out of the old well that Pa and I and a few others helped dig, I nearly cried as I see him pump the last stroke, now all of Pa's work is gone but the shed and that is leaking all over to, got to be reshingled. But the Bible says all things shall be made new, so when Pa come back (or is ressurected from the dead) he will see a big change here. L sees his mistake now—6 or 7 years ago I told him he should get someone to curb up the old well, yes, yes, and that always was his way. Now that he has this bill to pay he sees it, he is now piping it to connect it with the underground, above the ground into the old well to get it to the barn and water the stock. ... We are all well, hope you are too. Your Mother

More about Ennis' Watch

Mother to Leslie at Central State Hospital, April 2, 1929

Dear Leslie ... It said in the paper that Gov. Kohler said that he would denie every pardon that was brought to him (if that is true) then why didn't he write to the Lawyer on time, then they would not have been brought up to him. ... I know it is hard for you there but just be patient, it is hard for us here to, for we have a hard row to hoe to, the barn so cold that the cattle freezes. Well must begin to write something else, you asked about R. [Rob's] watch as I was their, yes we got that back as I asked O'Conner where it was—he cursed and swore at me, but Lamont was their too and stoped him, said why are you treating her like that, hasn't she got the right to ask for Ennis watch, he said yes, but he said he didn't know where it was, about 2 weeks after, the mailman came in and brought the watch, so it shows they knew were Ennis was and got the watch for me—if that isn't cheek what is it. ... L moved the windmill, he put it on slippers and boards and ankered it with fence wire and hay rope then pushed it with a crowbar, first one side then the other, so got it over that way. We are well, hope you are too. Mother

Finally it was unveiled that the pocket watch that was returned to Caroline from Ennis' possessions, was indeed the same watch that had belonged to his deceased brother, Robert Krueger. This leads one to believe that Ennis was indeed captured or shot and killed at some point. It does not necessarily show that the man who was shot in the barn in southern Taylor County, a week after the shootout at the farm, was Ennis. The denial of Ennis in the exhumed grave may have been part of the strategy to dismantle the case and help get Frank and Leslie out of prison. Recall back to the letter written from Caroline to Frank on July 10, 1927: "... I was over to the cemetery last Sat, toward evening and we had something done there that stired up an offul hornets nest a while ago, but will not say anything further about it, nor dont write anything about it, as we were in need of that on this case."

Another Failed
Pardon Attempt

Attorney Raihle had been organizing another attempt at pardons for Frank and Leslie late in 1928. He had a great deal of trouble in getting Frank to fill out another application, but decided to write and give Frank the date that the pardon would be presented before the governor in March along with the application that just needed signing. After much pleading, begging, and a little bit of the silent treatment from his mother, Frank did sign another application.

At this time Frank was feeling bitter about having built the large home and barn, suggesting that it might have been better luck to them if they had continued to live in the old log cabin on their homestead. Prior to the shootout, neighbors had been questioning the Kruegers as to when they were going to better their living conditions, build a modern home that was warm in winter, and straighten up their place. So they did, in a big way, and in all actuality, Frank thought it only brought jealousy into the neighborhood.

Unfortunately, this pardon was also unsuccessful after being presented to the governor in March of 1929. Attorney Raihle sent his sympathies to Caroline in a letter and suggested they try again in six months.

Caroline Has Trouble
with Her Hand

Mother to Leslie at Central State Hospital, April 24, 1929

Dear Leslie, your letter received yesterday, also Franks. He feels offul hurt about that Sheriff [Hewett] knocking me down that time, the next day after this trouble and now that hand troubles me, pains me so much two times I could not sleep a while ago. I got to keep it bandaged all the time. Dr. Neilson told long ago that time that I would have trouble with that later on, so Mon. I went to the Dr. and he too said the same thing, he cannot heal it, do anything for it, only hot water will kill the pains. Well we got in our last cow yesterday so we are thru with that, now to milk and that hurts my hand when I strip, only it don't hurt if I milk with both hands. ... L fixed it so that we got the water in the house again, and he piped it so that it runs thru the cellar into that pipe (that used to run the water up in the attic) and thru to that pipe that goes to the barn so all we have to do is to start the windmill and let it pump, now we have got the water in the bathtub again. All but in the toilet, they smashed that, but perhaps before winter we might be able to buy another one [Caroline told Frank they might order a new toilet from the governor—Kohler, I presume], he had to break up the bathroom floor to get at pipes that were busted but he has not got that finished up yet, well the paper is full. ... Hope you are well, From your Mother

Mother to Leslie at Central State Hospital, June 13, 1929

Dear Leslie, ... F. and the rest of the prisoners he wrote gets one hour outside every day. No the Gov. dont let any out, he dont do right their but he will see his mistake when it is to late—his Sectary told the Gov. not to let you out, now that is true, right from the Gov himself, he is from Neillsville. ... Well did you get your cookies, keep them in a dry place and they will last for 2 weeks or more. Got 107 chicks, going to dispose of all my old ones this fall, they make lots of work just now, hope you are well. I remain your Mother [Perhaps Caroline was referring to Arlo Huckstead, a representative from Neillsville in 1929. Huckstead's only son, Thomas Huckstead, an Army private, died in 1918 from meningitis while stationed overseas.]

Owen Bank Robbery

Mother to Frank, June 27, 1929

Dear Frank, ... Well the owner of the land northeast of us let us have the use of his 80 for pasture. O I was so glad I didn't know what to do with myself, our stock was starving here so we are helped out with that, the young stock we will have to get home now too for thier is lots of feed in thier but the fences has got to be fixed up first and L will have to start cutting clover. I did not hear lately how Leslie is getting along with his study, he is always cheerful but yet he wants to get out so bad. ... Well I am glad you are well which we are too. I remain your Mother

On July 3rd, Caroline told Leslie there was an early celebration at Owen when three men came into the bank and helped themselves to $8000 cash and about $7000 in negotiable notes, right in broad daylight. They escaped; she felt sorry for the youngest bank robber who was twenty-three years old. It seems this was the start of a lot of robberies and tough times for businesses and individuals in the Longwood community.

Later in July, Caroline deeded all of the cattle, livestock, hay and grain, machinery, tools and equipment on the farm to her son, Louis. Perhaps it was a formality or a way to protect the assets from further lawsuits.

Frank's Pet Cricket

Frank to Mother, August 18, 1929

Dear Mother, Another writing day so will write again, but do not know of much. … Where did you get the sticker you put on the back of the envelope? "Where and with whom shall we dwell In eternity." They hand out some queer things. It sounded like old times in my cell one night last week. A cricket got into the corner and sat there and chirped til he died. He starved to death, had no green grass to eat, so he went to eternity. He was happy tho till the last. … Am getting along well so far. Frank

While Leslie remained in the Central State Hospital at Waupun, he faithfully wrote letters home every Sunday to his mother and brother, Louis. In October of 1929, the state ran out of writing paper for the patients so Leslie traded another prisoner a few apples from home for an envelope and paper. Caroline hoped that wouldn't happen again and the paper shortage wouldn't continue. She felt very uneasy when she didn't get her weekly letters from Leslie.

Caroline Falls Down
the Cellar Steps

Mother to Leslie at Central State Hospital, November 6, 1929

Dear Leslie, your both letters received, am glad you are well now—about your eyes, just take hot water and bathe them, you can put a little salt in the water too, thats good too know. F. wrote that he got 2 of your papers, its called the Revivalist, he got the

last weeks and the week before that, you better ask for them—I
should think they would send them over their. Well last week Wed.
morning I took 3 pails, went down the entrance steps and as I
got on the second step my feet got out from under me and I tried
to hold me on the building but the first thing I knew I was laying
with my head on the cellar steps toward the South and I bumped
down one step after the other, 5 in all, real slow until 3 steps
from the bottom then my right hand and foot hit the cement
floor. Then I sat their, my 2 pails in the left hand yet, them
stopped me from going down fast, then I got up went milking but
I knew I was bruised all black and blue but it didn't hurt me, only
the flesh was bruised, but Sat. their was a car here from Owen
so went to the Dr. He examined me but nothing is broke so he
bandaged me so them veins would not brake more but then it
hurt until today—the swelling is gone down and it is not so tight
no more but my whole hip is just purple. I do all of my work in the
house, L does all the milking alone, feeds the chicks too. ... Well
must stop. From your Mother

In November, the neighbor's dogs attacked the sheep on the Krueger farm,
injuring two of them quite badly with cuts on their heads. Louis puzzled
with what he could do legally about the dogs, so he wrote a letter to the
district attorney at Neillsville. He received a prompt reply telling him that if
the sheep came under attack again, he could go ahead and shoot those dogs.
Louis did not want to chance causing troubles with a gun.

Leslie to Mother, November 23, 1929

... I received your letter yesterday and see that you are
getting along alright again. I also got the apples, they were in
pretty good shape. ... They killed a lot of rabbits so I suppose that
we will get rabbit for Thanksgiving day. ... [Rabbits were raised at
the prison for food and Leslie hated rabbit meat].

Kind Words in a Letter from Mr. Hewett

Mother to Leslie at Central State Hospital, December 11, 1929

Dear Leslie, Did not get a letter from you last week but as
you wrote to F. [in shorthand] its nice of you to. ... Well I got a

letter from that one [former Sheriff Harry Hewett] that knocked me down at the well that time. I will write just part of it, the rest I will tell you when I come down there. I will take the letter along for a purpose. "I suppose you know we lost our wife and Mother in Luther Hosp. Eau Clair March 19, 1926. Mrs. [his wife's name] was always a real friend of yours as long as she lived," and then he goes on … "I hope some Governor some day will pardon your boys out of prison and if I can do anything to help you obtain their release let me know, will gladly do what I can." (Then he goes on with something I dare not write) then he will say in conclusion "Mrs. Krueger I wish you the best of luck in the sundown of your life and we know that some day we will all get justice before the Great Judge of us all." What do you think of that, now their are 4 parties that was here and done us wrong that is sorry for it. … A man got boozed up here in the brick house [a new tavern just to the north of Kruegers], went home got on a ladder to put storm windows on and fell down and a few days was dead. Another got some their, run his car over a man that was driving his team but walked side of the wagon and killed him too. … Its getting offul, no one safe any more on the road. We are well. Mother

Frank Won't Sign another Pardon Application

Mother to Frank, December 14, 1929

Dear Frank, got a letter from the Lawyer this morning saying I have not received the pardon application from Frank and I wish you would write him again urging him to send the same to me, now what is the matter with you, do you want to stay their forever? It looks like it very much, now sign that Ap as soon as you get this letter so he will get it in on time to put it in the paper 2 times and it can come up next month. …From your Mother Mrs. Krueger

[On the back of this letter Frank wrote notes. The first was a sample document form of the discharge of a mortgage. His other notes went into great detail on the definitions of sealing wax and turpentine.]

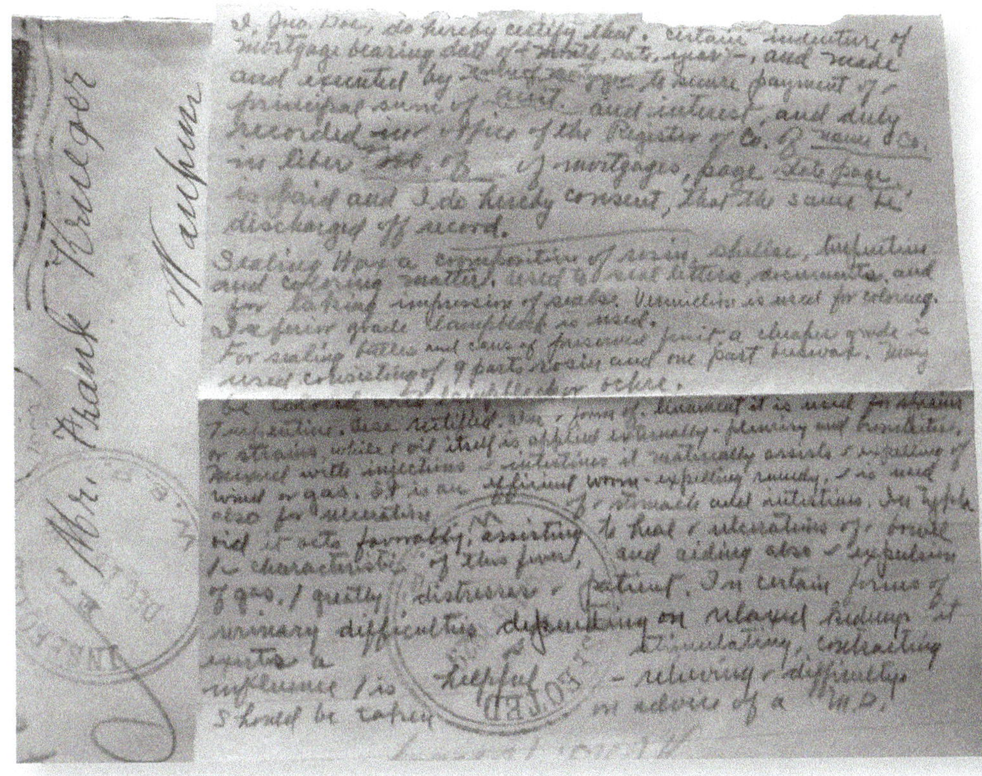

FRANK'S NOTES ON LAW, RECIPES, AND REMEDIES.

Mother to Frank, January 21, 1930

Dear Frank, Your letters both of you boys received today.
I do not know why it seemed so long this last 2 weeks, but as I
read that letter to L. O how mad he was … if you had to see what
we have too, you would sign up that paper quickly. Leslie said
I signed up, it don't do any harm and he is right to, he tried to
do something for himself but you stand and bock, I feel like not
writing to you at all any more, set their forever if you are bound
to, you wrote about the Attorney to go on if he don't get permission of you, you dummie, how can he. … As I told him what you
said, the lawyer said well if I were Frank I would feel just like him,
I don't blame him for not wanting a pardon for being guilty if he
is not, so he fixed it that way. L and I dont know what to think of
you, do you think anyone else will help you or are you not quite
----- [blank line in letter, something Caroline didn't want to say]

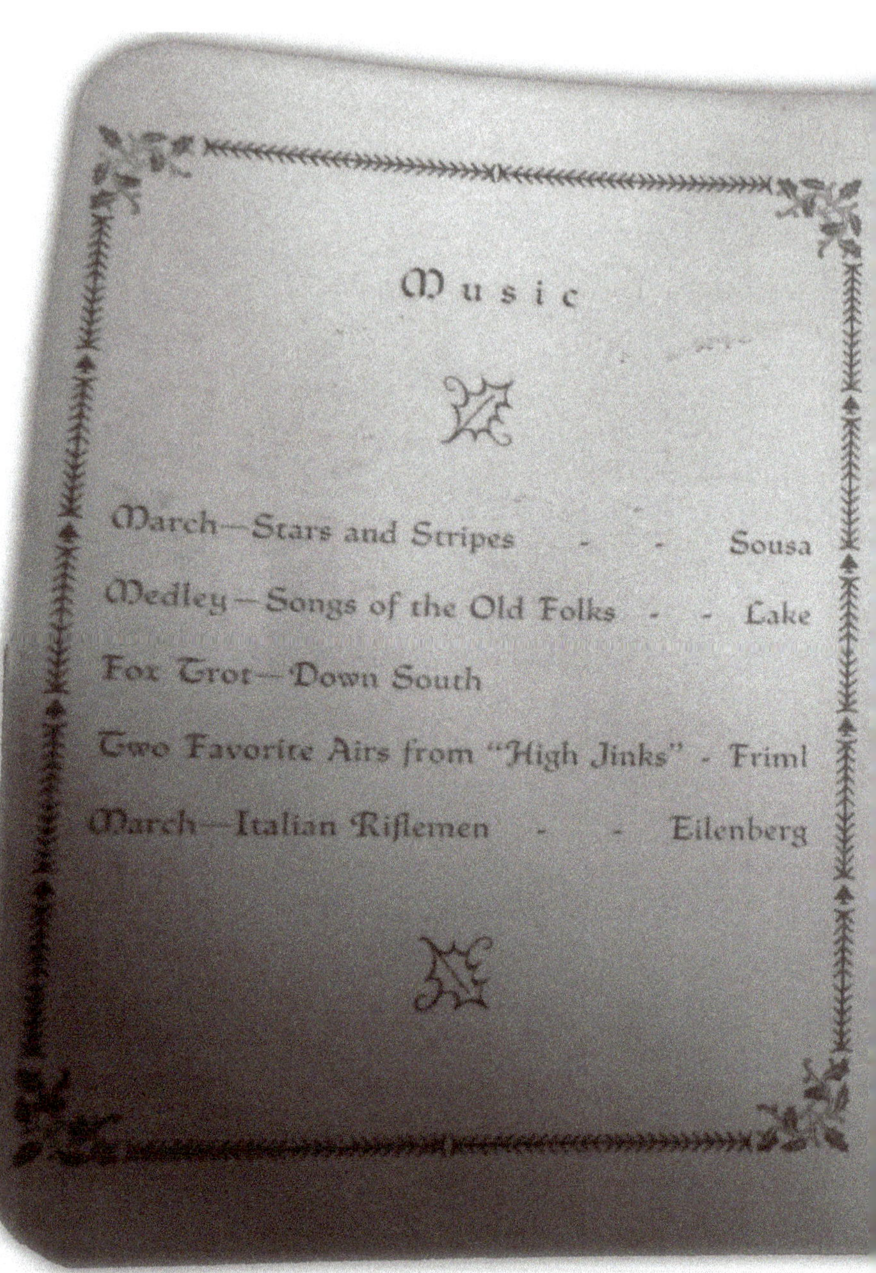

Music

March—Stars and Stripes   -   -   Sousa

Medley—Songs of the Old Folks   -   -   Lake

Fox Trot—Down South

Two Favorite Airs from "High Jinks" - Friml

March—Italian Riflemen   -   -   Eilenberg

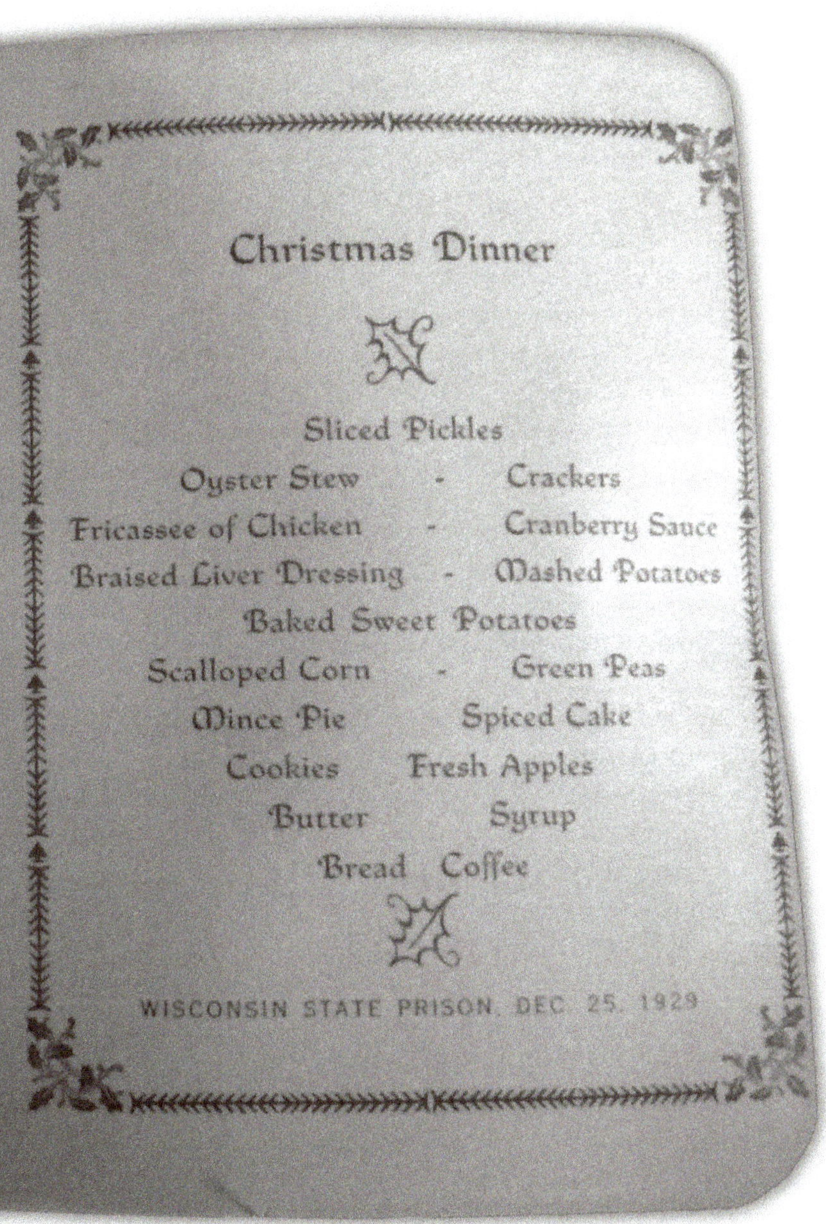

1929 Christmas Menu at the Wisconsin State Prison

L made me go to see you and to talk with you personally—cost
$15. and as I got their everything was no, no, your letter you
wrote such trips are getting harder for you, it taxes your nerves
so I wish the trouble would come to an end (then do your part to).
I left with the 11:20 train, up all night and day and then walked
home the next morning, walked to Withee, took the buss to see
the Lawyer, back at 5 and walked home again and all I hear from
you is no. O I am so disgusted, I am sitting here crying ... if you
only would do the right thing but its no, yes and as I went to
see the lawyer it was so cold, 16 below zero, but I walked down
their. O I must stop for it gets me, I'll have to lay down. Well you
wrote you had a cold, got rid of it quickly, now you sign up and
send it to the lawyer, it dont cost you anything. L is hauling out
Bornstead stove wood today. From your Mother

Frank's stubbornness or lack of incentive was probably due to his severe
mental breakdown. In 1930, with Attorney Paul Raihle representing the
Kruegers, he reworded the pardon application again as Caroline mentioned
in her above letter, and made out separate forms for Frank and Leslie. This
new wording did suit Frank, but he still felt as if it was some sort of apology
and he had nothing to apologize for.

Attorney Raihle wrote Frank that although Governor Kohler was very
sparing in his pardons, the Krueger case was a special case. He also reminded
Frank that he would not charge the family any fees for his services until he
was able to accomplish something good.

There were three points noted on the 1930 pardon application. The first
stated that Frank never committed the crime for which he was convicted.
The second said that the death of the man involved in this case was caused
by war hysteria and was not premeditated. And the third and last point
stressed that Frank had been punished already more than necessary for any
wrong done at the Krueger farm. He had already served nearly twelve years
of incarceration.

In February of 1930, Caroline wrote to Leslie that Frank was not well or
seemed sick from the way he wrote. She told Leslie that when his pardon
case came up at Madison she would appear before the governor for him, as
soon as the lawyer gave her a date. Although Frank had refused to sign an
application, Leslie went ahead with it alone.

Caroline mentioned that Louis and Ennis were also wishing this would soon come to an end, and that Ennis had been seen the previous summer, although she gave no details. Frank finally did sign and wrote a long letter home the last week of February.

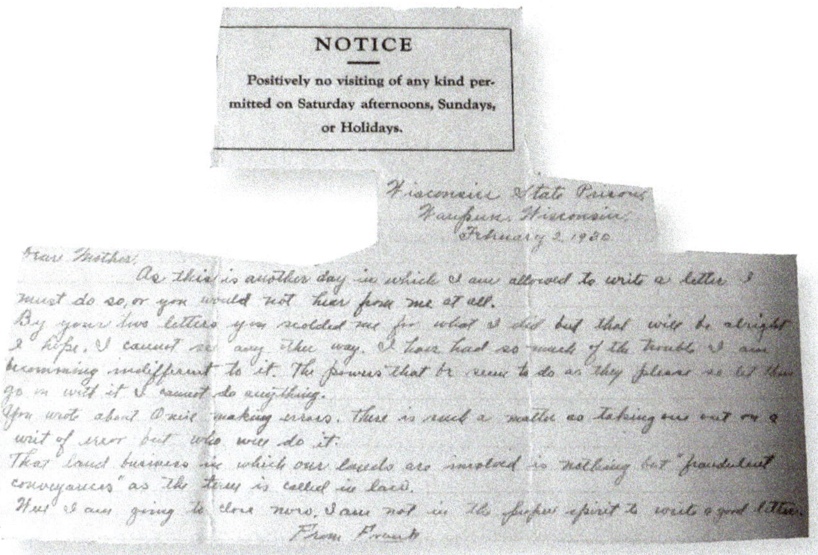

A LETTER HOME FROM FRANK, FEBRUARY 2, 1930, WITH ALL THE MARGINS TRIMMED.

On Horse Hair Chains
and Hair Switches

Mother to Leslie at Central State Hospital, March 5, 1930

Dear Leslie, Your and Frank's letters received yesterday, am always glad to get them in from the mailbox, well I must send you some horse hair so you get a watch chain, why don't you learn to make them, to have him [Leslie's fellow inmate] show you how, I always wanted to learn that but never had the chance, also I wanted to make a hair switch of my own hair but never was where I seen it done. ... Did you get that book, it is very interesting to find out what is comming very soon, then their wont be no more asylums or prisons or operations any more for He then will be Lord of Lords and King of Kings, then they will not throw the right ones into prisons

and the wrong ones go free, in fact the change has begun since
1918 since this trouble of ours has begun, well I hope the Lord will
down them quickly that has done us the wrong. You wrote a while
ago that they make rugs from wool or yarn, wish we could get $4 for
our wool, even 1 I would be satisfied. ... Is there a Hospital where
you are for the sick to, like at the prison, dont think that you will
ever go back to that place, never think of that, think of everything
else but that, scatter your thoughts, think of everything and I will
send you some cookies too, cake I cannot pack up so well but will
see when L goes down to town again what kind of box he will get for
it. Snow is nearly gone again, hope we will have an early spring like
20 years ago as Pa died. We are well, hope you are to, Mother

By March of 1930, the inmates in the insane asylum/hospital where Leslie
was incarcerated were given the privilege of having their own radios. Leslie
enjoyed this new freedom very much and a doctor told Caroline that he and
other inmates were improving in mental health because of the radios.

Mother to Leslie at Central State Hospital, March 25, 1930

Dear Leslie, got your letter today. ... did you read in the
Neillsville news where it said Ennis the younger brother escaped
and never was caught. Wonder who put that in that article,
somebody knows about him, perhaps he will tell the Gov. to, hope
so, if that is proven that will overthrow the whole affair and that it
was in the Neillsville paper, the very place where they were so bitter
against us and in another paper it said 6 of the jury men signed
up for to have you both let out and you know 1 died shortly after
that, he was for you boys to. He said their was a great wrong done
to them boys. Well will see you no doubt next week so will tell you
more, ONeil [Judge O'Neill who sentenced them] was for you to
before he died. ... Hope you are getting along alright to, just dont
think of the past, throw that away. From Mother

In April of 1930, Caroline questioned Attorney Raihle about getting Leslie
a chiropractor. Mr. Raihle told her that they would wait on that until after
they heard from the governor on another matter. He also mentioned that if
Ennis came home, he would have a right to his share of the Krueger estate.
So Raihle was not ruling out the possibility that Ennis was still alive.

Decoration Day 1930
at Riverside Cemetery

Nellie, the old Krueger work horse, was feeling good enough in June for Caroline to hitch up her buggy and have Nellie take her to the cemetery for Decoration Day. Louis told his mother to take the back way and she did, leaving at 8:15 in the morning. She tied Nellie up when she got there by the old Rapski house and there were already twelve to fifteen cars parked along the road. The speaker at the ceremony was from Colby and Caroline enjoyed his speech very much. She said he did not praise the big war men, but talked about those who suffer from wars: women, children, and the elderly, too. The speaker told of how rich men were the ones who started wars and said wars were all about money. Decoration Day services were special to Caroline and she hated to miss them.

Mother to Frank, May 28, 1930

Dear Frank, I must write again so you hear from us. … Got a letter from Leslie and sent him some more horse hair for that other party that makes them hair chains and L cut some of his horses hair and wanted a watch chain made of it for a remembrance of his horse and so he made it and Leslie sent it in this week's letter. It is nice too but I kind of like the black one best, but O such good workmanship, my its just fine, to bad for such party to be in such places like that, so now each one of you have one. … From your Mother Mrs. Krueger

Louis Takes a
Trip to Minneapolis

Mother to Leslie, September 3, 1930

This is L. birthday, time flies, the birthdays come around quickly it seems. He went to Minneapolis Tuesday morning, he wanted to buy things that he needed and it was excursion so he took it in on account of the fair, he dont care for that tho, mostly to get away once. He is comming home tonight but I am glad to, its lots to do and to look after and I get tired on my legs and back but it was nice weather …

Rumors circulated that Louis made a flying trip to Minneapolis to meet up with Ennis, but Caroline gave no indication of that in her writings.

THE WISCONSIN STATE JOURNAL—MADISON—JUNE 5, 1933 (pg 1)

ENNIS KRUEGER, DRAFT EVADER "SLAIN" BY GUARDS IN 1918, LIVES, ROAMS COUNTRY, FAMILY TELLS ATTORNEY

Mother Is Certain

[Excerpt] Subsequent development sustained her intuition, Mrs. Krueger said. Letters have come to her from New Orleans, Denver, Great Falls, Mon., and other widely separated cities within recent years. All unmistakably are from Ennis, she told her attorney.

Both brother and mother of the missing man are reluctant to reveal too many of the details of their contacts with him but did offer corroborative evidence of their assertions.

Three years ago Louis made a mysterious trip to St. Paul, Minn. Upon his return, he informed his mother that Ennis was in East Bend, N.C. Louis addressed a letter to his brother at that place and received a brief reply, which he exhibited to Raihle. It was postmarked East Bend, N. C., Jan. 18, 1932.

Once again Frank's lack of letters home was not a good sign of his mental state. Caroline complained to Leslie that although she wrote to Frank she hadn't received an answer back for some time, and no Labor Day letter, which was very unusual. She had sent him apples and plums for Labor Day and was preparing to send plums to Leslie as well.

16 SUE THE LAWYER

Mother to Frank, March 13, 1928

Dear Frank ...Well Rey. and his bunch must make it hard for the Gov., that cuss, the Lawyers looked up his work in our case and they all say it is something terrible, terrible, what offul work he done their, why its beyond believing the wrong he done us. I hope the Bar Association will tend to him like they did them Lawyers in Millwaukee. Well Rob. birthday was yesterday, when I think in what poverty we lived then but we were happy, had no trouble only hard work and we were not afraid of that, it makes me feel blue to think what we went thru since ...

In August of 1929, a damage suit in the amount of $5,000 was served on now Attorney General John W. Reynolds by Caroline Krueger. Attorney Paul Raihle of Chippewa Falls represented Mrs. Krueger in the suit. The suit, filed in Clark County, claimed Reynolds was excessive in his charges when he represented the family for their murder trial. Reynolds said the suit was brought about only to hamper his re-election campaign while running for state attorney general—Raihle being a progressive Republican and former legislator and he a Democrat.

Caroline clearly thought she had a case. She felt she was wronged in particular when Reynolds placed a lien against her sheep and cattle while she was in jail awaiting trial. The livestock were sold for $1450; Reynolds kept the money. He also charged an additional $3,500 of which he stated was not just for representing the family in the criminal trial, but for also taking it to an appeal at the state level, and for representing the family in the civil suits brought on by those injured in the shootout. Caroline said she dismissed

Reynolds after the trial but he continued to represent the Kruegers against her wishes, she couldn't shake him lose.

Reynolds was acquitted of the charges in Green Bay circuit court by Judge Henry Graass and went on to win his re-election.

Frank worried that Reynolds' power would make a negative impact on his and Leslie's pardon pleas. In December of 1930, Caroline wrote to Frank: "… you say R. can hold us back in the position he is in now, no he can't do that now like Crosby, he dare not have anything to do for or against our case as he was involved in it—so the same with R. They will have to get another Att. General in his place to do his work."

17 THE DEPRESSION HITS

Mother to Leslie at Central State Hospital, February 19, 1930

Dear Leslie ... L said a man came to the condensary in Owen and said give me something to do, give me a job for I and my family are starving, so he gave him one dollar and sent him to the cop—them are the times we are living in and our country gave Europe the dollars by the billions for a present, the outlook for the working class is bad. Well we got 3 new milk cows now, as I was gone 2 came in and another one overnight, so it will go better here again too, we did not have much income while the cows are dry either. ... When I get to walk to Withee I go on dry ground now all the way. Nellie looks poor and old again, the same way like a year ago, she likes to pick in the fields if the bars are let open, tired of hay. We are well. From your Mother

Mother to Leslie, July 10, 1930

Dear Leslie, Your letter received but not Franks this week yet, unless it comes today, it always comes on Tus. with yours. Well L will send for the book today if he goes to town. We had our stack open this morning and was going to top it off today and now their comes a quite heavy rain shower, it was all over in 1 hours time but it made the hay and stack wet so no hauling in today any more. I do wish you were home as it is getting hard on me, I am always tired and I often lay down to. I tried to get them few currents picked yest—but didn't get it all done and as I was sitting their picking, I thought why must it be that way. Leslie could do a whole lot of little things for me here but no, there he must sit and do nothing, also Frank. Well we will all work for the next Gov, if La Follette gets in he will let you out and lots of others, once I met him as I was in Madison, he said to me what an offul offul outrage that was done to you up their, it was a great wrong. Well we got our cattle tested yesterday again, a blood test this time, there is a sickness amongst the cattle that the people takes too, it costs 20 cents a head, we had 16 head but don't know how they come out yet, hope ours are all allright. ... I feel worried about F. he has not written, will be 4 weeks Sun. Well quite a few of them chicks are dying, I don't think I will send for anymore again, everyone is losing about ½ of them. One man had his 5 weeks then lost them so he sent 2 to Madison and they said that the last 2 days them chicks were in a incubatore was too hot and hurt the yolk of the eggs. ... Well must close. From your Mother, we are well

Mother to Frank, October 1, 1930

Dear Frank ... You wrote in your letter that you hate to see the cold winter come on, on account of us, you are right in that as we are so very poorly fixed for in the barn and I hope the winter will not be so cold as that is very hard on the stock, takes so much more feed and we have not got any too much. ... Well Kief, the one that run the boarding house in Owen, went into the bakery in Owen, rented it and he made his own oleomargirene and they found it out and they kicked him out last week. O he fed the people on some offul mess they say. L heard about it while their, so one after the other has to leave Owen. Kidd is only their once in a while, yet not much and others have moved away, starved out. Leslie slept in the cellar ever since early in the summer, he says he is not locked in either but he would like to come home tho, well he will when our new Gov. gets in ... pretty soon I will come down their to see you, now the work is getting finished up. I remain your Mother

The hospital where Leslie was kept was being remodeled so he had been moved to the basement (or cellar) for several months, as Caroline mentioned above.

Mother to Frank, September 25, 1930

Dear Frank, Your letters received from both of you, well Leslie wrote that the last plums did not make him feel so dizzy, got used to them, well its the last ones for this year. Now I send him appels once a week, 15 lb. costs 19 cents to send them by parcel post right from the mail box out here. I guess he must have set up all night of the election for he said at 11 in the night it was going all one sided, so he has his radio. I wish we had one too. You asked whether we thrashed—no we have nothing to, this year we didn't know if we could get that 80 of B. and so would have had to pasture this and raise a little hay so L did not plow up any, but as we got that for another year, L is going to plow some on the northwest of this 40 and he has plowed east of the orchard, but he is digging the taters now, they are fair not so big but quite a few under. Well a batchler, old already, in Owen he works in the plaining mill and he bought 3 acres northwest across the track from the mill, but he lives on this end of the town near Martisons, as he was working at the mill they saw a man with a wheelbarrow wheeling potatoes up to town so they said to him they are stealing your potatoes and sure enough right in broad day light to, about 8 bushels they sold to that restuarant, and one evening 2 men walked into the filling station on the northwest corner at Paulsons and demanded the money, they got $27. and started off. I told L we are lucky we have no money, so far this community was all right but they found it at last, dont see much money any more, all checks. ... From your Mother

Mother to Leslie, October 23, 1930

Dear Leslie, your both letters received Tus, but Frank is very discouraged just like you and I and everybody gets once in a while, the same weather to as their but no snow, yes our apples are just about gone, their are some left but not fit to send to you, but buy some once in a while, if you have no money I will send you a dollar every now and then for you need such likes to eat, your body needs them, so you buy some even if they are high priced. Phil Shettler has 2 boys, one is 14 years and he didn't want to go to school so he took poison but they got him in time

yet and he got over it, just think, rather die than to go to school.
... We are well, hope you too, From your Mother

In November of 1930, Caroline wrote to Leslie that someone blew up the safe in Owen's schoolhouse and stole $50, plus some class rings and other things, and that one of Mr. Dafner's boys stole a car and they locked him up at Neillsville. He and another young man sawed themselves out of the jail. That reminded her of when she and Frank were awaiting trial in the jail at Neillsville and Frank's cellmate sawed himself out while Frank kept quiet and didn't say anything.

A neighbor wanted to send Leslie a gallon of honey from his personal supply. Caroline enquired with the prison system and was told he could only be shipped one pint. She felt that was too little to bother with.

Caroline kept busy in December canning roosters. She packed fruit jars with chicken, filled them with water enough to cover, and boiled them in an open kettle for three hours. She used the canned chicken meat to make soup in summertime. It was more economical to kill and can the excess roosters than to keep feeding them.

Caroline wrote Leslie that she saw one deer go by atop of a car a little bit before deer season started. It was a small deer. The school children walking by her house told her it had been confiscated from some poor soul by a game warden.

The hardware store in Withee was robbed in December of about $700, but most of the money was recouped. Two young men were arrested in a hotel in Eau Claire.

Caroline took her eggs to town and sold them for 33 cents a dozen that winter, not much but she was pleased with what she did get. It was only the beginning of the Depression, with many local bank closings to come in the Longwood community.

18 NEW HOPE

Mother to Frank, October 29, 1930

... but when Phil. La. [Governor Phil La Follette] gets in he will see to it that you both will get out and many others to, as the papers stated, as he was their and went thru the prison he took notes down on some prisoners, you know he is the Crimanal Lawyers teacher in the University for those that are studying to be Crimanal Lawyers and I have been told over again and again that, that case of ours is worked on and all thrashed out, so Phil, knows it by heart already. He said things to me the time I seen him in Madison years ago that I would like to write to, but think best not to now, but we will have to put up another pardon in order to start the thing for the new Gov. and you must sign up for it to, no matter what they say what kind of record you have, dont pay any attention to that, the new Gov. knows different but he must have a starting point and we must hand it in, in the form of a pardon, I had just a chance to talk with the lawyer, this week so don't feel to heavy in spirit just cheer up ... they are telling L and me that now comes your chance. ... From Your Mother

Election Day for the Kruegers at Longwood, 1930

Mother to Frank, November 6, 1930

... On Election day got up early at 5 in the morning, got my washing down by 10 and had a call in the meantime and the milk

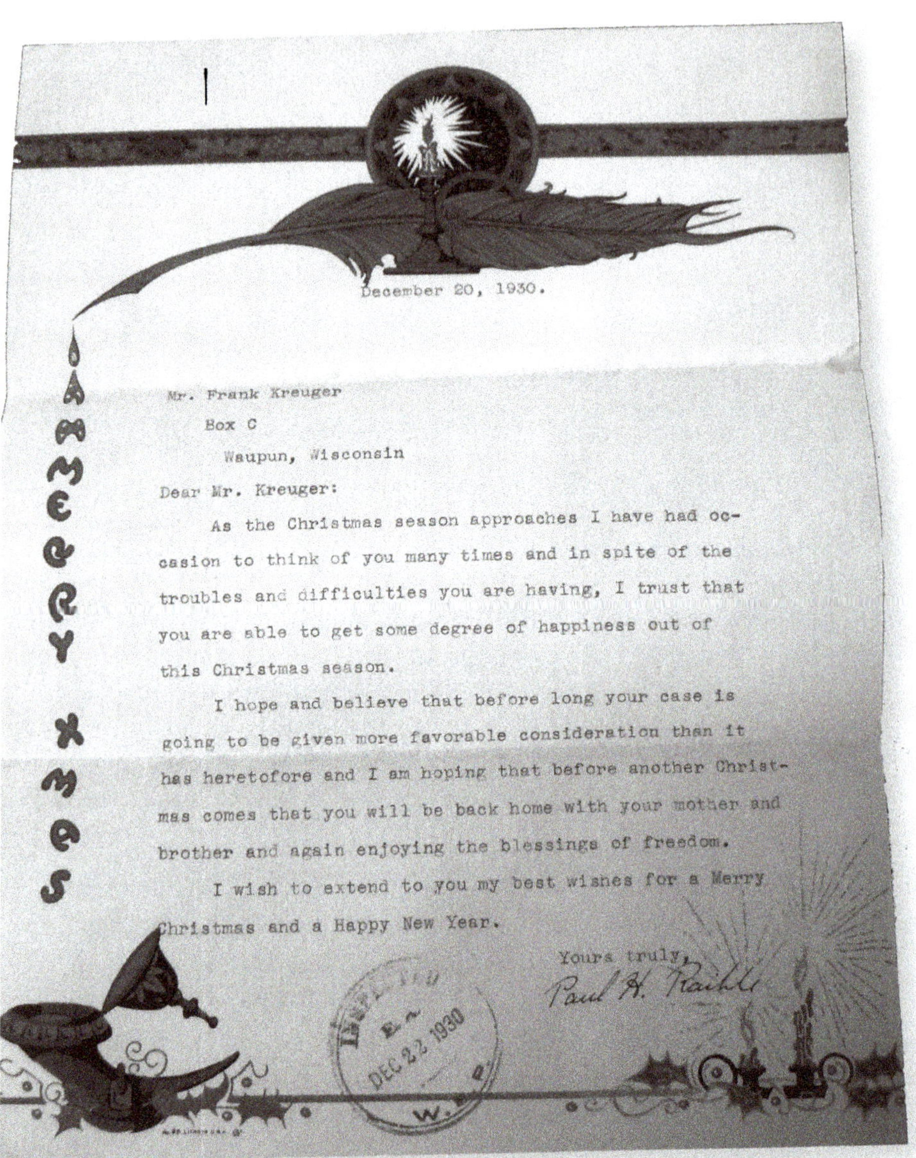

December 20, 1930.

Mr. Frank Kreuger
Box C
Waupun, Wisconsin

Dear Mr. Kreuger:

As the Christmas season approaches I have had occasion to think of you many times and in spite of the troubles and difficulties you are having, I trust that you are able to get some degree of happiness out of this Christmas season.

I hope and believe that before long your case is going to be given more favorable consideration than it has heretofore and I am hoping that before another Christmas comes that you will be back home with your mother and brother and again enjoying the blessings of freedom.

I wish to extend to you my best wishes for a Merry Christmas and a Happy New Year.

Yours truly,

Paul H. Raihle

1930 CHRISTMAS LETTER FROM ATTORNEY RAIHLE

gatherer came back and he took us along to Longwood (he said
he was going anyway and for us to go along), we voted and come
back and nearly had dinner ready at 12 in the afternoon. I ironed
and cooked some ripe tomatoes for supper... a good many now
say get right after Phil, right away so you will get the boys out. I
am glad Phil La F is in for Gov, but didn't Kohler get snowed under
proper, good for him he was all for the money men, the common
people he didn't have no use for, well they showed him the same.
... We are all well, hope you too. From your Mother Mrs. K.

In January of 1931 Phillip La Follette, son of Robert La Follette, took office
as Governor. Attorney Paul Raihle had high regard for Governor La Follette and felt more confident in achieving the Krueger pardons than ever
before. Raihle was determined not to give up the fight in freeing Frank and
Leslie. Along the road to their freedom, Frank was often the hold up. It was
always very difficult to encourage Frank to sign new pardon applications. He
couldn't see the point in creating another let down after another let down;
he felt it was easier to just accept things the way they were. Frank was clearly
suffering his worst lows in late 1930.

Caroline Gives Frank Words of Encouragement
She Says Someone Spoke with Ennis in Oregon

Mother to Frank, December 23, 1930

... Must write I must not do as I said as I was there, that I
wouldn't write to you again if you act that way, but I know and did
know that time that you was not feeling well nor did you look well,
for I do not want to go there and make life more miserable for you
then it is, it is hard enough already, don't feel so bad, it is always
the darkest just before the dawn and I know that help is near, only
dont let that trouble get ahead of you that they will have to put
you where Leslie is. ... Now when you are let out who owns the
land, its in Pa's name yet and not probated, so their is the first
wrong step the court took, they cant give a deed that way, then L
didn't sign nor E ... E was seen and talked with some time ago in
Oregon so we have proof that he is alive, now dont say anymore
[that] he isn't. Also Jensen is dead that's true to, for I told you

who killed him some time ago and he was seen being shot by the one that stood by him, don't let your thoughts run away with you and shatter your nerves—deliverance is near and lots more of the prisoners will be let out, so brace up. Well I hope you feel better than you did, I have felt so uneasy since I have been their I can't do any work at all ... From your Mother Mrs. Krueger

Ennis Kept Nearby for Two Years

Mother to Frank December 31, 1930

Dear Frank, Your letter received and am very glad you feel different then you did the day I was their, you certainly did look offul that day and I and L was so uneasy about you. L couldn't even sleep he felt so bad for you, but I do not know hardly what to say about your letter, one thing L has written to the new Gov but he has not got an answer yet, no doubt because he was not In Office yet (that I would like to see him on business) and if I see him I will tell him how it was and who it was, and about putting the injunction on it—no attorney will do it for I tried that. Yes there are lots of damage cases paid good and dearly, yes how much would we been worth by now if this wouldn't happened, my, my, but you are entitled to $2. per day for false imprisonment you must know to, but freedom is what belonged to us all—not such a mess for what another man done. Now about Jensen, yes his death was proven on the trial by Greib. [Greibnow] and other where he was shot thru, them can be held for withholding infor-mation. Whoever tells you that Jensen was seen after that trouble belies you, that must have been Ennis because he was seen in Owen that evening by some that knew him and you know them to, but they kept still. I would tell you more about this but think best not to. E was for 2 years kept not far from here, and as I was their you said someone told you about the house—that is a lie to, for it is just as you seen it last as we came up from Neillsville, nothing wrong with it, only it needs painting... From your Mother

Mother to Leslie, January 8, 1931

Dear Leslie ... was to Owen to hear the Inaugeration of the Gov. over the Radio Van—has a big one and you could hear everything so plain as Gov. said I do, it was plain to hear and I wish we had one to, but perhaps we will have this thing straightened up now pretty soon. ... I liked what he said in his inaugural speech (this is it the American people will be the actors in the greatest tragedy of the world unless the present economic disturbance is cured.) ... we had Dr. here for to have the horses teeth fixed up but Nellie's is no good anymore, some are dropped out in the back and the others are rotten, so we thought of killing her and yet we do not like to—she can eat second crop of clover yet so we would like to see how long she would really live, will have to give her a little ground oats, she don't eat much ... will send you some chicken next week ... From your Mother

More on the Shooting of Jensen

Frank had a notion that Harry Jensen, the man he was accused of murdering, never really died. He thought it was all part of the plot to put Leslie and him behind bars, a cover up of some sort by the government. Caroline never felt this way as she was sure Jensen was dead and said she knew, as did many others, who actually fired the shot that killed him. Her letters never mentioned the man's name.

Mother to Frank, January 22, 1931

Dear Frank ... I do not know why you can't believe that Jensen was killed. That time how you got it in your head that way or who put it their, a man that worked that time for Vater told L last Monday that he knows who killed Jensen and that he was shot just at the one fence at the end of our 80, all the people knows who done the deed, even the children, it was not at our place as you wrote and the new Gov. knows that (I don't like to see you so set in your way when its true) ... I hope you got my letter and the Paper I sent to you last Friday and that you signed it, for that is the only way the Gov. can do anything or start it, he can then have a retrial or writ of error or whatever he wants to do, its all in his power, and the Law. talked with different ones that is in or near him to know and they all say the same—start it now—sign up and send it to Chippawa and keep the copy if you haven't yet—no one got any damages yet of them men that got hurt so far nor want, that judgment was done wrong and the Judge says that himself that was done fraudently, his plan was that Fred would come and redeem it and that failed. I can have him kicked out of the Bar Association whenever I want to and he knows it to. Yes Rey was the fault of that—look up the laws of the Lawyers. … I feel so tired at times in my bones too but I go out, and its over again, I am spinning, to much sitting. I sent Leslie a box yesterday with 2 roosters and some cookies and 3 tablets so he can practice short hand. Well must stop for this time. L says I hope he will sign up, tell him too that I said it, so here goes—hope you are well again. From your Mother

Enclosed in the envelope with the above letter was a letter from Attorney Paul Raihle written to Caroline on January 28, 1931. In the letter Raihle pleaded, "I am waiting anxiously … Will you write to Frank and urge him to hurry the signing of it [a new pardon application] and send it to me?" On the bottom of Raihle's letter was a penciled message from Caroline to Frank. She told Frank how bitter Louis felt at his [Frank's] failure to sign, when he felt they were so close to freedom.

In an unsigned, typewritten letter from Louis to Frank, Louis tries to infuriate Frank so that he would go ahead and attempt another pardon: "When a man lays in a dump like you are [he] gets like a person lost in the woods, if he has no guide he will perish"—postmarked Owen, Wisconsin, February 26, 1931.

Spring Returns to the Longwood Farm

Mother to Leslie, April 30, 1931

Dear Leslie, Your letter received, see that you are well and that is a good thing to feel well. … Last Sun. it was so cold and windy and 2 little lambs come down in the pasture, but they lived it thru—one is a clear black one with a white spot on her forehead, it looks odd, we never had a clear black lamb before. L says we now have 31 lambs, well I have my garden all in that I want to put in just now, next week if its nice I will put in the rest, as it is in the right moon. I got the beef all smoked and my incubator will come of next Mon, so you see I am always at some work and L wants to get nearly all of the rest of the spuds in tomorrow if he

can. You asked that we must start this affair up, yes in a couple
of weeks then the Gov. will have at least nearly all of the laws
that he wanted past over with, that is what we have to wait for, at
least its best that way. ... well perhaps I'll soon be around their
and see you, this time if I get to Madison I will take the Northland
Grayhound buss right thru, don't cost so much either, it's 187
miles if I remember right. ... Hope you are well, as we are, my
hand is pretty good again to. From your Mother

Mother to Leslie, May 21, 1931

Dear Leslie, your both letters received, am always glad to
see them on Tus., yes everything is green and in bloom but these
2 days its been an offul cold wind. I see but the early apple trees
their will not be many of the Duchess nor big crabs but they have
been just loaded to breaking down these last 4 years. But Plum's
if nothing happens to them, lots of them and also the late apples
are just full of blossoms ... Frank wrote that he read about Hewett
dying, he wrote that we outlived him anyway, that is just what the
Bible says Psalms 37-35 that the upright will do every time. Well
the time will soon be here that I will go to see the Gov. No I do
not think our Law. dare to work for us just now but that is all R.
doing because he let out on because he took our cattle and sold
it or rather gave it away and that made R mad, him being in that
high office and them be shown up to him his dirty work but it
served R right, now R wants to come back on our Law. I see by the
paper some offul slur is thrown at him. ... We are well, hope you
are to. From your Mother

Caroline was referring to the death of Hewett who was sheriff in Clark
County at the time of the shootout. Judge O'Neill of Neillsville, who ran
their trial, had also passed away. The slur in the papers she referred to was
probably a mention in the press that Attorney Raihle had prior affiliations
with the KKK. This was noted in an article about the Krueger lawsuit against
Reynolds, in which Raihle represented them.

Mother to Leslie, May 28, 1931

Dear Leslie ... will say your letter did not find me as well as
usual, I have such a bother with the left knee sometimes, I have

got to bathe it with hot water to kill the pains. ...We sheared
our sheep these last 2 days, I think me standing so long on that
cement floor might have had something to do with my knee to.
Well Sat. is Dec. [Decoration] day, but I have no way to get over
their unless someone comes and takes me along. O I do wish E.
would come home so I could enjoy a few good days yet in my
old age. But I got it so far that I will write to the Gov. or to one of
them social workers next week and ask when I could see them,
make a date with them if they will let me, for I don't think that one
in Chip Falls dare to do anything in that line just now ... when I
get an answer I will see you both. Frank feels quite well again now
he wrote. Well must close, hope you are well, I remain your Mother

Frank to Mother, July 19, 1931

Dear Mother ... I have no faith in believing the governor will
pardon us so will not ask any more or sign pardon applications
for certain reasons I have. If he wished to do something about it
he can go on and do it as there is a good reason for him to do
something and he will not need to do any pardoning either, and
still get us both out of these places, in which we both have been
so illegally placed. Those pardon rules that the executive counsel
sent to you cannot be applied in our case. He knows very little
about the case and all he knows is those rules. Let them find out
where Jensen is and then do something about it. You have heard
nothing about Ennis yet? Suppose you try this. On the front end
of each of the two engines is the name of the place (the town or
city) where they are made. It is in large letters on the castings of
the smoke box. Write to the postmaster there enclosing a self
addressed and stamped envelope for reply, asking if he has heard
of such a person. It will not do any harm and maybe get some
good from trying. Something strange about that with him gone
and nothing found out so far. If you should find out something,
mention the place on the engine and do not write much about it.
... Am glad to hear you are getting along well in haying. Well I do
not know of any more so will stop for this time. Am glad you are
well. Use what I wrote you before on the eyes, it will help you ... I
am feeling good now, From Frank

Dear Mother ...You wrote you were going to send a clipping about pardon, etc. I have that here, so do not send it. They are of no value to us as they cannot be used in our case. What you wrote about in getting along in years and having to work as hard as you did when 35 is true, and I have often thot of that and how we planned to have something for later in life. But that is the way it goes when others mix into ones affairs and a trouble goes over the land as it was then when that happened at our place. It does not pay to plan for anything, the same way with an application, too many others to pass on it. I missed so much already so let it go.

Yes, it would be good if Leslie were home. It would take some of the work away from you. He belongs there, but it is the same as before. Too many others have the say. No I never got any papers back from Reynolds. I asked you about that once when you were here on a visit. I never got anything from him, only broken promises and that is about that mortgage we gave the day we left Neillsville. I will never give a paper to a lawyer again. I'll keep them myself. I have had enuf of them and only added trouble when I engaged one for services.

You say I should not say Jensen is alive? He is as far as I am concerned, and maybe enjoying prosperity. I did not do to him, what I am charged for. I know that. You must have not got the meaning what I wrote you about McCarthy. I saw in the Longwood news where a son of his went from here to visit his parents in Longwood. So I thot I would write and ask you. It is no good to me let it go. Just an item that is all.

Well I do not care to write about trouble all the time so will close for this time. Had some rain here yesterday afternoon and some during the night. ... Am in good health now, cannot complain, no pain to speak of. From Frank

At first I was puzzled at Frank's mention from time to time that Harry Jensen was not dead, that he had not been killed. In Frank's mind, neither he nor his brothers had shot Jensen, and the courts would not admit or allow the thought of anyone else having shot the man, so he must still be alive. Simple as that! Of course he wasn't.

Beggars Running Around, No Work, No Money

Mother to Leslie, August 12, 1931

Dear Leslie, must write again so you hear from us … it's the work at home and it's the busy season in the farm too, got to be right here and at it, the weather keeps on the same way every day but we do get a shower once in a while lasting about 10 or 15 minutes … we watched for them meteors too but we don't see them, they were supposed to be in the northwest last Tues and Wed. night but we didn't see anything. No they are not building any concrete roads in the Co. this year, they have enough to do to feed the poor, my what offul times it is—no work and men running round begging for to work, one was here Mon., he said I should think some farmer could take me in for my board and lodging, but the farmers are just as hard up as they, only they have their eats but when it comes to money there is none, everything is at the bottom, eggs 12 cents—why you cant buy feed for that and have anything left, and butter the same, but the Banks are so full of money they cant hold it much longer. They say something is going to happen, I am afraid of an offul crash between labor and capitol for it cant go on this way. I picked my pickles yesterday, I don't know why I put them up for we seldom eat them … I suppose they are all out on their vacations that's why we don't hear from them but this is a big case so it will take quite a time, hope they will soon get it ago. Well we are well, hope you to. From your Mother

Always Searching for Ennis

Mother to Leslie, September 16, 1931

Dear Leslie … do you have them sick spells often or that you don't feel well. I will send them horse hair tomorrow if L goes to town, are you in the new building that you write you can look out over the wall where you are sleeping. I wonder if that young fellow will make me a chain for around my neck. I would like them wheels made about so big or a little bigger and 22 inches long and if he has not enough black horse hair we will send him more as K, Nellie, Dixie, are away from home in a paster, so L can get some more for him and I will pay him for making the chain ... well we heard from that party at last, he wrote inside 2 weeks we will know if head quarters can do anything, he presented the case to them and they will see what can be done if anything. Frank wrote that it was said over the Radio that Jensen was alive and in a big western city, a Telegraph Operator, but that can't be. I don't believe that the way them swore at the trial like Grieb.—and them its almost impossible to believe. ... L was to the fair in Minn. last week and looked after some other things that he needed. Our new horse hurt himself, run against something and cracked the bone between his eyes, but its looking good so far. Dr. says it must not heal up for 6 months, good its not cold, the matter has to run out or it will kill him. ... I remain your Mother K.

It is possible that Caroline was referring to the International Labor Defense of Chicago as "headquarters." Louis wrote several letters to them in 1931 and 1932 asking for assistance to help locate his missing brother, Ennis. In September of 1931 the secretary of the Chicago District wrote to say that he had recently visited the national office in New York concerning the case and later turned records over to their attorney there. "We have not yet had an expression of opinion from them. Meanwhile you should keep in mind the location you mentioned but write nothing further to me about it for the time being except to keep in touch with me ... I know that we have kept you waiting a long time ... the nature of this case is such as to make it very difficult to move." The secretary wrote back several times to apologize for putting the matter aside, stating that the organization had been swamped with cases, over 600, but would get back to Louis.

Of course, most of the letters that Louis wrote are missing, so I am unsure of what location Louis was referring to and can only guess that he was somehow implying that Ennis may have been held somewhere by the federal government as a prisoner at some point in his absence, if he was indeed still alive. Apparently Louis thought he was definitely still out there somewhere. As late as 1953, Louis wrote to a psychic in Jackson Heights, New York, asking where his lost brother might be found. Louis wrote, "I have a brother that will not show himself back here where he left his place of living. Got any light or clairvoyant vision on him ..."

Frank to Mother, October 18, 1931

Dear Mother, Must write again today so you hear from me ... I see by both your letters you are still in good health which is grateful to me. ... I was talking to a man who came from Stevens Point and was acquainted with Mr. Hewett when he was on the police force there. He said he was asleep most of the time when on duty. He would be asleep in his chair. He was asleep in the chair in the baggage car when he brot me from Chippewa to Neillsville the time he was sheriff in Clark County. ... Mr. Hewett was a poor sheriff anyway. He gave no orders to protect property from the owners when they were in trouble, but he also had a judge over him who did not know what to do or was made to enforce any common sense when a country went partly insane. That decanter he had when in jail was his un-doing. A reason for being mopish. ... Louis should number the parts or mark the runners and take the sleighs apart in the spring. Take up less room in storage. Is Nellie having a good time this summer? ... Will close for this time. Am well so far. From Frank

People Live too Fast and Only Care about Themselves Nowadays

Frank to Mother, November 15, 1931

Dear Mother, I am going to write again today. Wrote last Sunday as I was allowed to do so on account of the coming holiday the 11th. It may be a holiday but to me it means imprisonment. If that court in Neillsville would have left us go when the war was put to a stop we would not be where we are today, that is Leslie and myself, and we would be better off as far as wealth is concerned. But instead of doing that they kept us locked up and wanted to have a big trial and get what little we had accumulated and tear us apart, so here we are. And no change made so far. Heap a lot of accusations against us. There is not much being done to correct the matters. I cannot help but sometimes think when some hinted at me that things should be straightened up at our place. What do you think about such statements. ...

Well I will not write any more about that, but answer

on some of the things you wrote about. Yes, we could have celebrated that day if we would have been at home ... Well I hope you stay there longer. You have seen quite a change in the physical features of the country and had some rare experiences. It does very little good to tell them to others, unless you happen to meet someone who has had the same experience, but the most of the generation of today do not realize or even get an idea of times as they have been. They live too fast for that, and it is getting like in the cities no one cares for another or does not even get acquainted. ...

If the weather stays as it has, the sheep can graze longer and perhaps you can come out fairly well by holding them. Well you will manage. A good time to get out the wood now and lay up when it gets colder. Disconnect some of the radiators in the rooms you do not use and save on the wood. Be better if Louis would cover the boiler in the basement that would help to. Makes the cellar cooler and would be better for the vegetables. Then again the floor would not be heated so well from underneath. Would have closed the south part off if I had been at home so as to make it cooler for keeping potatoes and such like. ... I am glad to know you are feeling as you do. By using what I told you, you will scatter that pain and if you keep after it will get rid of it later. ... Perhaps I will write again next Sunday as there will be another holiday a week from this coming Thursday. Do not eat too much chicken. Am well so far. From Frank

Frank to Mother, November 22, 1931

Dear Mother ... About that pardon business I sure do not know how we would come out on that. When you write and the secretary answers that is about all he knows is what he wrote to you. His word is of little account. I am quite sure the governor did not get your letters. That is what makes it so hard. Everything has to go thru so many persons hands. There are pardons there now that are not considered. Some held over from last month and some even from the time Kohler was in there, according to the papers. Quite a system that, I don't know what to think when one is drawn into a lot of trouble and then has to buy ones freedom, to which one is born here, from a line of men clothed with official authority. Chase after a judge that has assisted in depriving one of his inheritance. Looks a lot too humiliating to me. I wonder what we owe to such men because we did not go to Europe about thirteen years ago. In order to make out a pardon application that would be true to form it would be necessary to go to the cemetery and awake and resurrect that old fossilized, whiskered judge and get his views on the application and also the judge now in office.

Leslie and me were both sentenced for the same offence, and now I am here and he is in another place.

What I do not approve of when a lawyer sends an application to me to sign and swear to "that the following is true to best of my knowledge and belief" where I know that the charge against us is not true. …

If you could go back 50 years again and know what you do now you would not work so hard and try to get something for others to carry away and sell afterward. About W. C. Tufts losing in the bank, wish he would so he had to go to work or join the soup line. He probably would not destroy others property then. A job with a shovel would be a reward for him … Will close for this time. Am well so far. From Frank

Leslie Keeps a Diary

Leslie to Mother, January 9, 1932

Dear Mother … we did not start on our music this week but they started up school. I guess they furnish all the lesson and sheets. I had a dream just about like yours, I was up before a judge and he read off quite a little and then let me go, I hope that it comes true. I hope you got over with your cold … well the paper is getting full and do not know any more to write so will close, am well. L K

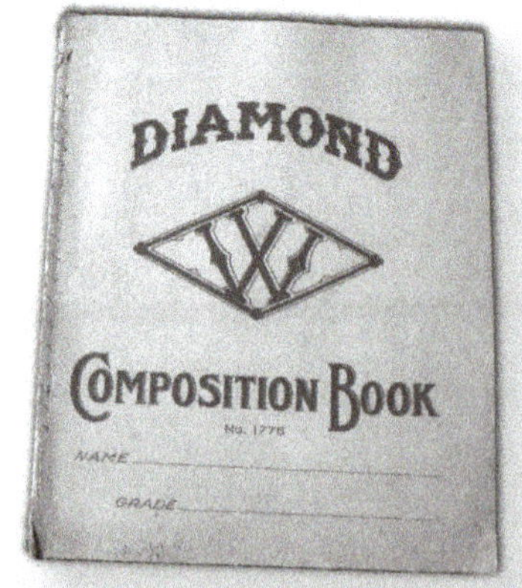

In a small composition notebook with lined pages and a spine reinforced with

white sewing thread, Leslie wrote daily entries from the winter of 1932 into the fall of 1933. He wrote with a green ink pen, the words now slowly fading. His entries were brief, especially near the end of the notebook.

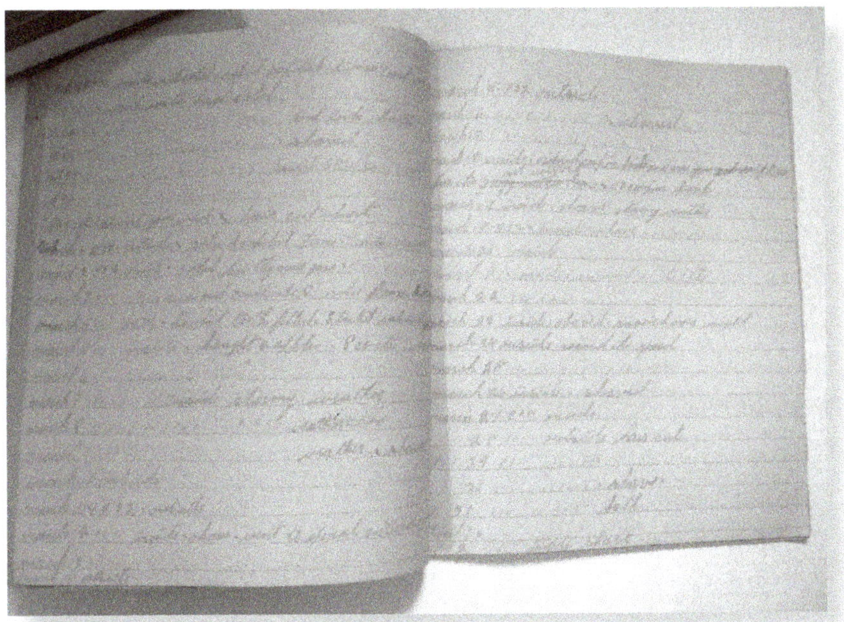

His first entry in February of 1932 told how he was reported for opening the windows in his room because the air felt stuffy, smoky, and hot. He had trouble with the assistant supervisor that day, who told him to move but didn't tell him where to move to. He ended up being sent from the basement to the fifth ward of the hospital in lock-up. He remained there for about nine days.

Leslie noted a few highlights in his diary entries: purchasing a copy of the Capital Times at the price of 7 cents, buying apples, toothpaste, and chocolate. About every third day he wrote that he had shaved, and once mentioned having a tooth filled.

On June 10th, 1932, Leslie noted a visit from his mother. A few times he said he received a dollar from home and once a box of apples from home. He spoke of two visits from doctors, two blood tests, and a visit from the Organization on September 1, 1933. The bulk of his hum-drum entries simply said "Outside" or "Inside," indicating the days he was allowed to go outdoors and that was quite often. The time must have passed very slowly for Leslie.

Dear Mother ... Yesterday I started to work again but on a different job. I am working in the dining room. I bought some apples last Saturday and they cost me seven cents apiece, they know how to charge here. I received the Milwaukee Sentinel. I got to pay again as much here if I order it. Last week my hair began to itch and come out so I had them cut off short but I did not catch much of a cold after it, they feel good now, it is early yet but I don't think it will hurt anything ... the paper is getting full am well. L K

19 ANOTHER PARDON ATTEMPT

Frank to Mother, March 20, 1932

Dear Mother, Well writing day again, so must write another letter ... During the cold spell we had a short time ago I often thot of the cattle at home in the makeshift of a barn you are trying to get along with. Glad its warmer. So Leslie is working again. He has worked at that before, or in the kitchen as I found out a while ago. He should not buy any apples, go without them at that price. He can learn how to do institution cooking, and maybe army cooking too ... You mentioned the kidnapping in both your letters. I do not read much about it, only some of the headlines on the paper. Why should I be interested there, when that very thing is done in our own family, under the name of law, Only in our case its abduction. To steal a child is kidnapping. Take a grown person is abduction. Take the case of Ennis, where is he? One they consider wrong and the one done under the court is considered correct ... Those men that presided at our trial know that two men should not be sentenced to life imprisonment for the killing of a man when a mob had a hand in the case. But they want to be bull headed about it. Rush the prosecutor knows better than that. They wanted a big trial and made us the victims. Now they say get down on your knees and beg pardon from us for the lie we charged you with. That court in Neillsville and the lawyers Rush, Crosby, Reynolds, and David of Green Bay and the judge in Green Bay and Stevens Point, and Neillsville all victimized us in grand style. Those men and many others in that neighborhood and who knows what men in other places took us for a bunch of fools. They did not think they would show themselves up as they have. Defraud family out of their small amount of worldly goods they had accumulated in a long period of time in the name of the law.

Last month twenty seven pardon applications were before the governor from this place alone as I read in a paper. How can he consider a case like ours. Where does he get the time. Simply cannot do it. That is all. I have little faith in getting anything that is beneficial to the two of us as long as that Progressive Attorney General is in there. He willfully defrauded us out of a share of our estate, and I have no faith in him. There seems to be no appeal to any other court. The whole trouble sets me to thinking how terribly angry and determined the whole mob on September 14 were to destroy us, and later the representatives of the law made a worse case of the whole thing just because we refused to take a hand in war across the ocean. I wonder if it has benefited them. I speak very little about it as it does very little good so there is more satisfaction in keeping quiet. There are many persons who are terribly jealous and very quickly charge one with knowing too much ... I am going to close for this time. Am well so far. Frank

Frank to Mother, April 17, 1932

Dear Mother, Must write again. I feel downhearted and disgusted with such trouble as has been foisted upon us. I sometimes feel, when writing day comes, to write only a few lines, only so you hear from me and how my health is and closing the letter ... It is too bad you lost the year old heifer after raising her, and on account of the condition of the barn. No one feels the loss of the barn as the owners do. The men who burned it have nothing to lose or inconvenience to suffer from the act. They little realize the years of saving and work they destroyed in their patriotic frenzy. Now in regard to the pardon. What are you doing? Paying your hard earned money to that lawyer in Chippewa? Or is he going to do as Reynolds did. A little work and later present a big bill? ... I am about filled up on these men good and plenty ... I do not know what to do. So I prefer to sign no papers to present before the attorney nor judge that beat me out of what was mine to make a living from. I would like to be home and work there to make a living but how can I when there is nothing to make a living from. I am not going to write more about it ...

Well I must close for this time. Now do not carry on a lot of correspondence with that lawyer. If he wishes to know anything let him go somewhere else and get it ... Do you not wish sometimes you were in the old log house? We could have repaired that and got along and perhaps got along better. At least we were not bothered as much as later where everyone walked all over it and thru it. We should have let the neighbors build new houses and we stayed in the old one and not fallen for the talk of "when are you ever going to build." I am well so far. Frank

Yes, Frank was very bitter and refused again to sign another pardon application. He didn't want to deal with any more lawyers, anyone at all. His lengthy letters continued.

Caroline wrote a letter in April to Leslie in German script. She included a listing of the alphabet. Leslie was interested in learning to read and write in German, he had not learned it as Frank had when young. At the end of the letter she told Leslie to keep an eye on the sore on his leg that did not want to heal. It may have been the beginning of diabetes.

The Sticker on the Back of the Letter

Frank to Mother, May 1, 1932

Dear Mother ... I see by your last letter you are somewhat downhearted at the time of writing. One gets that way when thinking of the trouble we have had and are still in. I get that way sometimes but have to get over it and take things as they are. I do not wish to start anything as it turns out only in disappointment. I am not going to write anything about the pardon. I have never got even a response from the others that were handed in. I am getting so used to trouble I do not care to even respond or correct anything ... Is there much work to do in your spring cleaning? How are the walls? Don't glisten any more like they used to, I presume. Quite a while ago since they were finished. How does the varnish last on the doors and casings and on the colonnades and stairs? Do not work too hard as you can take one room at a time and not do it all at once. I could help you well on that now. That is about all I have been doing since I was hauled away from home. So have learnt some about it and forgotten some other things I used to do. Have to please others also in life. So have to wait till they get work enuf out of me ...

You will not miss much when the mill gets moved from the town next to yours. I wish I had not gone there as often as I used to. They used to brag what a good thing it was for that town. It certainly cleaned up around there and other places. [If] That riff-raff had not come from there that day in a patriotic fever I would not be where I am now nor have lost anything. Also those that defended them. What does Leslie want to learn German for? To get more enemies? ... Be a good thing for you to hire the man for a time so you do not have to work so much outside. I read it was a good spring for making maple syrup. Made me think of home and the trees we used to have. If you get any more of those stickers, like the one you sent on the back of the envelope of the last letter, *"As For Me, I Will Call Upon God: And The Lord Shall Save Me. Psa. 55:16. He Shall Save The Humble Person. Job 22:29"* throw them in the stove and make wood out of them. The treatment you got when in trouble after giving your time and money for such likes is enuf to turn from it. Hope you have good luck with your incubator. Will close for this time. I enclose the card given me for Mothers day. Am well so far. Frank

Mother to Frank, May 5, 1932

Dear Frank ... you say of us to get that man again but why when you could be at home, he is an offul eater, he eats as much as L and I together at each meal and that means for me to do a big cooking again over that hot stove all summer, but it seems to do no good to say anything to you, you got into that rut and wont get out, or think of anything else, or as you say take things as they are ... Well the cow is dead—it rained Mon night so L got her in the barn and then she could not get up in their so L killed her, she was very weak anyway. ... The house cleaning is to go over the whole wood work, the walls are just as they were but the gloss is off, the varnish is nice yet but not on the floors, it is dull from washing it over. Leslie wants to learn German for he says he has plenty time so he has something to do. Them stickers were given to me but don't think if you fight your Creator that you will come out ahead and don't write that to me no more. The shingles on the house roof is getting so rotten that it rains thru, we must reshingle it pretty soon now... Well I got the card you sent to me and thank you for it, it's a nice rememberance of our Mothers also in the past. Well we are well hope you are too. I remain your Mother C. K.

Frank wrote in June to tell his mother about new excursion rates that he saw advertised in a Medford paper. The Soo Line bragged up special rates for the summer on Friday and Saturday trips if one returned by midnight the following Monday. The cost was 1 cent per mile round trip to Chicago or Milwaukee. In a separate June letter, Frank again stated reasons for his refusal to sign another pardon application. He felt that, after fourteen years, if the county couldn't have straightened up the matter by now they never would. He said it was hopeless and better to carry on in the circumstances he was in and say no more about it.

In June of 1932, Attorney Paul Raihle again addressed Frank Krueger at Waupun to sign another pardon application. He sent Frank a pardon blank begging him to sign again, to make another attempt with the new governor. Raihle had very high hopes for success for both brothers' release and justice this time. It was going to be different this time, it was going to work.

Mother to Frank, June 29, 1932

Dear Frank, rec. your letter the usual time but O what a letter, if you would have given me a blow over the head it wouldn't been any worse and L. O my my, he said he had a good mind to sell all the cattle and leave, for what am I trying to uphold this thing for if he don't want to do anything for himself, he is more dumb than an animal that at least tries to break lose but he don't and that is true of you … you simply say no like a drowning man, I do not understand what ails you, not a right mind and just look out, you say this letter is a hard one to write, why its only yourselfs doing, your indomniable self will you say of obligations where isn't obligations. I'd throw the obligations and would not stop for that, after you are out what difference does it make, you say about the wrong the Clark Co. bunch lied, yes but do you think they will come to you and say or beg you. No, they are glad you don't want to get out. And the Government they wont come to you either, their will have to be a complaint brought in first and you have got to be out from that place first, then we can help ourselves, now let bygones be gone and look for the future and sign up that pardon app. for that's the only way out for you and the only way Gov. says so to ... Well we are well but disgusted. My Father would be 102 years today had he lived but he is gone 42 years already ... well we are well, hope you are to. From your Mother

So Close, But Yet So Far

Frank to Mother, July 3, 1932

Dear Mother, Got your letter and see you are very much dissatisfied on account of the paper I did not sign. I have not much to say about it but let the officials look after that as they see fit. I took the law for the case and will have to take what is given me. If I can be of no service to the state but here, why here I will have to remain. There seem to be enuf men who wish to make life hard for one, and I am getting used to being abused and handed hard knocks. I am getting so I do not feel bad about it one bit. I do not care to start anything, in fact I do not care to see things go as I used to drive my affairs where I was free to do so before I was sent to this place, and if that is the wish of the state I will say that they have succeeded in getting me down. I was called up to the record office last week and asked if I wished to sign an application and I told him, No, sir. So he can send the paper back or send it where they see fit or file it away and I will say that I will not start anything. This knocking a person down and putting things against a person and then see how wonderfully he overcomes them does not appeal to me. There is a limit to such likes under which a person can stand up. I do not like the statement that Crosby made about the organizations. I never belonged to any and I do not see how I am supposed to go to them for help. I wonder what else is going to be brought up.

You wrote about looking to the future. What did I do when we were all at home? What did we build for? What did we conserve our woods for? And what did it bring us? There was not even security for us. Men whose official duty it is or was there when the trouble occurred to protect property didnt even do so, but even assisted in disrupting it. I am not planning anything whatever for the future. The "all wise" judge that sent us here planned the future for us and as he is now gone those that succeeded him, seem to be unable to change his decision. The judge that never made a mistake or wrong decision. I am sorry to know how the property is going to pieces. I cannot fix the roofs on the buildings and be here. If the rain leaks thru, the only thing to do is to take it as it is. Leave it go. I have been thinking if it were a good plan to sign only papers which are of good value otherwise one may be picked up for forgery. I have signed some on the advice of others very much to my grief later... You wrote in the letter that a complaint must be made. To whom, I would like to know, the government? Would it be considered? And how many would it take and how long would one have to wait? I cannot write any more so will stop at once. From Frank

Mother to Frank, July 7, 1932

Dear Frank, rec. your letter yesterday but not anything good in it to look to for, in the future for me, I suppose you like that dump their so well that if I died you would not even want to come to see me once more, this has been pretty hard days to go thru with, with L, sometimes I feel it must feel good to be where Pa is when one has such stubborn human being to deal with that pleases others more than himself or his own folks, well go to it, time will tell you what you have done. I am very tired this evening but will write just the same, we shocked up quite a piece of hay yesterday and today he cut down some more and tomorrow haul in and put it into the barn or stable and its heavy for me to handle it. Am not strong any more but I have got to whether I can or not—well the sooner I'll be out of the way ... the grasshoppers are getting offul bad. L said there is a nest of them up in the woods and the trees and leaves and ground and fence and logs and everything is just covered with them ... had a ride to Greenwood Sun. but the corn looks very poor, our's is the nicest I seen so far, well must stop, we are well hope you to. From your Mother

La Follette Mentions Krueger Pardon during Marshfield Speech—Frank's Spark

Mother to Frank, July 27, 1932

Dear Frank, must write again so you hear from us. I feel pretty good again but L was pretty well done up—too hot Fri and Sat, but Sun he rested up and so he is all right again. Well today we will finish up our haying then L will go up north of Owen and cut a few loads of marsh hay to cover up the stack with ... if you should happen to see a recept [recipe] of drying and canning sweet corn send it to me if you are allowed to—our sweet corn is nice to, so I thought I would try it once Well now I am going to write something which I hope will wake you up out of your sleep and I hope you will do as all say you should, last Thu Lafollette was speaking in Marshfield (I did not know it or I would went their to) on his tour or speaking tour outdoors and their was an offul mob of people their and as he was talking and raking down the war and the wrong and injustis done to the people, he commenced about pardons and a party in the one cornor of the back said What about the Krueger Boys, why don't you let them out and his answer was that their has been no Application of Pardon presented to him so far and without that he can not do anything for them, their must be a complaint of some kind brought to him and then he can act upon it, otherwise I am powerless he said, but as soon as that Application of Pardon is presented I am able to act for this war was an unjust one and he just raked it down just offul.

Now you want to know how we found that out—2 men from down that way, totle strangers to us, come and told us late Fri evening they wanted to do something for you, they said they would sign up or go or do anything for you. ... Now this is what the Att. wrote to me that I should write to you. "The reason that I wished especially to have this Pardon matter taken up at this time was because LaFollette is now in his political campaign. If we would file the app at once it would be heard in Sep just shortly before the election and I personally believe that LaFoll. would grant the Pardon. On the Appl. I asked for pardon on the grounds that F was not guilty of the crime charged (which I believe would meet with his satisfaction)." Now he told them in Marshfield he did not dare to start it himself but as soon as a complaint was brought in he could ... Now if he said that to such a lot of people will he not do something? I have an idea he will just say it's a miscarriage of justice and against our constitution to go across and them boys were and done right and you are free. Help you he will if you will only do something for yourself, now sign up and be set free. These men said after this party had said this (about the K.B.) everybody was for you to be let out—make up a pati [petition] we'll all sign and so forth, now don't stand like a bocky horse and linger for everyone says its your last chance. I say it myself. From Mother. Its mail time.

Caroline wrote a letter to Leslie the day after the above letter to Frank. She told him the same story about Governor La Follette's speech in Marshfield and the positive words he had to say about giving the Krueger brothers a pardon. "... perhaps he [Frank] will sign up now, now in your next letter you write to me, tell me what I shall say to him ... From your Mother"

Mother to Leslie, August 3, 1932

Dear Leslie ... You asked why I did not send you an app. of Pardon. I did not know that R. made out one until afterward he wrote to me, but you cannot have a Pardon made out while you are at that place, the Gov dast not act on that. I wrote to you to have an exam. As I was their Dr. D [Deerhake] said to me you didn't have an exam for a long time, he thought he would have to give you one for you wasn't bad as you come their, but he don't do that, so its up to you to ask for it, then we will see, then I suppose it will be handed in to the Board of Control ... I picked 2 bus. of cucumbers today and am selling them to Owen store tomorrow. I can not use all of them and I picked peas and canned some, will pick more the next 2 days and can them, they take lots of time ... only half of the taxpayers of Longwood paid their taxes

... well we have and will again, I'll see to that. Well must close for this time, hoping you will do as I tell you. From your Mother, my back hurts me very much.

Frank on Canning Corn and Signing a Pardon!

Frank to Mother, August 7, 1932

Dear Mother ... I read once how to dry sweet corn but have forgotten now. You can can it by taking the corn on ear and dipping it in boiling water long enuf to set the starch then take a sharp thin blade knife and cut the corn from the cob, then put it in the can with some salt and maybe a little sugar and then process it in hot water or in the oven long enuf to kill the bacteria. When you process it in hot water take the wash boiler, put some narrow sticks in the bottom so the cans do not touch the bottom of the wash boiler, set the cans on the sticks, then put in water in the boiler but not so it runs in the tops of the cans. Leave the screw caps on the cans loose until processed. Cook until thoroughly heated thru or cooked. Then remove cans and seal tight. Perhaps you could dry it slowly in the oven after cutting if off the cob and keep it that way. Be sure to get it thoroughly dry or it will mould. Then you can cook it afterward when needed in milk. There is a cyclopedia here that tells how to can anything, even meats, chicken etc. You should have let me know before this. I remember reading—put in a teaspoon of each sugar and salt when canning. Maybe I will copy some if I can get that book. You could write to Washington and get bulletins on home canning. Probably cost 10 cents or some such price.

Well I will have to write more on the pardon business again. I do not know what the record office clerk did but I suppose he sent it back to the lawyer. If one would get consideration from that place in Madison one would be encouraged to try but I never heard from there in any of my previous applications. Perhaps it makes little difference whether one swears to a lie or refuses to do so. Have to go thru a lot of examinations and other red tape, foolishness again. If the governor would cut the sentence to twenty-five years I would soon be thru serving time if he cannot give one a release or pardon. To ask for either one is to put the O.K. on the courts sentence. Write to the lawyer and tell him to send the same application here and I will sign it. There will be plenty of time before the next pardon hearing in September. I wonder what difference it makes if everything has to go by such and such time. I have seen so many leave here on similar offences or charges that it aggravates me to ask anything. ...Well if he sends the papers here I can sign them and make another attempt at it. Will close for this time as I have written almost both sides of the sheet. Am fairly good in health at present. Had a cold I guess, From Frank

Attorney Paul Raihle sent a letter to Frank dated August 11, 1932, to let him know that Caroline told him he agreed to sign another pardon application. Attorney Raihle made it clear to Frank that he would word the pardon to say he was innocent of the crime charged. He asked Frank to have the record office clerk send the application back to him at once after signing it and he told Caroline not to worry about the charges on this matter. Raihle again stated that he had very high hopes with Governor La Follette and that the last attempt with former Governor Kohler was very close. On the bottom of Attorney Raihle's letter Frank wrote in pencil, "Pardon application signed Aug 12, 3:15 p.m. at Prison Record Office, Before E. M. Larson. Short interview later with Krouse Record Office Clerk." This was the fourth governor that the Kruegers had applied to for a pardon.

Mother to Frank, August 11, 1932

Dear Frank ... It was a long time to wait for your letter but as it come and I had read it, O my how glad I was, of course you never did com. the crime but there is no other way to get you out and it will come to light then who did commit it. This way they just say it right out, they are safe that they will not be sued as long as you are their and they are right in that, But O how glad I am that the Gov. can not say anymore that he had no complaint brought to him from you. Well I am going to try that corn, perhaps it will be good by next week—that is the field corn but the sweet corn will be coming along so to, that is what I want to put up the most, yes haying is done with, am glad to, its getting to hard work for me, even the running after everything—cattle, chickens—and all the cooking is getting to much in such hot

weather. I have had such pains in my back yest. it hurt me so
bad I hardly could do my housework, but today I do not feel it so
much because I am sitting still more, mending and writing letters
this afternoon ... Well must stop and hope you will be home next
month, hope you are well. From Mother

Leslie could not be pardoned while a patient of the insane asylum and he
and Caroline were working on a plan to either have him re-examined for
sanity or returned to the prison. She felt that soon both of her sons would
be released, one way or another. Caroline told Leslie she had plenty to eat at
home for when the time came. In the meantime, she sent him a large box of
homegrown plums.

Local Banks Closing

Mother to Frank, October 20, 1932

... Well I suppose you read about Owen Bank locked up and
L heard they were 78,000 short but there is so much talk can't
believe everything, but as soon as the Examiner got to Owen he
got a car and went to Withee and told Beilfus not to open for 10
days—well that caused almost a panic but it opened up again this
morning. ...

Mother to Frank, October 28, 1932

... Well the Withee Bank went down too, first it said they
were only going to lock up for 10 days, but now all that had
money in it have only 5 cents on the Dollar coming, or wait 4
years and then they will get their money back, and Abbotsford
done the same thing the same way as the Withee Bank. But Owen
is a goner, someone else is trying to start up their now. L heard
Mr. Van. H. lost 300 dollars their tax money and others lost all
their living money for the winter—now on the town all of them ...

Mother to Frank, November 3, 1932

... just think, the Withee bank is gone to, everybody lost in
that to, some their whole life's savings just as in Owen. Oscar G.
took out $10,000 just before it went down and A. R. O. took out
$40,000 and left for Florida, and another one took out his—forgot
who it was. Wm T. sold the O. Bank $30,000 unworthy bonds and

Withee B. [bank] 9,000, there is W. C. T. for you—he and Bob M. is
in the real estate buissness in Minneapolis now, wonder if he can
get away with that. Well a man was here from __ he is hard after
the Gov. to let you out. Leslie is now in the new building where
the kitchen and the dining room workers are, they have hot and
cold water in every room ... that man from __ is head of a big
Organization so you might know who he is—hope you are well,
from your Mother

I believe Caroline was referring to the International Labor Defense of Chicago when she mentioned the "big Organization." Louis kept in contact with
the Chicago headquarters but little was mentioned in letters to prison about
the I.L.D. or what role, if any, they played in the release of Frank and Leslie.

Leslie to Mother, November 5, 1932

Dear Mother, I received your letter about half hour ago so
will answer it. There are a lot of automobiles going by, I suppose
going to Madison to here the president talk. I am on the top
floor, I can look out over the wall. This is a better place than
the other place. I think they made that into a sick ward, quite a
few have the T.B. so it is best I moved. This is the new building
west of the one I was in, it is not the one with the wall around it.
Radio starts in the morning when we get up and stops when we
go to bed. We go out for walk every day. Well I have not heard
what was done about the pardon, I suppose that he will say it is
a government case and will have to be straitened up just like the
others did. It will take a good lawyer to do that. There are 3 or
4 planes out there every Sunday taking up passengers, looks as
though they are busy all day. Well it has been kind of cool this
week, did not have any snow, it rained a little last night. And the
paper is full—am well. L K

Mother to Frank, November 9, 1932

Dear Frank ... you asked if Leslie has a pardon up, no the
Dr. their said that as soon as the Gov. gives him the order he will
let Leslie go, not before. I have an idea that when your case is
looked up by the Gov. he will see what they done to Leslie to and
let him go to without any further trouble. ... From Mother

FRANK'S INCOME AND EXPENSE LEDGER FROM 1923 THROUGH
AUGUST 1932, WRITTEN IN SHORTHAND (AUTHOR'S PHOTO)

20 OUT OF ONE IRON CAGE INTO ANOTHER

Frank at Central State Hospital Waupun to Mother, November 19, 1932

Dear Mother, Must write another letter so you hear from me again. I am writing on a different date than I used to write previously and also from a different place. Suppose it will be a surprise to you when you read this letter and see where I now am located. The powers that be have seen fit to transfer me to the same place where Leslie is. I wonder if that is all I am going to get from the application. I did not expect to get this but have to be satisfied as it is. Am doing no work so far but am on the ward passing away time.

I suppose you wrote a letter this week, and I will perhaps get it later, sent here from the prison, so cannot write much this time. ... Have seen Leslie several times and visited with him. He is the same as before but has put on more weight.

I will not write any more this time. Hoping your health is good. I am feeling well so far. I was transferred here the 15th. From Frank

Leslie at Central State Hospital to Mother, November 20, 1932

Dear Mother, I received your letter half hour ago so will answer it. You asked about F, they dragged him in here this week too so now we are both to gather again—he looks to be in pretty good shape. I do not know how the pardon came out if he got anything done. They say and it was in the paper that 400 pardons were up, only 6 got anything done. I do not know what to do about it. I was thinking if you could get one of that

organization lawyers they would know how to get after it. I know
that if they take it up something will be done because they do not
play around with it. ... Next week is thanksgiving day I guess we
will have chicken. ... Well I am going down and see F, he is on a
different ward. And the paper is full, am well. L K

In September of 1932, Frank was interviewed and examined by doctors
at Waupun, but he refused to answer their questions. Rather than receiving
a pardon, he was transferred in November to the insane asylum known as
the Central State Hospital at Waupun—the same hospital that Leslie had
been incarcerated at for the past several years. Caroline became aware of
Frank's uncooperativeness and scolded him. She pleaded with him to cheer
up, stop being blue, and answer all questions when the next group of doctors
scheduled an exam with him.

Caroline wrote to the Board of Control in late November to see if they
would re-examine Leslie as well. Having both sons now declared insane
meant that neither could have their freedom. In order to be pardoned and
released, they had to be sane.

Frank's reasoning for not answering the questions from the examining
doctors was in part stubbornness. He was tired of all the red tape but should
have known it was coming. In a handwritten note to himself he said, "... I
applied a petition for pardon not an application for a civil service examination or a doctors license. If the governor knew what he is about he would go
about it in the proper manner ..."

Attorney Raihle wrote to Caroline and sent four blank petition forms
along with his letter for her to fill out and mail back to the governor's office,
along with personal letters requesting Frank's pardon. Raihle felt that four
separate petitions would make a bigger statement than one large petition.
When the date for the next pardon hearing was announced, Raihle promised to let Caroline know. He also informed Caroline that a group called the
German Society in Milwaukee had passed a resolution urging a pardon for
Frank and sent it directly to the governor. This society was to play a major
role in gaining freedom for both Frank and Leslie.

Mother to Frank at Central State Hospital, November 24, 1932

Dear Frank, received your letter but Oh, Oh, what shall
anyone say to that. I suppose that was the work of them 2 Dr. I
told you that time, what was on record as I was their that shows

either do what I tell you or you must take what I give you. Or did you have any trouble their, write and tell me just the plain facts or I can not do anything for you if I can at all, it looks as if I can't, yes that is the power that is ruling now and its going to be lots worse before long. Well what does the Dr. say that ails you their, and was [warden] Lee in favor of that? Or don't you know, where you are now we can write a little plainer than where you were. ... But what surprises me so is what La Follette said in Marshfield and what he said to the Law. and me in Madison as he shook hands with me, he said something is going to be done for them, well perhaps he will yet but I have little hopes ... well just cheer up, perhaps its best the way it is, at least you'll have more freedom their, well this is Thanksgiving day but not for us as I am here alone today and must do all the chores. L has been gone since Mon. will be home tonight ... am having a rooster for supper tonight and dressing with it and taters. ... We are well, hope you to. Mother

Frank Refuses IQ Test

Frank at Central State Hospital to Mother, November 27, 1932

Dear Mother, Got your letter yesterday so must answer it today. ... About me being here, I do not know who gave the orders to have me brot here. I know the officer who brot me here from the prison.

About those two doctors in Madison. I refused to take what they call the "intelligence test" and that would offend them. I told them I did not want to answer their questions, that they were not capable of taking my intelligence. They have a psychology (pronounced sick-ology) test, by which they think they can test a persons mind. I wondered whether the two were more sick than I. I knew they could not read my mentality by the questions they asked. Anyway I did not ask them for anything. I signed a paper asking the governor for a pardon on the grounds of being not guilty, so had nothing to do with the doctors. Perhaps the Board of Control had a say in getting me here. Am not certain tho. About Mr. Lee being in favor of it, I do not know either. Had no interview with him nor did I get into any trouble as I know of. ... I have little faith in the governors statement he made to you "do something for you," such remarks are of little value. If I were still at the prison it would be "doing something for you" leaving me there. One wants what is satisfactory to one and what is due one. Should be more definite, more explicit, more bussinesslike, or nothing. Well I hope Louis got home O.K. I do not like to see you alone at home so long, especially now in the winter when it is cold. Cannot blame him in a way either. ... Am getting on in health as before. From Frank

Louis left home to go deer hunting with a group of men from the Popple River Dam area. He hunted north of Redville and shot a forked buck, which he brought home to Longwood. Louis needed a break from the farm and felt much better in spirit when he returned, also knowing that the venison he harvested would be a real treat.

Leslie to Mother, December 10, 1932

... I see F right along, went to work last week. It is something funny that a person can work in here and when it comes to let a person out, they will say he is not fit or also do nothing. If a man is able to work in here and they have no complaint, there is no reason why they should hold a person around handling all kinds of knives and things. ...

Attorney Raihle and Wife
Visit the Krueger Farm

Mother to Frank, December 15, 1932

Dear Frank ... last evening the Attorney and his wife came from Chippewa and brought us the glad news that you was granted a conditional pardon so that you might be treated for mental disorder. O but we're as glad, my my I can't tell you and so was the Attorney, he was tickled all over, but in one thing he is afraid for you when they examine you, that you might not answer and be friendly their, you might make the mistake for your life, his wife was working 9 years in such a place and she said she see many they would not answer the questions that the Dr. asked them and the Dr's said then stay their and they were perfectly well but they were to stubbern, now don't you be that way. Raihle said he did not know where they were going to take you for to be examined, but now do as we tell you, you are free from the life sentence, you will never go their to prison again but there is danger for you to have to stay in an Insane Asylum, so do your best and may God help you. Now the many letters that you got from here I think I would throw them in the furnace their, all but the valuable ones, so you wont have to bother with them or send them home in a box and I will write to Leslie this afternoon to and tell him what will be done in his case to, well its offul cold this morning again just bitter and did you see the moon and the moon dogs last night, don't see them very often, we are well, hope you to. From Mother.

Frank to Mother, December 18, 1932

Dear Mother, Must write again today. Got your letter Friday and also one from Raihle yesterday. Conditions are different here than they are at the prison. Here I am privileged to write every week. Both your letters contain good news for me and if I were at the prison now, or rather when the conditional pardon was granted by Governor Phillip La Follette, I would be released from that place, but being where I am now I do not know what the outcome will be. Well am pleased as it is and will have to wait until other changes are made. The attorney wrote what one of the conditions were and the rest of his letter contained about the same advice you gave me in your last two letters. Will have to make the better of things when they come. Will not write any more about it this time. Am getting along well so far and hope you are in good health when this letter reaches you, and continue so. From Frank

Did the State Board of Control foresee a pardon for Frank Krueger in the fall of 1932 and put him in an insane asylum beforehand to prevent his release? It would almost seem so, as he was examined and declared insane a month before the conditional pardon was granted, not long before La Follette's governorship was about to end. The conditions of the pardon were that Frank would not carry firearms after his release and that he would seek treatment for his "nervous condition." Attorney Raihle felt that Frank's condition was not serious and told him so. Raihle and his wife were planning a big reunion and a chicken dinner with Caroline and her sons upon their release.

Leslie to Mother, December 17, 1932

Dear Mother, I received your letter yesterday and so will answer it. I see F got a pardon. I made mine out this morning, he says he will act on it sometime this month. I suppose that if he acted on his he will do something with mine too. If we get that settled we can get this other fixed up to. Three had trials last week, one went out and two came back. It has been kind of cold this week. ... Now next week winter begins and a week from today is Christmas, the greatest day of the year. I proble be out as quick as F will if he acts on my case this month. Well I do not know much to write, they cut out everything in the paper about our case. I did not see it but I found it out just the same, am well. L K

Letters Home No Longer Censored— Ennis Did Not Fire the First Shot

Frank to Mother, December 23, 1932

Dear Mother ... In your letter of last week you wrote something about what to do with my old letters. I haven't them in my possession now, but they are in the box and put away so will take care of them later and some are good to keep as reference. ... Yes, it is better here as for living conditions and also not so restricted, and more freedom for conversation. Can also look about more. I can see the sun rise and also go down. Something I had not seen since I was removed from Northern Hosp. There I could see it in the early morning across the lake. One misses those changes in nature when down in closed walls. Can watch the changes in the weather as rain and snow and lightning. Raihle wrote me the conditions the governor set for me. Good enuf but how about others using them on us in case of trouble. First compel one to take up arms for ones country and later restrict one entirely. I had decided to do that anyway, even in hunting. Puts me in mind what Attorney Kountz of Neillsville said to me when he called you and Ennis and me to Neillsville the time we went there [the summer before the shootout]. He asked me whether we had them, and I said, yes, always have as long as I remember. That was also Hewett's reason he went thru the house one time when you was out picking berries. I would not let anyone do that again without papers.

That "first shot" was not Ennis that did that but the man down the road that hit me, but we will have to let that go I suppose. Shows how much some know about it. What Kountz asked me gave me the impression they wanted a reason to start trouble to get a "case." Well they got one and a good one. Want to "straighten" up something already in good order. You will probably hear news from Leslie as he said he signed papers for a pardon. He told me so should write it to you. So there may be some chance for him as far as the charge is concerned. I wrote you about that before, cannot let one off without the other as we were sentenced on that. Nothing definetly proven, so therefore the only alternative is to remove the charge from both of us. That I will abide by as we know that. Must write on something else.

Those berries shurely kept well, 8 years. You must have got them perfect, a good preparation, a good rubber and also a good seal on the can. You never lost much canned goods anyway as I remember. ... I always get two sheets [of paper] here, but not on the other place without special permission.

Yes, I am on the working list, have been since the 9th of the month. Have a task on the ward here, I stay mopping and cleaning for a short time in the morning and now and then at different times of the day and a little time in the evening. Just keep things clean about the room. Work along the same lines I have done in the past, since being in these places.

Am going to close for this time, so according to custom will wish you a merry Christmas and a happier and more prosperous New Year Nineteen Thirty-Three. ... I am getting along well so far. From Frank

Frank's referral to the "first shot" in the above letter was prompted by a letter that Caroline wrote to him the day before. She stated that in a letter she received from the governor about Frank's pardon, Ennis was blamed for firing the first shot. Frank disagreed with that statement.

Frank to Mother, January 1, 1933

Dear Mother ... Hope Leslie got something also as he is entitled to it as well as I. I have different work now, am working in same place as Leslie is. In the dining room. See him three times daily and speak a little now and then but we have not much to say, only what takes place at home and how you get along. He got your letter yesterday or was it the day before and he stated a few of the articles you wrote about. The work is something different than I have been doing, but have done some of the same kind before. Have to help run the elevator to get the food and dishes from one floor to another before meals. The elevator works the same as ours in the house only the platform is larger. It is made by the same company, Rosenberg, Milwaukee. ... Do you use the one in the house now? Hope Louis can keep it in good working order, tell him to look it over carefully, once in a while especially the wire rope and brake lining. ... I better stop or someone will think I am off or see too much. Am getting along well so far and feel good in health also. From Frank

Leslie Gets a Pardon, Too

Leslie to Mother, January 7, 1933

Dear Mother, I received your letter just about half hour ago. I see that you are getting better which is a good thing. I also see that I got my pardon which is another good thing. I heard it last Sunday—a fellow seen it in the paper but all the rest of the papers that came in here it was all cut out. Frank had some kind of examination last week. I do not know what they are going to do, so far as answering a few questions I can do that. ... Well I hope that I will be home to eat some of that venison, have not had eny for a long time. What did he do with the hide and the head. Well today we do not go outside until Monday, there is not much snow so it makes walking good and the paper is getting full, don't know eny more to write. Am well L K

When the neighbors became aware through the press of Frank and Leslie's pardons, they assumed they were both released and at home. Some stopped to visit at the farm thinking they could see the brothers. Caroline received cards in the mail from friends congratulating her on her efforts in gaining their freedom and wishing them all good luck in the future. But they were not yet free.

Louis said that when he went to town everyone questioned him about his brothers, when they would be coming home. They wanted to know if Frank was really that sick and felt he would recuperate much faster if they just let him come home. Public sentiment began to heat up with anger as time passed and the boys were still not released. They wondered what a pardon really meant or what good it was.

Frank to Mother, February 5, 1933

Dear Mother ... Maybe I should have not put my name where I did on the other letter and I thot of it too but what difference does it make. ... No one sees it but the postmasters or the mail clerk and the mailman who delivers the letter. ... We have had enuf trouble heaped upon us. A lot of jealous persons who could not bear to see us keep what we owned. Now that we are down they should be satisfied. As for their sympathy I don't need that, they can take a walk for themselves. I can find that word in the dictionary. The envious, jealous, greedy, trouble making concerns in that neighborhood as well as in other places who sided with them.

I did not get the article you said you sent but I have read about the organization you refer, maybe it is of some benefit if it does not consist of some of the same persons that have made trouble in other ways. I don't ever care whether I prosper again or not. It does not pay to be too ambitious. ... Last Tuesday three doctors from Madison were here and called Leslie and myself up for an examination. I have not heard anything from them again. They were sent here by the Board of Control to interview us on different matters, went into the case some, and had some papers pertaining to our case, some from the judge, and some from the warden of the prison as well as other papers which I did not get a chance to see. They do not know all then. I told them about our youngest brother and that was not known by them. Its on paper that he is dead and they said it must be true if the newspapers said so and he is buried on the lot. So I told them what you had done to the grave and that I did not believe he was buried there and that it took different evidence to convince me. Now one can see after all these years what the secret service and all such likes are used how little they can do to find out the true facts. Well I must close as I will soon have to go to work again. Am getting well in health so far. From Frank

Frank to Mother, April 9, 1933

Dear Mother ... I do not know whether it is in Warden Lees' power to hold one in prison in my case, but I think they could have at least waited until the pardon application was considered by the governor. If no action had been made on the pardon by then, move one somewhere to another place. Looks to me as tho the governor is not the chief executive of the state but that there are other men who have more power than he, and that it becomes almost necessary to make out another application to beg pardon of them. The thought comes to me that Reynolds had a hand in this, as he does not wish us to get home again and thus keep his, and others work covered up so we have no chance to defend ourself. Well that is our officials that were in authority at the time. Some irresponsible shysters who live on someone else. There is only one way and that is one has to let them go is about all I can see. One can protest and they don't know how to consider that. What beats me is how a lie can be upheld and how powerless they all are to give the case a good thot and reasoning. It does little good to write about it. ... I am getting along good so far. Well I will have another birthday anniversary shortly but will not write the date as I do not care to have many know that. From Frank

Frank to Mother on Easter, April 16, 1933

... Well this morning is a time in the churches the land over. All merely a custom perpetuated. It does have some significance however in nature, as in plant life for instance. They commence to grow after lying dormant for the winter. A resurrection but in a different form of state or nature. There is some church service on the radio now ...

A BOX WITH MANY OF FRANK'S LETTERS (AUTHOR'S PHOTO)

Leslie to Mother, March 4, 1933

... I have been here five years and I would like to know what them Drs mean when they say a man is crazy. Not one treatment have I got since I have been here ...

Much Excitement for Caroline

Mother to Leslie, March 15, 1933

Dear Leslie ... excitements I should say so, the Banks got lots of money now again, a good way to get in the gold, but by them Banks closing the papers don't say how much the people lost, nothing is said of that, last week will long be remembered by the people that lost their money in them banks, that is going down into history. The Withee bank did not bust, they just come and closed it, that is all and the people that had their money in it gets 50 cents on the dollar, but it opened for business yesterday for good again. Owen business men are all doing their business now. Well last Thursday as I was writing your letters a man came in asked for L to help him get his horse up, it had slipped on the ice out on the road at the mail box so they got it up, then an Indian woman came and wanted to sell herbs for medicine—well finally she left, then our dog barked so much on the south side in the orchard I went to call him back, but he kept right on, so I looked again and their was Larsons house afire on the south side on the roof, but they got it out. Cars my my, in just a few minutes, from here until over at his house and his yard all full … that was a close call for him … has Frank a radio in his ward to? … I am feeling much better since I have them new glasses. Hope you are well to. From Mother

Frank placed some notes in an envelope with a letter from home that he had received in April (presumably for safekeeping). One of the notes bore the signatures of three doctors and a date of 3-28-1933, blood test taken about 2 p.m. A lengthier note read "Attempts are even made here, by men in charge to force upon a person acts that good reasoning and sound thinking would quickly forbid. I have experienced such before by observation and cannot see it tried upon me, especially if it is of doubtful value. Strange, how some men will adhere to custom and you should do this because he is getting it done to him. Because someone else ahead of him did this so we should do the same. I suppose you do not know what I refer to, but I will not write it in this letter." Frank said suggestions were also made about taking a spine test of some sort when he had the blood test.

One Good Feature
about the Asylum

Frank to Mother, April 23, 1933

… where one writes one hears that [the radio] besides all the rest of the noise in the room, talking, card playing etc. Quite a place, it has one good feature about it as it passes the time easily. Can look outside which is worth something ...

Back at Longwood, farmers were talking of a milk strike. Louis went to a meeting in Owen in late April. The milk strike was scheduled to take place on May 3rd, and Caroline felt that more tough times were ahead for them. She said the farmers were on their knees and hay was selling for just $10 a ton.

Hospital Sends Frank's Letters Home

Caroline received a box of letters belonging to Frank in late April from Waupun. Frank had requested them to be sent home, but he was not specific as to what of his personal contents should be mailed out. His most prized possessions in prison were his tin box with a hasp on it in which he kept letters from home, his dictionary, drawing board and tee square, his watch, two watch chains and two charms. He also kept a Milwaukee Sentinel Road map, other old maps, a World Almanac, a Scripto automatic pencil, a slate, and other important papers of which he kept an itemized list. (Frank was quite bitter that these were never returned to him.)

Frank told his mother that he had kept all the letters she ever sent, very few envelopes were tossed and those letters doubled up. Most were arranged in packages, tied up, dated, and placed in order by date. After questioning Caroline about what she received, Frank felt that all the letters did make their way to her at Longwood.

Frank to Mother, May 7, 1933

Dear Mother ... the World Almanac I had as a reference book, I had tore out some of the pages. I wanted to keep the rest, I did not care for to take along if I were moved but when the order came I went and the cell house runner packed it and sent it along. It describes all the countries on earth and how they are governed, under new rulings since the World War, so comes handy when one reads. I had a "Scripto" pencil in which I used the lead you got, but I suppose he did not send that. Its an automatic pencil, put in the leads and write. Never needs sharpening.

The long glass cases with perforated aluminum caps and "Owen" on the side were tooth brush holders. They came in them if we bought one of those make of tooth brushes. The letters marked I-8, I-9, I-10, I-14, indicate the cell I was in when I got the letters. Those I got when I worked in the hospital are marked Hosp. Looks to me as tho you got all my letters including those I got when in Winnebago. The box I will not enquire about, if one cannot be called up and told about when one's property is sent back, I will not run after him on them. I would not like to lose the jewelery tho, as that is all I have as keepsakes. Among the letters you have should be two red papers giving the number of the watch case and also the number of the works. I can trace it if too long. Should you come here I will send it back. That old pocket book is the one Sheriff Hewett gave me in place of the one he kept or lost, mine was a black purse and opened in halves. Don't know what he did with mine, whether he kept it or whether the hospital in Chippewa kept it when he got me I do not know. It was a case of grab, grab, and keep. He either traded with me by force or lost it. The old soak and wonder how many more such man one has to contend with. Must close for this time. We hear some good pieces on the radio here. Violin and other instruments. Someone just played on the pipe organ. ... Am glad you are better, getting along O.K. myself. Frank

Mother to Frank, May 11, 1933

Dear Frank ... About them pocket books, I got them both, yours and mine as the bank was cleaning up their bank, they found a shoe box with all of our files in it and also them pocket books and a piece of a table cloth and I forgot what else—all our deeds. So the Cashier asked the District Attorney what to do with them, he ordered them to be sent home to me, that was six years after this happened, they were sent from Neillsville here. I told you once but no doubt you forgot it. Well the Governor is going to close down every cheese and condensery and butter factories in the State Saturday night at midnight, so they did force him to do what the Farmers holy day Association wanted him to do, that will avoid blood-shed because none dare to take any farmers milk. I read in the papers yesterday that quite a number of the old Veterans in the soldiers home has got to go back to their relatives to live on account of economy, old people between 65–80 years, the State can not keep all the inmates of our 17 penal and Charitable Ins. ... Well I feel pretty good now again, planted my onions last week to, hope you are well, From your Mother

Frank Places High
Value on his Prison Letters

Frank to Mother, May 14, 1933

... Be careful about the keeping of those letters and papers, if you should leave the house or even nights as one cannot tell what plans others may think of an attempt to carry out. The thot came to me some time ago of taking your letters and copying the principle news and events in them and then tear up the letters but I did not do it, but left them as they were. One does not approve of the stamp in them put there by the institution and causes inquiry should others get hold of them, in some cases tho they may also be of value as they prove where one was on that date in case someone wants to make trouble. Ones record is hard to get from men in these places, on account of changes from time to time ...

In June of 1933, Caroline received a letter from Attorney Raihle in regards to her sons' last examinations at the Central State Hospital. Dr. Lorenz said Frank and Leslie were still both insane and he was unwilling to release them at this time. Caroline felt the State Board of Control had no right to keep holding her sons, that if they were insane, they should be transferred closer to home to the Clark County Insane Asylum at Owen. Frank felt that the pardons were of no use, nothing but poorly issued pieces of paper. He said he would have to look out the window and find consolation in the beauty of nature.

More on Ennis

Mother to Leslie, June 1, 1933

Dear Leslie ... The Lawyer and his wife were here Dec. [Decoration] Day and he wanted to find out something of a party 5 miles from here, so they had me go with them and he found out just what he wanted about E. O I do wish E. would show up, that would over throw this whole affair, then they can not get out of the people seeing what fraud was committed, the Law. says I am going to get them boys out. Van. H. got me with their car Dec. day so I got over on the cemetery, but such a crowd, someone passed as it was getting dark and their were 6 cars their yet and so many new graves …

Leslie to Mother, June 3, 1933

Dear Mother, Received your letter and so will find something to write this week. We had a nice week, everything is starting to grow, the trees are all through blossoming. I see that them fellows are up to there tricks yet, they are not through yet. Well the Dr told me a different story, but I do not take there word anyway. I am on the best ward in the institution, I do not know what kind of ward, they call it the trusty ward—in the night the night man only comes around once a hour to punch the clock. I have been working right along around dangerous people and weapons and I seem to get along with everybody, so I do not see where they get there insanity stuff. Nobody can say that I was dangerous in any way … L K

In June, the newspapers ran several stories on Ennis Krueger and mentioned that his mother had received letters from him from various locations throughout the U.S., some just recently. Mrs. Krueger wrote to Frank about the news articles and said the purpose of them was to get Ennis to come home. She hoped he would read the articles and "come to his senses" and stressed how certain she was that Ennis was not in the cemetery.

Caroline also wrote to U.S. Marshal Cyril Marks in mid-June concerning the recent write-ups in the papers. "… You claim you did not see the body of the man who was buried as Ennis Krueger, but affirmed a conviction that the man had facial characteristics which would make identification positive—how comes all that. How can you make identification positive if you never saw the party. … Ennis has been seen and talked with since that time … Mrs. Krueger"

Frank to Mother, June 11, 1933

Dear Mother ... I do not know about Ennis but perhaps he too, is in a place where he cannot send out a word unless someone else has a look at it, so one hears nothing from him. I told that to [Dr.] Lorenz when he was here and Lorenz made no reply. ... I have been branded as crazy before I was brot here in irons, or to prison, was called that when home. When we together built our new house and when threshing was "crazy" because we owned so much land, because I did not drink, etc, etc, etc and on and on and on, so had to argue and dispute nearly all my detail acts when going thru my routine of work which I did when at home. Now I have nothing to do but look after myself, my personal body, and the routine work assigned to me. Home, freedom, home ties, relatives, everything is supposed to be forgotten and I am to do nothing but let someone else "gap" at me and "watch that fellow close."

If I were you I would make no effort to do anything to get us out of here but leave it to the, Oh well! I don't know whom to ask, I am sure, as none of those officials have any responsibility, and do all acts in the name of the "state" or the government, etc., as lawyers start with the "State of Wisconsin" versus etc. and then the "trial." It's a trial well and true for the person convicted, as I have experienced. Well I am a "patient" now and have been for how long. You know that as well as I. You wrote I should not think much about such. I have plenty of time to think and will as long as I live or is breath in me as that is what my mind is for. When I cannot do that I may as well be buried. There are many factors that enter into our troubles such as jealousy, at what we had at the time and prejudice on account of our language we spoke. Quite a hatred at that time and not gone yet either and will not be in our lifetime. Our laws are built around the capitalistic system and one can be robbed with impurity by the courts and the law and enslaved besides. Will close for now. Am well in body and you know how I feel mentally by reading this letter.

Dr. Deerhake, superintendent of the Central State Hospital, sent a letter in June to relatives of inmates kept there. The message informed family members that patients would only be allowed to write letters on the second and fourth Sundays of each month and legal holidays due to "limited appropriations." Prior to this, they could write every Sunday.

21 **THE GERMAN SOCIETIES** In late June of 1933, Caroline began to talk more seriously about the "organization" and how it might help with the release of Frank and Leslie. She was referring to the German Societies from Milwaukee who banded together to seek the boys' freedom by organizing what they called the "Krueger Committee" of the Central Federation of German Societies. The leaders of this group were G. Osterwyk, E. Aumann, and Paul A. Kaufmann, all of Milwaukee, Wisconsin.

Attorney Raihle wrote to Frank on June 30th with good news. The Federation of German Societies had obtained permission from the governor to have an independent examination of Frank to determine his sanity. Raihle encouraged Frank to cooperate with these new doctors who would be his "friends." He told Frank to try and forget his bitterness during the examination and throw away any wild ideas. Raihle did not know when the doctors would arrive but felt it would be soon.

Frank had jotted down a recipe for floor wax on a small scrap of paper and enclosed it in the envelope for safekeeping with the letter from Attorney Raihle. "In a vessel set in hot water away from stove melt ¼ lb. bees wax and 1 lb paraffin. Add ¼ pt. raw linseed oil and 2 pints turpentine. Stir thoroly and pour into tightly covered container. This makes 3 pounds of <u>floor</u> wax."

Frank to Mother, June 18, 1933

Dear Mother … I see someone is at Owen instigating or enquiring, well they certainly have been waiting long enough, and I doubt if anything will be done of benefit to us, as we have waited so long already. … Perhaps when they give John S. [John Servaty had accompanied Joe Gantz to Taylor County and back

when Ennis was supposedly shot in the barn there] in Owen a
good grilling they will learn more and enquire further and it will
help, let us hope so. ... When you write to us both you could
enclose both letters in one envelope and save stationary and post-
age. We both get together three times a day where we work and
get time to say a few words and on week days every afternoon
outside when the weather is suitable. If we do not get separated
here such can be done and save you some in letter expense. You
could send it to me one week and to Leslie the next. ...

Mother to Frank, June 20, 1933

Dear Frank ... in another paper that was sent to us here it
said if you 2 boys was not let out, that Organisation would ask
the Gov. if they can send Drs. their from their own Organization
and they said that they will work until you both are out. O it was
quite an article. Huffy my my, Also Crosby [current Judge of Clark
County] said or wrote to the Gov that it has never been really
desided who done the deed ...

Leslie to Mother, June 24, 1933

Dear Mother ... A week ago Monday Palmer [Dr. Plahner] and
two more Drs. were here to see me, said they would get me out
but do not dare to write it, they probly wrote it to you. The other
two asked me if you got that insurance money, they said it was in
some bank. I told them I did not think you got it, they said they
would see about it. It is two weeks ago, getting about time I hear
something, said I should stay in Milwaukee a month before going
home. Well I do not know any more to write, things are getting
dry round here again, need rain, am well. LK

Frank to Mother, July 4, 1933

Dear Mother ... I see you could not order the newspaper for
Leslie, he is just as well off if he would not get it I told him. Those
papers wrote enuf about us when the trouble was on that were
not true happenings, so what is the use of having them. One has
no chance to defend oneself in those papers. Everything printed is
as the reporter sends it in and often that is changed by a re-write
man. So it is as well to go without. I see them when in prison and

then they are censured and cut up so one does not get what one
pays for...

Mother to Leslie, July 10, 1933

Dear Leslie ... I can not write very well. I fell and hurt my
right hand and elbo and shoulder, the back of my hand is swelled
badly and the 2 middle fingers I can't straighten them out yet,
happened last Sat. O I wish I would not have to work outside eny
more, its getting to hard for me, glad you get your paper again,
hope them Dr. will get their pretty soon and find you fit to be let
out. ... Perhaps them Organ. is looking up the whole thing before
they send them Drs. their, but when they come be your best,
don't talk to much, tell F to answer on this if you're their yet so
long, when they get their it will go quick, either one or the other
way with you. Well we are well, hope you are to, from Mother—my
hand hurts from writing.

His Name is Narkofski

Mother to Frank, July 20, 1933

Dear Frank ... Well I don't know much to write so I will copy
a little more of what it said about E [Ennis] in that paper, that is
how it starts, "the stranger than fiction tale of a living "dead" man,
a principal in one of the nation's notable cases of war hysteria,
was released to the United Press today" and then it goes on telling
all about the trouble that was here, then Crosby answer what I
wrote to you, sometime ago you wrote about judgments against
us when you get out, no you are not right their, La Follette took
that all off as he pardoned you and as Dourthy Stanly and Ryan
were in as Attorney General they took that all off and sent the
letter to me stating that, so don't worry about that anymore, there
is nothing against any of us. Well I am tired myself of waiting
for them Drs., if they have not been their yet, what is the matter
with them [no money] ... A week ago I had a ride to Hanable and
Gillman and thru their just for a ride, so I see the place where they
shot that man, his name is Narkofski instead of E [Ennis] ... we are
well, hope you are to, Mother

I have heard nothing from Oosterwyck [Krueger Committee chairman] since the last time I wrote you. I am writing them today and asking them the reason for the delay. ... I do not know why the United Press agents were at Owen ..."

Perhaps Attorney Raihle's letter prompted Oosterwyk to take action, or he was waiting for the proper timing to conduct the independent examination of Frank and Leslie. In August, the Krueger Committee wrote to Frank for the first time by the request of Caroline Krueger. The committee had recently visited with the State Board of Control on the Kruegers' behalf. They explained their German group was a society comprised of forty-six organizations and wanted Frank to know they had taken up his case. They said a commission of doctors would soon be visiting him to make an evaluation and stressed full cooperation, just as Attorney Raihle did in his late June letter to Frank. The group tried to assure Frank they were his friends, as were the doctors they were sending to see him at the hospital in Waupun. Their ultimate goal was ensuring freedom for both Krueger brothers.

The Worst Drought

In late August Caroline wrote to Leslie about how dry it was, as dry as she had ever seen it since they moved there in 1884. She spoke of how the blue jays were ruining the apples by pecking at them. She tried to can the fallen apples that weren't too damaged by the birds and the chickens. Nothing was wasted. The potatoes Louis planted in the spring were only the size of marbles. Caroline had some potatoes left over from the year before that they were still eating. The corn was drying in the field, turning yellow from the bottom up, and farmers were cutting it and placing it in their silos. Caroline and Louis shipped out their sheep but those under 70 pounds were refused and brought back home.

Mother to Frank, September 6, 1933

Dear Frank, Must write again so you hear from us, well it sure was hot today again and dry, my my I never see it so dry but once since we live in C. County and Sun. evening a wind like a cyclonic wind for a short time but no rain. Well L picked our apples today so they will not fall and get bruised up that they

wont keep and our 22 sheep brought us a little over $45. The
freight was $16.45, its terrible the way the farmers are treated.
Them men said that they were going to go to see you both and
they said they want to see how insane you both was and the
Attorney and wife was here to. (them men wrote to him to be
sure and be here as they wanted to see him to) he said to them,
well you will not see an insane man in Frank for I have seen him
and no one can make me believe that there is anything wrong
with him. Leslie he said I did not see yet, you wrote how many
Ex. [examinations] you will have to undergo, well I don't know
but I guess the ones that will come next will not ask you how old
you are, that will be no visiting that will be an Ex. and I hope it
will be the final one in the K favor. I wish I could write what they
told us, but I dare not do that ... but what fires are raging north
of Redville they say is all burnt over and we could see the smoke
to and about 2 miles north of Withee also. Well we are well, hope
you are both too. Remember 46 organizations are back of you
both. From Mother

In late September, the three doctors enlisted by the Krueger Committee
hadn't arrived at Waupun yet to do their examinations. Caroline wrote to
Leslie and said they needed more money to make it happen. The committee
had raised half the money and called a special meeting to help raise the rest.
Caroline thought it wouldn't take long.

A bachelor near Owen gave Louis two bushels of beans so Caroline said
they would not starve.

Milk Strikes Ongoing

Mother to Leslie, October 27, 1933

Dear Leslie ... This is going to be a tough time to live thru,
not one cent coming in now that the strike is on, we can not sell
our milk—the condensery is shut down, all cheese factories, not
much travel on the roads now. L was in Owen the other day and
Grei [Griebenow] was so mad, my he said it is offul, no teams or
cars on the street to be seen and one of the store keepers said
not even the town people comes in and buys. ... They will open
the doors of all these institutions soon. I have to churn every day

now and use the butter instead of lard, well I hope you will soon be home, that them Drs. has been their and found you all right. I am not so well, pain in my shoulder. From Mother

Mother to Leslie, November 9, 1933

Dear Leslie, I must write again, this is the third letter I am writing to you 2 and no letter have I gotten of you or F. What is the matter, have they even stopped you from writing to us? Well I hope not. ... I don't hardly know anything to write, O yes the National strikers were in Withee, about 40 men of them and they stoped all outside trucking into Withee and last week in Owen and Sat. they were in Neillsville, the papers said 150 men but that many went by here alone, truckloads after truckloads, the first truck had 30 cars follow him then more trucks and more cars, a party was here stopped in from south of Neillsville to feed their baby, they were going a long ways and they said all roads were blocked and people in town, all of 3000, every place were full of people and they had to go around quite a ways to get thru. The papers lies so about that strike, they are striking all over the U. States. It is hard for everyone, I have to churn every day. I was in Owen last Thur. and a woman came up to me and said what is the matter with you farmers, what shall we do for something to eat. I said go to A. R. O., she said he wont give us anything to eat. I said you had big wages after the war, 5 and 10 a day, what did you do with it—run around with cars, dressed in silk, she didn't like it. Well I suppose there will be Excur. Thanksgiving on the R. Roads and I will come and see you if you are their yet. We are well so far and hope you are to. From Mother

Frank Asks for Sewing Needles

Frank to Mother, November 11, 1933

Dear Mother, Must write again as it has been three weeks past since I wrote to you. See by the letter you wrote to Leslie that it seemed quite a time and it is a long time when one has to wait always according to certain rules laid down.

Leslie is not going to write to you this time as he is going to do the same as I did a short time ago—write to the party in

Milwaukee [from the German Societies], he wrote to me and wanted both of us to write to him. I wrote about a month ago and Leslie is going to write him today. Well on the 30th of last month three men from Milwaukee were here and examined us again, asked us questions about the cause of our trouble, etc. Have not heard anything from them lately or what they have decided on. So will have to continue to wait as usual. ... Must be quite exciting times in the community around there, while the milk strike is on ... a farmer is also a worker making his own living. Some of these legal and so called professional men seem to have the idea that a farmer is of little value to the community. Some queer ways some men have nowadays to send food stuffs around to different Towns and back again before they can be used. The food you raise on the farm has to be sent away and then back before it can be used as food. If one suggests something he is judged as out of his head. ...

I am going to enclose a needle I broke yesterday. If it goes to you, try and get me two or three and send them to me in your next letter. This one was just the right size for number 3 thread which we use here. I need them for sewing on buttons, etc. ...
I see you are still having trouble with the hand, the injury the

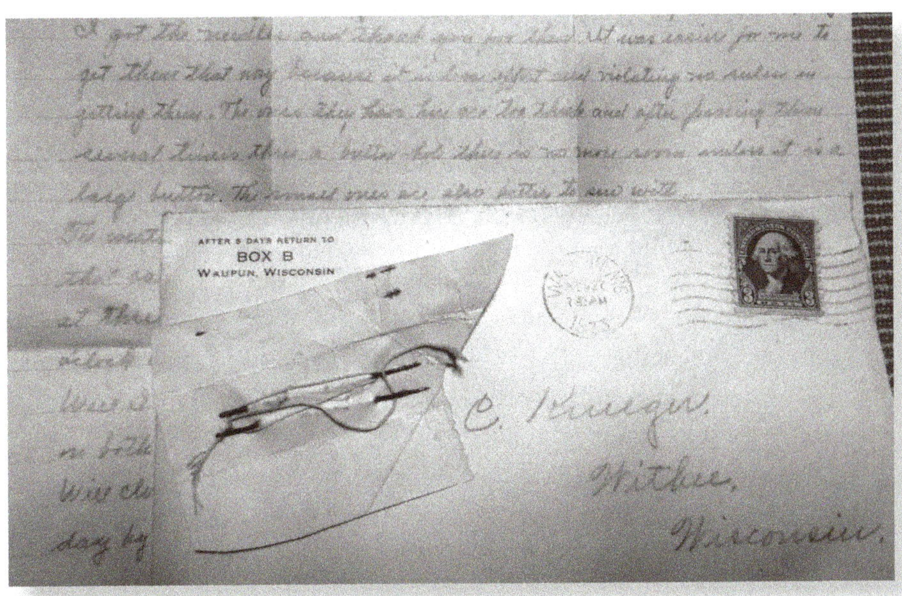

sheriff gave you when the trouble was at our place. Have to work with an injury on account of such men clothed with authority. Well I will close for this time. Am getting along good so far.
From Frank

Frank did receive two needles from his mother in a letter. They were still inside the envelope, coated with rust, when I found them. Perhaps he never used them, but the prison system did let them pass through to him.

Leslie Declared Sane

On November 11th, Caroline received a letter from Attorney Raihle about an upcoming hearing on the status of Leslie. He had been found sane by the team of doctors who examined him, but Frank had not been as fortunate. Attorney Raihle did not know the true condition of Frank, but felt his depression probably had a hand in the doctors' decision. The State Board of Control scheduled a hearing for November 28 to decide Leslie's fate. Raihle suggested Caroline attend that hearing at Madison. He felt that Frank would improve with time being in the better environment that he was now living in, and it would help him to know that Leslie was now declared sane.

Mother to Frank, November 16, 1933

Dear Frank ... well I am glad 3 men were their at last, will see what the outcome will be the 28th, they are going to meet with the Gov. and Board of Control, see if Hanna will fight it again. But that Orga- said here that they will fight for you both until you are out. ... We had a pie social in our School, 5 cents apiece, each ask of the other what they were doing now days—churning, churning, was the answer, well the Condensery started yesterday again. The patitions were sent to the Presadent and if 32 States fall in line it will be made a law that the farmer will get better prices for his produce, then their will be set prices on what milk. That is why them patitions. ... Well last night I went to Longwood to a meeting of our County Agent and I put in my application for 15 ton of hay and 1000 lb of corn. Our Co. got $208,465 for drought relieve so I sayed to L, I am going to ask for help too, the Co. took enough from us. ... Well must stop. From Mother

Frank to Mother, November 26, 1933

Dear Mother ... am glad others are taking our case up and pushing it but do not see how I can repay them. ... Your having to go to a county agent to get hay and corn aggravates me. When I think of the land we used to own and the plentiful crops of hay we used to put up and have plenty to feed our stock thru the winter and have some to spare and sell. There was no agent to see then and we got along then also and were better as we had to rely on ourselves and not gravel at the feet of someone else. For us, certainly a deplorable condition indeed, to have to share with other helpless creatures some of our accumulated wealth, earned by our own incentive, ambition and foresight. I think you will have to pay (perhaps will) for the hay and corn later. Yes, indeed the County got enuf from us. ...

While I think, write me in our next letter again about the drawing board I wrote you about before. I am enquiring about it here and they told me to ask you again. Also about a tin box about 1 foot long and 10 inches square at the ends. Will speak to you about it when you come here, and should I forget, remind me. Wish you did not have to come here any more, but we two go where we belong. That would be possible if we got what is due us. Make trips here every now and then and practically work for the railroad or transportation company. I got the needles and thank you for them. It was easier for me to get them that way because it is less effort and violating no rules in getting them. The ones they have here are too thick and after passing them several times thru a button hole there is no more room unless it is a large button. The small ones are also better to sew with. ... Will close for this time and am getting along the same as in time past, day by day. Am feeling well in health so far. From Frank

Leslie to Mother, November 30, 1933

Dear Mother, It has been so short time and seeing you that it is hard for me to find anything to write. You had nice weather and it is that way yet, no snow. I did not expect you at that time of the night. I would liked to have been at Madison and heard the argument, I suppose that I will be there pretty soon. And if they give me a fair decision I will soon be home. I am glad to get rid of this bunch and I think F will go soon too, I told him about it. I suppose that I will not be here when I get the answer to this but what train do you take out of Madison, but I think I will find a way out. Well today is Thanksgiving, got rabbit to eat. But I do not care for rabbit. What time did you get home, did you leave here that night, and do not know anymore to write. You better write to F, he is not going to write, has nothing to write, so he told me he feels good that one is getting out. L K

Caroline's Meeting with the
Board of Control at Madison

Mother to Frank, December 2, 1933

Dear Frank and if Leslie is their yet its for him, as I am answering his letter to. Now I am going to write some things that Dr. Dearhake [Dr. Deerhake, head of Central State Hospital for the Criminally Insane at Waupun] said in Madison, so you can see that the same element that worked against the Kruegers in Neillsville there is now working thru Dr. D., and Lorenz Reis had not much to say for as soon as it was over with, he [was] up and out, but Rosenberg was not present. Dr. Dearhake said that I was to blame of you 2 because I put you both up against him in my letters. Now that is a lie and I was the cause of you 2 being their (just like they said that time in Neills. The old lady is to blame, get her, if we get her we will get the boys all right) so that Dr. Dear. listens to that element, he is snaring himself, but it seems as tho he dont see that yet. I seen it right away as he said what he did. He also said that Warden Lee had to keep you in a private cell the last couple years you was so insane, just think what he said, wonder what Lee will say when he hears that, for I was their, not the last time but before that, and asked him, Lee, about your record and this is what he answered—F's record is an A-1 100 per cent perfect. He answered that way every time I asked him and Leslie's to the same way. Dr. Dearhake also said Leslie boasted what a nice home and farm and cattle we had. I supposed all what we had here and

Raihle spoke up [and said] now I have been their quite a number of times and I will say that they have a beautiful farm located on such a nice high place, as nice a place as can be found. And about the home can say he explained it just as it is and the cattle also, now because Leslie said the truth, Dearhake took him for insane, now who is the insane one.

I wrote a letter to Lee that time, why he let them 2 Dr. in to talk with you just the week before the pardon came up and who asked them Drs. to go and see Frank as long as the Prison Laws forbid such likes, and a few other questions nothing out of the way and Lorenz brought the letter their for Raihle to read and he did read it. Well Raihle says I don't see anything out of the way, hasn't she the right to ask Lee questions, there is nothing to that, Lorenz had no more to say, he sat down. O Dearhake said that he wanted to Ex. [examine] Leslie last night but he [Leslie] just got up and went out, but I am going to Ex. him for 3 hours. Yet now what a sense—he was Ex. of 6 and himself is the 7th Dr. and yet he isn't sadisfied. Well this time I told them also that them boys did not kill that party, the one that did kill him is walking the streets in Owen and everyone knows it up their too. Now this is all on record, and one of the committee from Milwaukee asked for it then, we will see it in print. I was also asked if we got our insurance on the barn, also what insurances and how much in each and Dr. Plahner from Mil. said that he was going to see to it, that you get Doctored rightly.

Nor did they like it that their were 48 organizations backing this up, for as it was over with and we [went] out they called Raihle back and wanted him to promise them he would drop them 48 Org., and Raihle said he would not promise—that was their doings. Lorenz was so mad he said he was going to resign from the Board of Control. Now it was left that they can get 3 disenterested Dr. to Ex. Leslie, but first take him to a Madison hospital or put it into court. Now as I see it, it would be the best way out for them. Let Leslie come home, and take you out from their to another Hospital and be Dr. until you are well and then send you home also, for you are both free from the State and they have no right to keep you their, if anywhere, you belong here in Clark Co. Hospital at Owen.

Well I have written about the most important things, will see what they will do now. ... That Organization says they will not give up until both are free and at home. ... Now I want you to keep this letter for if they see something in it they don't like well and I will also keep a copy of it. Well I wrote a long letter, hope you will improve in health as Dr. Phlaner says as he left, he will. We are well, From Mother [On the edge in the margin Caroline had written: Do you get medicine, answer me that and did he do anything for you lately ... if Leslie comes home, tell him not to talk to anyone as he looks bad, so fat they will mistrust him.]

The Fallacy of the Whole System

Frank to Mother, December 10, 1933

Dear Mother ... So the gossip is going around yet about you being to blame. The persons causing and carrying such gossip cannot usually do a piece of necessary work themselves. That story is still being circulated after so many years. They cannot do the work you have in times past. They cannot spin a fleece of wool and knit it into mittens and stockings. But here is what they can do in that county as they did before. Those so called professional men. They can circulate a petition among the residents and business men of Clark Co. to get your two sons into a penal institution, into involuntary servitude or slavery, to extort work from them. An institution that is connected with outside business interests within and outside the state. Such acts such people can perform and find enjoyment in, and gloat over. What the Superintendent said, Leslie had told about the cattle and home he had when he was on the farm does not surprise me in the least, that he (the Sup't) tried to make out as a boast. Would you think it were possible to convince such a man of the work and events and the personal property we owned during our long stay on the land that was our home? Do you think you could make him see that. Impossible. He has been in that neighborhood, he has told me so himself. One can see how little they know of ones past life and how talebearers and persons against us can hurt things for our family. ... One can see how the heads of these places work to keep them up. "Institution minded" men. They think if an inmate has a bed and something to eat they should be satisfied like an animal. Wonder if they think we two have a better life here and the years we were in prison then we had when free to roam about our lands and could go out of the house and in when we pleased. Could work with our machinery and tools wherever we chose and produced our living from the land. Where we could go into the house and spread butter, real butter, sweet cream butter, on our bread as thick as the bread itself. Now we get something they call butter, on Sunday morning only for breakfast, the size of the pattie which is about 1¼ x 1¼ x 5/16 inches. So the letter you wrote to Lee about the two doctors examining me while my pardon was applied for was presented also. Every cell in the prison has a rule book in it giving all the laws pertaining to pardons and parole of convicts. I have read over many times, these laws, and see nowhere, that doctors are required to examine convicts making applications for pardon to the governor. Raihle can look that up in his law books.

You wrote about Leslie being examined by 6 doctors and the Sup't being the 7th, that is not all. He was examined by doctors while in Camp Grant in 1918 and the beginning of 1919 and upon entry to the prison and by the different doctors in prison as changes were made and by Superintendents in this institution that proceeded the one that is at the head of it now. Leslie is well enuf in health, that little extra weight he has will soon come down when he gets home where he belongs and gets outside into the air and at physical labor with Louis. He has a good appetite and eats plenty and it puts weight on him. When not performing his special "assigned" duties in the dining room he sits in a chair or in his room and perhaps sleeps also during the day. He is not supposed to exercise by walking or move about, because if he did he would be judged as nervous and uneasy. I have told him to reduce the quantity he eats but he pays no attention and I don't coax him either. His weight has been put on by his long stay here and besides he eats candy, all he can get. ...

One can see the fallacy of this whole system shove one away from his home by force and in irons to institutions and then

to another for sanity trials and then back to the court and a jury
for a trial again. When the war was on the cry was "Down with
Autocracy." Looks tho we have legal autocracies here that need
attending to. Looks also as tho there is "Doctors Autocracies" as
well that need attending also. I do not see where I need further
doctoring as some seem to think. I don't need medicine of any
kind nor do I care to take any. I worked in hospital before and
studied the effects of the different medical treatments and come
to the definite conclusion that I do not need them. The less
medicine for me the better. I am above weight now according to
insurance table of weights if they can be taken as a guide. ... The
feeling of being where I am contented and where I am pleased to
be is a good treatment in itself. ...

 Well I tried to find out about the drawing board and box
but no results. My personal effects are mine and looks to me as
tho they were safer when I had them in my cell when in prison.
No one held them back from me there and inmates were in my
cell when I nor the officer in charge were not near. I lost nothing.
I am also short some money on my monthly statements. Money
that belongs to me. I kept a copy of this letter so can refer to it
anytime. Am getting along same as before and well also. Frank

On December 21, 1933, the Central State Hospital for the Insane received
$2.00 from Caroline, $1.00 to be credited to each of her sons' accounts. She
told Frank to use the money to buy grapes for himself and the same for Leslie,
rather than candy. She said Leslie was so fat that anyone would be ashamed
of him and she worried about his obesity affecting his heart. Caroline also
told Frank to stop brooding, as he was only hurting himself by doing so. The
16th of December was Ennis' birthday and Caroline wished he would come
home for Christmas; she wished for all three of her sons to come home.

Leslie Moved to Wisconsin
State Hospital at Mendota

Frank to Mother, December 31, 1933

 Dear Mother ... This will be the last letter I will write this
year. ...Yes, I see Leslie enuf before he left to say good-by to him,

but hope it should not be necessary and that we will not be apart as long as we were before I got here last year. Maybe will soon be back to you if those in charge come to a sensible conclusion. ... You wrote you did not like to see Leslie taken where he is. I told you that was not necessary when you were here that evening last. Entirely unnecessary and I told him while here but he could do nothing but obey and that is all. One thing—he has not the name on him of being in an asylum. A sort of stigma, or infamy. If it is his mind they want to pass on, that should be done and nothing else. He may have some imperfections otherwise but those are to be left. The state does very little to help persons to advance further as no one seems to care or assume responsibility. Being taken from one place to another gives one some experience but that is of little value also. No, I am not doctoring as you asked, unless ordinary "necessary" work is considered such. I am thinking I do not need doctoring. ... I will again wish you both a Happy and Prosperous New year. Its mild today and foggy and the water is standing in the low places.

Leslie was taken to the Wisconsin State Hospital for the Insane at Mendota, Wisconsin, in mid-December of 1933. He hand copied a letter from the State Board of Control about his examination there at Mendota. "We have today examined Leslie Krueger transferred to the Wis St. Hospital on Dec 11, 1933 for observation and examination. We find him extremely cautious, guarded in all his remarks with a pronounced prejudice with respect to various organizations and individuals, particularly Physicians, somewhat slow in his responses but calm and composed, fairly agreeable, possessed of almost average intelligence, the intelligence quotient being 85 and without any clearly defined delusion or hallucination. At this time we are reluctant to come to a defined decision regarding the presence of a major phsychosis and we pray that he may be kept under observation at this institution for a period of one month or more if necessary. We feel it would be well if we could have an opportunity to examine his record while an inmate at the State Prison and a patient at the Central St. Hospital. Respectfully Yours, August Sauthoff MD; Peter Bell MD; A C Washburn MD"

Another letter sent to the State Board of Control addressed to Dr. Frank C. Richmond, Director of Psychiatric Field Service, from Peter Bell, Supt.

of the Northern Hospital for the Insane at Mendota, Wisconsin, was hand copied by Leslie. This letter was dated December 24, 1933, and gave details of the initial examination of Leslie Krueger. "… Throughout the procedure the individual was very evasive … at times almost impossible to penetrate. His manner was superficial and he appeared very guarded in all response to inquiries … impossible to elicit any well systematized persecutory delusional trend …"

The letter went on to say that Leslie showed anger toward the doctors doing the exam and referred to a conflict that existed between his family and a competitive logging company prior to the incident that left him imprisoned. It sounded to me like they were confusing him with John Dietz, a man from northern Wisconsin who became engaged in a battle with law enforcement over logging on his property, and was imprisoned after the shooting death of a law man. The statements appeared to be doled out in an almost routine lingo, one that may have been repeated many times for other patients.

Dr. Bell said he felt that Leslie was full of delusions but was stifling them the best he could, knowing the detriment they would bring to his gaining freedom. Bell noted that Leslie needed more observation and doing so would give the necessary time to procure his records from the State Prison and Central State Hospital. It seemed there was never any intention of releasing him at this point, no matter how the initial exam went.

The Waiting Game Continues

Frank to Mother, January 14, 1934

Dear Mother … You wrote you had a steer to kill. Well if I was there I would get a good steak from the hind quarter or the round. Something that does not get in these places. Always the trimmings or hearts in stews. … I see you heard from Leslie. What was the idea of sending him to that place. That institution is along the same line as this or the one at Oshkosh. I understood he was to be examined by doctors not connected with the state doctors. The place he is at now is controlled by the Board of Control and State doctors. I suppose a lot of more examining and questioning. … There has been time enuf for all the examinations necessary. … Am getting along day to day as usual and feeling good in health. From Frank

Mother to Frank, January 25, 1934

Dear Frank, Must write again so you hear from us, don't know much tho, got nice weather again after Sun and Mon rain, it took all the snow away but left ice. Well got 2 letters from Leslie, one was written the 19th I got that Mon and the other was written the 16th got that on Tus. They don't attend to the letters their like where you are, on the 16th he wrote that he had one Ex. [examination] but would have to have another one he thinks this month, and things are different their than where he was with you. They do not read the letters that comes in, but them that go out they do, and in the 19th he writes I should read the letter then burn it as there are contagious diseases all over so I did, he said not to send any of his letters to you and that he feels good as well as usual. He also got 2 letters from the Attorney but he told me to write to him that he received them, seems as tho he dare not answer them. ... Got a card from the Organ. saying they was going right on with this case and that they were going to have a big business meeting like last week for the K case, but have not heard any more about it. I see by the papers that the Institutions where you are Officers are hailed up before the law to, their were 4 big articles in the paper about the ill treatments the inmates got. What has become of the paper Leslie got when their, do you get that yet, or is it run out. ... Am Spinning now days, got a few roosters to can yet next week, so it will soon be spring and you both will be home is my wish, we are well, hope you are to, no L has a little cold but not I. From Mother

Mother to Frank, February 1, 1934

Dear Frank ... See you feel the same as usual which is good, but one mistake you are making just now and I am afraid it might hurt you later and that is try to forget the past and look for a bright future, now don't think I don't like your letters for I do and how you explain them as they are so well explained that an insane person could not do so, that is one thing in your favor, for they want a letter once in a while their ... well hope you will be alright again soon and out from their ... Mother

Attorney Raihle explained to Caroline the necessity of a jury trial to determine the sanity of Leslie. They would have to bring a lawsuit against the state. The German Societies would need to re-examine Leslie and give this information to a jury. Raihle said it would cost a few hundred dollars, considerable money, and he hoped that between Louis and the Krueger Committee, enough money could be gathered to pay the expense involved in bringing this forward. He wanted no pay himself, only enough to cover the court costs.

From Gerhard Oosterwyk and Ernst Aumann
[Leaders of the German Society of Milwaukee]
to Leslie Krueger at Mendota State Hospital, February 8, 1934

Dear Friend, Your letter from 13 January received today and can tell you that our meeting on behalf of the Kruger Fond was a big success. D. Plahner gave us a fine lecture and I told the people what the Krueger Komitee has done, and what we suppose have to do In the future. I am very sure, that you will have a fair deal, don't worry about that. Today I got a letter from the Lawyer Raihle. You can be thankful, that he is working for you too. ... He does what he can do, we the German Komitee were ready to go in the court, for a jury trial. He said, wait until February, and now he wrote to the State Board of Control, to get her decision that you should be released. We are waiting with great hope to the letter from the Board because we are sure that you are perfect sane and fit for society. Now, dear Friend, I hope you will be out soon, and your first step must be to come to Milwaukee see us because we have to work in behalf of Frank, and for that we have to talk things over with our friend and society's delegates.

With Mr. Raihle I am still in connection with him asking questions ... to get this case settled ... Isn't it funny. You got the most time and nothing to do, I get no time, and lots of work. ... If you come to Milwaukee, you get a place where to sleep and to be home in my place. Don't believe you are without friends, you got more friends than you know, because everybody is willing to help you, and I call them therefore friends. ... Be hopeful and trust yourself, like we do it. Your friends of the G. A. Society

Dear Leslie ... I wrote to you the 7th and also send you 2 stamps envelopes and paper, will this time too if our state is too poor to supply with such likes at least once a week ... no doubt they wont let you out to go home, but in the meantime just be yourself as usual, don't say anything against any one or the Drs., just be on the jolly side,... do you get as good food their as in the other place? Will send you 2 dollars you asked for, buy yourself fruits as that keeps your health and strength up, got a cold in my bones and in my head a little, not bad, its that way all over. Your Mother

From Mother to Frank, February 15, 1934

Dear Frank ... Drs. made it offul bad with him, saying he remained evasive and cautious in his replies and is unusually stubborn, something Leslie never was, if you want me to I will copy the whole article ... last week Thu. and Fri, my it was cold and the Barn was cold, the cattle humped all up and just white with frost. O it's a pitty but what can we do, got to live and as I was milking I thought my fingers would freeze, well only a few more weeks then the hardest is over ... well about the corn sheller, I guess you are right but it came from Moo. [Moody] Place and I thought it was from him, and the girl that married out west farther. I have often wondered if his conscience don't bother him when he thinks of how he lied about Ennis being dead, where he knew it wasn't him, that is what he left for, they forced him to lie, but I blame him for not have said enough to stick to the truth, such a coward. ... Leslie wrote home for me to send him 1 dollar as they will not give him any of his money, he wrote he asked the Dr. and he said they were waiting order what to do with him ... he don't like it their at all, he is working at the same job as he did where you are, he wishes he was with you. Well I wrote enough for this time I guess all right. Mother

Leslie Recalls his Examination Questions

On a torn half-sheet of writing paper are a series of questions and answers written by Leslie, most likely from memory. The sheet is in an envelope postmarked March 2, 1932, along with a letter from Caroline to Frank. "Where was this man hit. <u>Side of neck.</u> What would do if it happen again. <u>Leave the state.</u> What gun did you use. <u>No.</u> Did you know this was coming. <u>Yes.</u> How did you know. <u>Friends told me.</u> What did they do it for. <u>Don't know its that way business was not for liquor.</u> Do you have eny enemies <u>No.</u> talk behind your back. <u>Yes.</u> How no. <u>Friends tell me.</u> How sleep. <u>well.</u> dream much. <u>Very seldom.</u> hear any noise. <u>No.</u> are you nervous. <u>No.</u> get excited. <u>No.</u> Do you believe in killing. <u>No.</u> Why not. <u>gainst the ten commandment and not human.</u> Do you believe in got. <u>Yes.</u> Does he ever talk to you. <u>Not yet.</u> Have you a poor conscence. <u>Clear conscience.</u> How long go to school. <u>until about 18 years.</u> When start. <u>As soon as I was able to walk.</u> Pass grade. <u>Yes.</u> Do you believe in law. <u>The law is alright but the inforsment is not very good.</u>"

Frank on Income Tax Returns

Frank to Mother, March 11, 1934

Dear Mother ...Yes, soon another birthday anniversary will pass in memory of Robert. Well he has been gone quite a while and also missed plenty of trouble. May he rest in peace. ... Tell Leslie in your letter I am the same as when he left here, same job, same bed, same place at the table etc. Tell him I said he should keep away and off the lake, should such be permitted. Can't tell what may be done in these tricky times and the state of condition people are trained to nowadays. You wrote about income tax report. I believe you do not need to make out one as your income is not enuf. I think it is if below $800. one does not have to fill out the blank. Better find out. I heard it announced on the radio today that the report has to been in before a certain date or be fined 25 percent. I thought 25% of what? He did not say either. I do not have to make out any and I would not if outside. I could not give a true report of all my detail affairs and I would not "perjure" myself under oath. I'd fight him before I fill out a paper for any man. It's a graft anyway so someone finds out your business. It's a part of the capitalistic system. Gives a job for a large clerical force of office men.

And I question if the income derived from the tax pays the cost of the assessor. One hears nothing of how much comes in and how the money is spent in the state. If a business man builds up a large business by his own initiative and is rewarded by a large income to himself and the shareholders, the income tax will take a large amount away from him. So he would be working for someone else mostly. Better to stop work altogether and make the other fellow do some too. They are all dishonest anyway and make a fool of one who tries to get along in a peaceful manner, even if they have to make up a war to do it.

I wonder where all that examination papers go like Leslie and myself. Probably filed away somewhere and forgotten or buried in an office in the work and forgotten about during these hustling times. Well I will close for this time, am getting along from day to day, and hope you get over the cold soon. Will wait anxiously until your next letter comes, so keep up courage and gut as that helps to keep yourself in condition. From Frank

Leslie Moved Back to Central State Hospital at Waupun

Frank to Mother, March 25, 1934

Dear Mother. Well must write again. Have some different news this time but perhaps you know about it already or will before this letter reaches you. Leslie was brot back here last Monday the 19th. You will get a letter from him I suppose. I have spoken to him only a few minutes, so do not know much to write. I do not understand why he was sent here but could have been sent home to you there to stay. ... Yes, it is now two dozen years ago since Pa left us, and a sort of responsibility fell on the rest of us when he left, but we recovered and went on till this trouble came on us and which we are not over with yet. Perhaps we will get through this also but of course quite a loss to us in worldly wealth, such as lands and property and time which we could have put to better use. ...

I was called to appear before the committee. Mr. Lorenz was there but there was not much done, only a questioning about the treatment of the patients of this institution by the attendants. Such as unnecessary roughness. He did not go into the particulars of individual patients cases. They did however read off the different institutions I had been in and the date of transfers. They also made the statement that we had been framed, and a few other questions. You mentioned the superintendent of this place in your letter. I am inclined to think he formed his opinion about us, me anyways, just a little too soon, was too hasty in his judgment, he however had plenty of time to pass on Leslie as he was here longer. A sort of belief is in the minds of these men that an individual committed here is not even of a "near" correct state of mind. Especially at the front office does this prevail. I noticed it at once and it was proven to me by the handling of my personal belongings I brot along with me, and not even adjusted properly yet to date. The work expected of me must be done as a person of a correct state of mind would be asked or told to do it. ... Will close for this time, am well so far to date, bodily, but not satisfied mentally with the state of our affairs. Hope you get over your cold entirely by taking care of yourself with the weather this chilly. From Frank

Mother to Leslie at Central State Hospital, March 28, 1934

Dear Leslie ... so you are both back again where you were. Well I wrote to the Supt at Mendota the same time I wrote your letter and this is what he answered I will copy it. "Dear Madam: Replying to your recent inquiry concerning Leslie Krueger beg to advise that he got along very well during his stay in this institution. He was always willing to visit with others and help with the light work. On March 19 1934, he was returned to the Central S. Hosp. at Waupun, very truly yours M. K. Green, Supt." Now if such good standings, what did they mean by sending you back their again where you are now. O such an outfit eny one can see how them leaders stick their heads together but its going to be stopped, will now have to see how this is all coming out first before we can do eny thing more and that investigation wont take much longer and then perhaps they will let you out themselves or we will go on everything is ready. I got a letter from the Org. saying that. ... Hope you are well, going to cook some molasses candy for my cough today. From Mother

Dear Mother ... Them Drs that examined me last was Supt. Green, Dr. Sauthoff and Dr. Silvestor about a month (Feb 26) before I left there. I do not know what they did, looks as though they did not do anything, they are all working for that institution. I am working at the same job I worked at before I left here in the dining room, see F every day same as before. What was the name of the hair tonic you used—my hair itches but they will not give me anything for it, they are coming out too, don't like to cut off short now. The investigation bunch was here yesterday, think they will start Monday, did they throw out any of the Dr at the other place. Lorenz was here and his bunch but they did not do anything, examined the records that's about all. Well I don't know any more to write, am well, L K

22 HOME AT LAST

On May 1, 1934, Louis Krueger sent a money order for $1.50 to Waupun along with a rare letter to Leslie. He wanted Leslie to use the money to order a bottle of hair salve from a company in Chicago that he ordered for himself. Louis told Leslie this hair salve would clear up the scalp irritations that he had been complaining about. He typed the same phrase he mailed to Frank the year before: "… when a man is thrown in a dump like you are …" as part of his brotherly advice and "there is going to be nothing left undone before I get thru with this case here …" Louis always came across in his letters as the tough brother who was going to straighten things out, one way or another.

Attorney Raihle sent a petition to Leslie on May 7th, and asked him to sign, notarize, and return it quickly. Raihle had recently met with the Krueger Committee at Milwaukee and plans were made to have the question of Leslie's sanity taken up in the County Court at a hearing, as mentioned to Caroline back in February. As soon as Leslie's case was settled, Attorney Raihle promised to work on Frank's sanity case as well. It seemed that without the extra push from the Krueger Committee of German Societies, nothing would get accomplished in obtaining the brothers' freedom.

Leslie to Mother, May 12, 1934

Dear Mother … I received your letter this afternoon … did not go outside but once this week and that was today, … I did not order that hair tonic—can't before the 20th, the order day. … When I was at the other place they told me that they would not declare anybody sane at that place. I would have to go back to the court I came from and then take another examination by the county Drs. and if they settled it, I would not have to go for trial, that is the way the S.B.C. does than say the way they do. Well this week was my birthday—years come and go, that never changes, and the paper is getting full, am well. L K

Mother to Leslie and Frank, May 23, 1934

Dear Leslie and Frank … Well we got our corn in and L is sowing a new kind of hay seed, it is recommended to stand dry or rainy weather but best dry, he is sowing it with the garden planter in rows apart, like onions only wider apart, he sowed some a week ago and its sprouted already, he likes to experiment on such likes. … Frank wrote, he wondered what the performance is going to be when Leslie is called to appear in the Clark co. Court. As I was in Neillsville different times they always said to me if that was to be done over again your boys would not be put their, that was an offul injustice, an offul wrong done to your family, a black deed committed that is going down into the History of Wis. Their couldn't been a blacker deed done. So he will be received better this time … One of our last year lambs has a lamb and its so little that people laugh about it, but O how lively it is. Well we are well so far and busy attending to cattle and field work and the ole hen and everything else. Hope you are well to. I remain your Mother.

Frank's Notes on the Back of an Envelope

Test May 28, 1934, and Visit to Dr. Reubly. Test again June 11, 1934 and Interview with 3 state doctors plus 3 German Society doctors plus three members of the Krueger Committee. Mentality test June 27, 1934, also Leslie. Finger Tip test June 30, 1934.

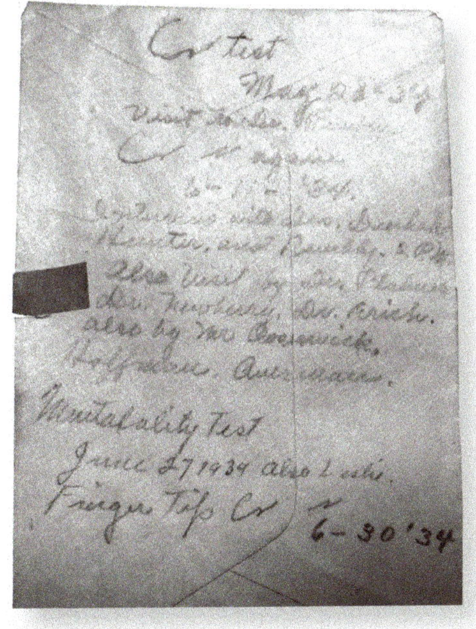

Frank's Notes on Tests & Dr. Visits

Mrs. Tufts Heard it via the Radio

Mother to Frank and Leslie, July 4, 1934

Dear Frank & Leslie This will be the last letter that I can start like that and I am not a bit sorry in that one way, but would have much rather seen you both come home. But the way it is, its no doubt for the best. But O how glad I was as I heard the Gov. had at last set you free from that place, and that Authority. It was not 8 o'clock in the morning eating our breakfast in the kitch, I said to L a car is come in and who was it but Mrs. D. Tufts and Mother. She had to go to Neillsville and got her car filled with gas at the filling stating in Withee and he [the man pumping her gas] said what he heard over the Radio just a little while ago that you both had got a complete pardon, and O she said she could not get down here quick enough to suit her and tell us and tickeled happy all over and also lots of others, not forgetting L and I they say now if another war would break out they would fight to the last ditch, all giving you right for standing for the right, now they see it well. Jesus suffered for what wrong he did not do to, and got his reward for it, well them Dr's did not come their for nothing, they must have had quite a time with the Gov. as it started at 1 then again at 1:30 o'clock. They send me 3 German papers, wish I could tell you all they wrote and in yest. Daily Wis. News they are going to make an effort to find Ennis, but I will send that article to you after I get your Address from the Hospital where you are going to be Dr. up in shape again before you can come home, their where you are now I dare not do that and from now I/we can write whatever we want to, that makes me feel good even to think of it. [Frank was required to spend several weeks at the Milwaukee County Hospital in Wauwatosa to help make his transition to the outside world somewhat easier, if that was possible.]

Well a party stopped in last week from Loyal, he said well how long will they have to stay their yet, everybody wants to see them out. 2 men and 3 woman from Perkinstown said the same thing, it just seemed as if it was in the air that something was going to be done for you. The one that you got the window frames from, his wife and her sister and brother-in-law was here to, said the same. Well this is the 4th and its raining just little showers every now and then, spoils lots of young peoples fun, if its called fun, also some accident and then mourning. L is cleaning the Barn make ready for the testing of Bang's disease in the cows, they just come tell you they will be here in that time for you to have the cows here, the owner has nothing to say. I don't know about a few of ours. Get $30 if they are no good any more, did you get the money back that $1.50 that L sent to them their for your hair tonic? You demand that.

I should think that them Dr. Dearhake, Lorenz and others that ex- you would feel cheap now in the German Paper—it askes the question (did them Brothers stay their 15 years + over for nothing?) I suppose you will be able to call on Frank when you are their, but one thing while you are under them 3 men's hands, do just what they demand of you all, but not on liquor, they are an offul people for drinking and the old sayings is 1 glass is to much and 2 are not enough. You never begin, need never to be ended. Well you might not have to stay long to. I hope our cows will be alright now that they give so much milk. I want to go down to see you both this Summer and I will think of you both the 8th Sun. It says your Address and the party you are going to stay with he went to Waupun with us that time Raihle and the rest of us was their from Madison. Well this is Thu. morn. and I must go out an pick my currens, there are not many this year but have to pick what there is, and then go in the Garden again, its to bad you both was not in Milwaukee over the 4th. They always have such fireworks, had chicken to eat the last 2 days, got to get at them now. I put up 35 qts, they taste good that way and keep well to, well must stop, are well only for my knees they to are getting old and wearing out. From Mother

One can feel the excitement and anticipation that Caroline was going through in her lengthy letters to her sons. As she said, she could "just feel something in the air" and she was correct. It wouldn't be long before the family would be reunited again at home on the Longwood farm.

Raihle Receives Letters in the Krueger Brothers' Favor

Mother to Frank and Leslie, June 28, 1934

Dear Frank & Leslie ... We had an offul down pour and wind last Sat., broke down another big limb of our last 2 late apple trees and one of our old plum trees out past way, but L with the horses pulled it back again and the trees were so loaded with apples but the ground is all covered with them now. ... Another down pour Mon. and rained every day since a little, but yest. I washed and then went up in the woods and got a cow with her calf and when eve. came I was pretty tired, but their will be no haying—the first time I ever see that, maby later in August their will be some as it is making good head way now and where them dead spots were, clover is com. as thick as hair on a dog, oats is heading out nicely, our cow is up and walking all around and gives ½ pail of milk, but do not use it as long as she gets medicine. ... Hope I will get the insurance as we are very much [in need of] something for a stable for to house the stock for the winter for as that day the Dust blew so it moved the north half quite a little east and its hard to do anything with it. [The Krueger Committee requested addresses of both companies that the barn was insured under back in 1918. They wanted to contact them and try again to get the Krueger's some compensation, so Caroline sent along the addresses.] ...

Well here is for Leslie—see you are their yet but got a German Paper and in it, it said that they were their to see you both (that is the committee) in Waupun and what was desided to do and that they took it up to the Gov. the 25th, they are in hopes he will let both of you out. Raihle wrote last week and in it, said that he is getting many many interesting letters in both your favors to be let out and they are going to get you out to, whether the board of Control and Dr. wants to or not. ... If they want you to go to Milwaukee then go for a month—of course I know you would like to come home too but they are doing so much for you, you will have to give in to them. ... L got a hole lots of pie plants [rhubarb] so I canned them, got 14 qt. put up, going to get some more, when you both come home we will need more sauce. Are well, hope you both are too, From Mother

Frank at Central State Hospital to Mother, July 8, 1934

Dear Mother, Well have to write another letter as it is my turn this time. I did not write on the 4th but let Leslie do the writing. ... See you wrote about the committee sent here by the different Societies. I am very grateful to them and all the members who are taking a part in the attempt to move us from here. I see they are trying to get us from here to another place. I am sure I do not know all about the move but will try and make the best of it when told to do so. There may be obstacles come and temptations to be faced which both of us will have to use our own minds to face and get away from. One you wrote about, one glass is too much and 2, etc. rather hard at times and one sometimes loses friends by refusing, but guess we will get along.

A newspaper came out with an article stating the present governor had removed the conditional pardon and granted us a complete pardon from the sentence imposed upon us both by the Clark Co. Court. We will have to be thankful for that ... I will have to make the best of it when I get to another place. ... Among these official men it is always spoken about taking over to another place for treatment. I do not understand what treatments I need. If there is something wrong I would like to know what it is and maybe I can do more for myself than others can do for me. There is something wrong with all of them too, but of course one is not supposed to see that I guess. Well I hope your cows came out well in the test. Some more of Madisons huey that those fellows got up. Something one never heard of years ago. Well it gives a job for some even if the work is of doubtful value. The country is full of that humbug stuff and hot air. Well must close for this time, am getting along good so far ... From Frank

Caroline received a letter from Governor Schmedeman the second week in July stating that the petitions for executive clemency for Leslie and Frank were granted by him. He said the petitions were presented to him by four of Caroline's friends from Milwaukee. The governor had different

plans for each of the brothers. Leslie was to stay at a farm near Milwaukee under the care of one of the petitioners of the Krueger Committee for one month while awaiting Frank's release from a Wauwatosa hospital, where he would get special treatment for his mental condition. Another of the governor's conditions was that the Krueger home and farm had to be made reasonably free from evidences of the disturbance that started it all. With bullet holes still visible throughout the home and the barn a shell of what it once was, it would have been nearly impossible to accomplish this condition.

In addition to the stipulations Schmedeman gave Caroline, he also congratulated her for her efforts in the long years and those of her friends who helped to bring the family together again without any hope of financial gain in the matter.

MILWAUKEE SENTINEL, JULY 17, 1934

> "… Frank walked through the gate with bowed head. Leslie came out smiling and happy. The years of silence had left a deep impression on the elder of the brothers but they had not broken the spirit of the younger. … Both had been outfitted in new light suits, new shoes, and caps. Their meager possessions they carried in boxes and bags as they emerged from the inner doors of the penitentiary. …"

On July 18th, a letter was sent to Caroline from Ernst Aumann of Milwaukee to let her know that Leslie was staying at his home and Frank was nearby in the county hospital at Wauwatosa. It was at last real, they were free from iron bars that encircled them for nearly sixteen years. Mr. Aumann assured Caroline that both of her sons would be back home in one month.

Well It's All Over

Frank at Milwaukee County Hospital, Wauwatosa, to Mother, July 22, 1934

Dear Mother, Must write you another letter so you hear from me again, but am writing this one from a different place. You no doubt have read some about Leslie and I being transferred from Central, the 13th of this month to the prison and then of two of us again being taken from the prison. I to the Milwaukee County Hospital for Mental Disease, Wauwatosa, and Leslie to Milwaukee. You have heard from Leslie so know where he is located and in whose care he is. We were both taken from the prison on Monday, July 16, after being there more than three days. Those three went slowly and a thrill of gladness went thru me when the prison guard placed the key in cell door lock, unlocked it, opened the door and said "Well its all over." He then turned us both over to a deputy who gave us our clothes, we were then paid our money, plus transportation money back to Neillsville and then turned from the front gate, from where you also so often went with a heavy heart.

Outside our pictures were taken and two automobiles were there waiting to take us where we now are. The trip was a pleasant one and the day fine but warm, which we did not notice so much when the car was traveling. I am now getting along well, and adjusting myself to the new place and conditions. The three men from Milwaukee, who you know, and Leslie were here and visited me last Friday. I will close for this time, will write again after next Tuesday. My present address is, to myself, Care of H. M. D. Box "A," Wauwatosa, Wis. Hope you are well in health. From Frank

From Leslie at Milwaukee to Mother, July 24, 1934

Dear Mother ... this last few days I have been on the go quite a little. Last Sunday was to the Singer Fest at Wauksauk [Waukesha], there was a large crowd there, shook hands with the governor [Attorney Raihle wrote to Caroline that more people shook hands with Leslie than the governor] he gave a speech there. Last night was to the Gold Smith building see Palmer. In the morning I was down and see F, he likes it there says it is like a hotel, he expects to be out in about two weeks. ... They are going to have a farewell party about the 18th of next month so they told me to wait until they let you know, the Milwaukee Sentinel will pay your fair and after the party they will take us home. ... the fellow I stay with delivers eggs and butter and I go with him, so I see the town quite a little. They expect to receive an answer from there letters, so you will have to answer them, don't know any more to write. I will write again when they get ready to have you come down. It is hard to find work. Am well, Leslie Krueger

From Oosterwyk and Aumann at Milwaukee to Caroline, July 25, 1934

... If you can come here on 15 August we can leave here at 19 August, after a nice farewell partie with the members of the societys who want all to see you, Frank, Lesly, Raihle. Everything is settled already, a big Hall, singing society, lunch ... and that will be the end of our work for 2 years. You believe me, Aumann and myself, we are glad it is over, it was a terrible thing, and it would have been a crime, to let it go ... we're glad, that we could do what we did, and believe it, because we show results ...

There was a bit of rapid correspondence between Caroline, Ernst Aumann, and Gerhard Oosterwyk in anticipation of the reunion between Caroline and her sons in August. They asked her not to talk with anyone on the train to Milwaukee, but to give her first interview to the *Milwaukee Sentinel* since they gave the best press coverage in favor of the Kruegers' release. Aumann and Oosterwyk wrote about the choir that would be singing at the farewell party. It featured about seventy-five singers, the nicest in Milwaukee. The Society wanted to do its best to celebrate Leslie and Frank's freedom.

Mother to Leslie at Milwaukee, July 29, 1934

Dear Leslie, got your letter, see you have good times for which we are glad, and that you are both getting your bearings, well its quite cool today, got our little oats cut and set up but its full and nice, heavy... I see that we will not meet until 2 weeks later, well that is all right too, see your faces in the papers all over and you look as fat as ever, when you get home I guess I will have to feed you on sour milk—well you will lose that very soon without anything extra. L says as soon as you are home he is going to look up butternuts, he had a ride with someone that wanted him to go along to Neillsville and he went their, he says the trees are just loaded with them, he is kind of tired sitting at home always too, his fingers are healing just fine... will no doubt see you the 16 in the morning as I do not like to go with the day train that stops at every station, that is what I think unless there is a change in the train service. Hope you are all well down their, give my best regards to all that know us. From Mother and Louis

Frank at Wauwatosa Hospital to Mother, July 31, 1934

Dear Mother ... The haying season seems to be getting shorter there every season, but this year it was on account of the dry weather. I thot you were not permitted to pick berries on the 80, that the present owner would drive you off, maybe he is not clearing there anymore. Picking berries is a task you always liked anyway. ... Used to like to do that myself. Makes me think of the many blueberries we use to pick on the sand country, west. I can clearly understand how Louis hurt his hand in the chain on the binder. The clutch lever is in a dangerous place and one has to be careful when one reaches for it when the binder is in gear and the chain running. I often thot of that when I run it and was careful. I thot of changing it but was always so busy at that time haying or repairing threshing machinery. Well I hope he gets better soon and his hand be none the worse after the accident. I hope he will not have to do all the work alone very soon if our affairs go as they are planned.

I am working again since last Tuesday at the same work I did when in Central. In the dining room here. Am getting so I like that kind of work. Its as good as any inside job, and clean work, and also a necessary work as we must all eat. ... Dr. Plahner of Milwaukee was here and visited me last Sunday afternoon for a time and we talked about how he worked to have us both removed as has been done in the past, and maybe he will work some more in our behalf. ... I am getting along well so far from day to day. This institution has been started many years ago and has large trees standing on the grounds, and lawns well kept so makes it more cheerful and nature like. From Frank

From Oosterwyk to Caroline, August 1, 1934

If you believe that you are the only one who is glad the boys are out, you are mistaken. Thousands and thousands of German-Americans are glad that this is over.

"Lesly Don't Need No Buttermilk"

From Oosterwyk and Aumann of Milwaukee to Caroline, August 10, 1934

... Enclosed you will find a Railroad Ticket (Round trip) Withee-Waukesha. <u>In Waukesha we will pick you up</u> because it is easier for you, and Frank and Lesly will be there, and will be glad to see you there, too. ... Now, please, don't forget the letters to bring along which you sometimes ago get from <u>Ennis</u>. With the help and advising of the Sentinel and the American Weekly, we will try to find him, too. But bring everything along, what you get. If Mr. Raihle get them letters, let him know, he should bring them papers along. I got a letter from him yesterday saying he will be here by Soo Line, Saturday 18 August. ... Yes, we worked on it, and we want to finish it. Frank signed this morning the paper, that he wants to leave the Hospital, the rules and regulations are, that if a patient wanted to go, he must inform the attendant on D. [duty] 5 days before. ... Lesly is very good weight 214 Pounds, beating Mr. Aumann by 10 Pound. Frank weight 175 Pound, but he will pick up, give him the buttermilk you wanted to give Lesly. He don't need no buttermilk. ..."

Kind Letter from a Stranger

From Florence Wing at Rhinelander to Caroline, August 25, 1934

... I suppose you will be surprised to hear from me, a perfect stranger, but I could not resist writing to you, and congratulating you, on the return home of your two sons. I was living at Neillsville at the time of the War, and as the Captain's wife, of The Home Guards there, was a very dear friend of mine, I heard a great deal about it, and I saw the boys when they were taken to jail. There were a great many of us that knew at the time, that it was an unjust arrest, but in those times, we could not say our soul was our own, even. This was another affair like the John Dietz, of Cameron Dam, poor man, he was unjustly kept in prison, until his family was all grown up and he missed all those happy years in prison, which he should have spent in raising his family and with his beloved wife. ... Everything I saw in the paper about your case, I would cut out, and save, and I always had the assurance that they would be released. ... I also know a man living at Neillsville, who told me how your home had been robbed of many things at the time of your trouble. He mentioned silverware in particular. There is plenty of Law, but very little Justice. ...

MILWAUKEE SENTINEL, *AUGUST 19, 1934 (pg 3)*

"... Several hundred persons last night attended a reception at Jefferson hall to rejoice with Frank and Leslie Krueger at their release after 16 years behind bars for the "draft battle" on their Clark county farm and their reunion with their mother. The reception was given by the Federated German-American Societies."

Back Home at Longwood

In the last week of September, Caroline Krueger received a welcome letter from Mrs. Ernst Aumann of Milwaukee, thanking her for the apples and pickles from the farm that were sent along home to her with Ernst. Mrs. Aumann said she and her husband were always thinking of her and the boys and wondered how they were all getting along. She hoped that she and Ernst would be able to drive up to Longwood the following summer to the Krueger farm for a good visit.

This was the first of several letters exchanged between Caroline and Mrs. Aumann, who would remain friends for life. Mrs. Aumann sent the Krueger family two bags of clothing containing two overcoats and a ten-dollar bill the following winter. The items and money were collected for the Krueger family by the German Societies. Also donated to the Kruegers was a large toolbox full of tools the Aumanns planned on bringing up the next summer.

The gift that the Krueger Committee and Attorney Raihle gave to the Krueger family could never be repaid, and would not be forgotten.

PATRONS ARE REQUESTED TO FAVOR THE COMPANY BY CRITICISM AND SUGGESTION CONCERNING ITS SERVICE

WESTERN UNION (48)

The filing time as shown in the date line on full-rate telegrams and day letters, and the time of receipt at destination as shown on all messages, is STANDARD TIME.

Received at Main Office, 320 E. Wisconsin Ave., Milwaukee, Wis. ALWAYS OPEN 1934 AUG 18 AM 1 53

MB23 145 NL=THREELAKES WIS 17

MINUTES IN TRANSIT
FULL-RATE   DAY LETTER

MRS CAROLINE KRUGER=
  CARE DR CHARLES L NEWBERRY MILW=

I REGRET BEING UNABLE TO ACCEPT THE INVITATION TO MEET YOU
PERSONALLY SATURDAY EVENING I CAN ONLY IN PART APPRECIATE
THE HAPPINESS THAT IS YOURS IN BEING REUNITED WITH YOUR
BOYS FRANK AND LESTE FOR WHOSE FREEDOM YOUR EFFORTS HAVE
BECOME A CLASSIC EXAMPLE OF A MOTHERS DEVOTION IT WAS ALSO
A PLEASURE TO HAVE MET THE MAN OF THE COMMITTEE YOU ARE
WITH WHOSE EFFORTS AT GREAT LOSS TO THEMSELVES FINALLY
BROUGHT FULFILLMENT TO THE TASK WHICH THEY SET THEMSELVES TO
AND WE ALL ARE ALSO HAPPY THAT WE HAVE HAD A MAN AS GOVERNOR
SCHMEDEMAN TO PRESENT THE MATTER TO FOR COURAGIOUS
SOLUTION I WISH TO EXPRESS MY HOPE THAT YOU MAY ENJOY
MANY YEARS WITH YOUR BOYS AROUND YOU IN RENEWED PROSPERITY
AND HAPPINESS I SHALL ALWAYS BE PLEASED TO BE AT THE
SERVICE OF YOU AND YOUR BOYS IN THIS MATTER=
  WILLIAM I HRIG.

THE QUICKEST, SUREST AND SAFEST WAY TO SEND MONEY IS BY TELEGRAPH OR CABLE

MILWAUKEE ATTORNEY WILLIAM IHRIG PETITIONED GOV. SCHMEDEMAN
FOR KRUEGER BROTHER'S RELEASE

How and Why September 14, 1918, Happened

The Krueger brothers had a few strikes against them along with failing to register or follow through with the draft laws. Although they were all Wisconsin born, including Mother and Father, they still spoke German and were identified as German in a mostly Danish community. As elsewhere across the U.S., people weren't tolerant of Germans, who were viewed as the enemy, no matter who they were. The Kruegers were set apart from the community that they lived in for various reasons: strong religious beliefs, nondrinkers, and successful farmers who bonded together to build a very unique rural farmhouse that attracted much attention. Frank often suggested their success caused jealousy and misunderstanding by others.

When they refused to register and Louis fled the state, they were all branded as "slackers," someone to be hated, especially during wartime. It probably didn't take much to raise the mob and its mentality into the frenzy it became on September 14. Frank Krueger called it a "patriotic frenzy." This day was most likely looked at as a social event, a rare opportunity to be armed for a worthy cause, a chance to get in on some real action … just down the road.

Were Leslie and Frank Krueger Guilty of First Degree Murder?

My opinion is a definite "No." They did not seek out Harry Jensen in hopes of shooting and killing him. I don't believe Mr. Jensen was shot by any of the Kruegers. He was standing behind his car loading his gun when shot.

He was parked on the highway fronting the Krueger farm and was between a quarter and a half mile from the Krueger buildings. Although the Krueger letters never gave the name of the man who shot Mr. Jensen, they inferred over and over that they knew who did the deed, and said everyone else knew as well. I believe it was an accident and Harry was shot by one of the crowd. Harry's unfortunate death was seen as the way to put the Krueger brothers away, a way to punish them for evading the draft and resisting arrest. Charging them with first degree murder allowed the most severe punishment.

(Note written by Caroline Krueger, date unknown)

On the morning of Mr. A. Replogle Auction in Withee, I went to see him about what he knew of the shooting of Harry Jensen, Sep. 14, 1918. I asked him if he knew who shot H. Jensen and he said "Yes. But I did not see it. Had I seen it I would have said so on the trial in Neillsville. But this is the way I know, Buxton and I were at Vaters and as the crowd kept comming we decided to go into Vaters Stable out of the reach of shooting, we might have been their maby one half hour when Mr. Taylor came in and told us who killed Harry Jensen and that he seen it done. Mr. Taylor the Auctioneer and as I understand Mr. Johnston Sr. up north knows all about it too."

(From Mother to Frank at Waupun, March 14, 1921)

... I think that there is a show that you both will be set free of the charge entirely as all of them knows who done it, they have told me that the bullet that killed that man never came from the south ...

Was Their Time Extended Intentionally by Insane Asylum Placement?

Yes, I believe it was. If it weren't for the prodding of the German Societies, the Krueger Committee, and Attorney Paul Raihle, Frank and Leslie may have never been released from the Waupun Prison System. It was ironic that both brothers were placed in the insane asylum just before their pardons were given, not allowing them to have freedom as a result. Questions given to them at examinations seemed repetitious. Reasons given for pronouncing their continued insanity status were ridiculous. Who would not be evasive, and mistrusting, when questioned so many times after being incarcerated for so many years?

What about Ennis?

Only theories can be given on the life and death of Ennis Krueger. I had hoped the letters would shed more light on whether he was killed in Taylor County, Wisconsin, on September 22, 1918, or not. Part of the reason for lack of information on the subject was that family members had to be cautious in what they wrote to one another, as most letters were censored by the prison system. I will list a collection of facts and give my opinions in italics.

1. A man was shot in a barn and killed near Polley, in Taylor County, Wisconsin, on September 22, 1918, by U.S. Marshal Joseph Gantz. At first the news media was told that a fictitious marshal named Jones from Montana shot Ennis. *Why was this cover-up necessary?* The body was propped up in the vehicle on the return trip to Withee, made to appear as if alive, driving at high enough speeds to cause some damage to the vehicle. *Why was this high speed necessary? This behavior showed fear and makes one think that they were unsure of who they had killed and were afraid someone would see the victim, recognize him, and cause them to be in serious trouble.*

2. The man claimed to be Ennis was buried on the Krueger lot at Riverside Cemetery near Withee. No one from the Krueger family was allowed to view the body or attend the funeral.

3. Caroline Krueger requested all items recovered from Ennis' body in 1921 and received his pocket watch and a money order for $8.40. The pocket watch was a Hamilton that had belonged to the deceased brother, Robert Krueger. Although this watch was returned to Caroline, there was some argument upon her request, some confusion as to where the items might be located, but they were sent to her in the mail two weeks after her request. Along with Robert's Hamilton pocket watch, Frank had also given Ennis about ninety dollars before he ran away. *One would think Ennis should have had more money left after only one week's time had gone by. The fact that the unique watch Ennis was carrying was returned to Caroline leads me to believe that he at least had been in custody for a period of time. He could have been captured at another time and released with the understanding never to return home in order to preserve his freedom.*

4. In the summer of 1927, the supposed grave of Ennis at Riverside

Cemetery was exhumed and observed by Caroline and Louis. They both said that the body was not Ennis. Attorney Raihle and others claimed the body was that of a Polish youth, Narkofski, who had disappeared from the Polley area after the shooting in the barn there. I questioned a practicing undertaker if it would be possible to identify a body that was exhumed after nine years and he felt the body might be unrecognizable, although he really wasn't certain.

5. Caroline, Louis, Leslie, and Frank believed that Ennis was alive and had created a new life in a new location to avoid being incarcerated as they were, and because of his fear he refused to return home for the remainder of his life. The family said they received letters from Ennis from various states including North Carolina. In the collection I only found 2 empty envelopes I felt were a part of "Ennis' letters." They were addressed to L. E. Krueger at Withee, Wisc., and postmarked from East Bend, North Carolina, 1932. One envelope had been folded, the handwriting on it was Louis', so it most likely was sent to someone by Louis using his self-addressed envelope for their reply. The 1930 Federal Census lists two single sisters living together near East Bend, North Carolina: Eris and Rena Kruger, in their forties, both born in North Carolina. In the 1920 census they can be found near the same location with their parents on a farm. Perhaps Louis wrote to "Eris Kruger" hoping she/he was Ennis. He was said to have found out that Ennis was living in East Bend, N.C., after a trip to Minneapolis in 1932. All of the letters supposedly received from Ennis were given to the Krueger Committee of the German Societies, who promised to continue the investigation and attempt to locate him after Leslie and Frank regained their freedom in 1934. There is nothing to indicate the Committee had any success, and it seems the unity of the committee fell apart not long after the brothers were set free.

6. Caroline made a statement to Frank in a letter dated December 31, 1930, that Ennis had been kept not far from their home for two years. I wasn't able to find any further information on this statement but at the time she made it, it seemed like a new revelation for her.

7. Louis wrote to psychics at Imperial Beach, California, in 1946, and again to New York in 1953, asking for help in locating his missing brother. Undoubtedly, Ennis was on the minds of his mother and brothers the rest of their lives. They never gave up hope that he would return to Longwood; they were most certain that he was not killed in 1918 in the barn near Polley,

Wisconsin. Who could be the better judge of Ennis' demise than his own family? I will leave it at that!

Caroline Krueger's Thoughts

Caroline Krueger to Dr. Green (Superintendent at Central State Hospital, Waupun), December 28, 1933

Dr. Green Dear Sir, I will try and tell you just a little how Leslie got to Waupun Prison with his Brother Frank in the war time because we were Germans. The people mobbed the Krueger's and while this mobbing was going on, one of their own men shot one of their own number by accident, as I was told afterward by one of the Officers. And this crime was laid onto the Krueger Boys but they never committed that crime because the man was too far from the Kruegers home and over a hill, but on the trial the sentiment was so overwhelming against the Krueger's that Leslie and Frank was sent to Prison for life, one bullet killed the man and 2 men were sent to Prison for life, their they spent over 15 years of their life for a deed they never committed.

Now how Leslie got to the Hospital of the Crimanal Insane Asylum was this way—as ex-Govoner Zimmerman was Govenor we had a Pardon made up for Leslie and just one week before the Pardon was presented to the Gov. they took him out of Prison and put him into the Asylum, for they feared that the Gov. would let him out, and he would turn on them and sue them for false imprisonment, for their was not even a warrant sworn out against him, and as we had a pardon made out for his Brother Frank they done the same way with him. The Thursday before the next Wednesday as the Pardon was to be presented to ex-Govenor La Follette they took him out of Prison to the Insane Asylum. The party that com. the crime does not live far from the Krueger home. Now Leslie was shut in so I never told him much of anything of this trouble, as I thought he might take it hard, now this is only a touch of this trouble that I have written. And so cannot answer all of your questions.

Yours Truly, Mrs. Caroline Krueger, Withee Wis.

Leslie Krueger's Thoughts

Leslie's speech at Jefferson Hall at the German Societies' party celebrating the Krueger Brothers' freedom on August 18, 1934:

Ladies—gentlemen—dear friends

Your society has done more for us than any other society-club church parties. There is one society that worked in our behalf. When I was taken from the prison I thought things would go better for me. Instead things were going worse. When I heard from this committee, Oosterwyk, Aumann, they asked what they could do for me. I said get me out of this place. They said in about 8 days they would have a Dr. out here to examine me. Which they did. Things looked different to me. I thank you for all your society has done for me. They did nothing wrong. I will assure you that I am sorry there was no such society 16 years ago. My brother and mother who are here today did everything in their powers to clear me of this trouble but it all failed, but still my mother and I had hope that we would get our freedom and for your work we are thankful through our attorney Mr. Raihle, through the Governor restored to citizen of this country which did us a great injustice. I have talked to a lot of people since this war, telling me that Wilson said he would keep us out of war. When a country goes to war nothing is gained and a lot of people feel that they will never be paid for their service. I thank you.

Frank Krueger's Thoughts

Frank from Wisconsin State Prison, Waupun, to Mother, March 4, 1928

I do not want to find fault with the law on that [registration for the draft], but will say as I said then, let those sign that wish to and excuse those that did not care to put their names down for such a purpose. To sign your name was almost the same as enlisting to be a soldier to go and fight someone you did not know. The public mind at that time was quite well "filled up" on the word "murder." The newspaper spread it over the land in profusion, in fact it was the "going thing" at the time. All we can do is wait until it blows over or wears itself out, of course it never will entirely.

There are only two gravestones for the Krueger family in the Riverside Cemetery. In the photo below is the stone for Louis Krueger, last family member who died in 1963. Just northeast of his grave, in another row, is an old stone for his paternal grandmother, Friedericka Krueger, who died in 1895. The cemetery sexton said there are other Krueger family members buried in the row with Louis, although none have a gravestone. The sexton was uncertain who was buried where.

RIVERSIDE CEMETERY WEST OF WITHEE, MAY 2012
(AUTHOR'S PHOTO)

The Brook

I come from haunts of coot and hern;
I make a sudden sally,
And sparkle out among the fern,
To bicker down a valley.

By 30 hills I hurry down,
Or slip between the ridges;
By 20 Thorps, a little town,
And half a hundred bridges.

Till last by Philip's farm I flow,
To join the brimming river;
For men may come and men may go,
But I go on forever.

I chatter over stony ways,
In little sharps and trebles;
I bubble into eddying bays,
I babble on the pebbles.

With many a curve my banks I fret,
By many a field and fallow,
And many a fairy foreland set
With willow-weed and mallow.

I chatter, chatter, as I flow
To join the brimming river;
For men may come and men may go,
But I go on forever.

I wind about, and in and out,
With here a blossom sailing,
And here and there a lusty trout,
And here and there a grayling,

And here and there a foamy flake
Upon me, as I travel,
With many a silvery waterbreak
Above the golden gravel;

And draw them all along, and flow
To join the brimming river;
For men may come and men may go.
But I go on forever.

I steal by lawns and grassy plots
I slide by hazel covers;
I move the sweet forget-me-nots
That grow for happy lovers.

I slip, I slide, I gloom, I glance
Among my skimming swallows,
I make the netted sunbeam dance
Against my sandy shallows.

I murmur under moon and stars,
In brambly wildernesses;
I linger by my shingly bars;
I loiter round my cresses.

And out again I curve and flow
To join the brimming river;
For men may come and men may go,
But I go on forever.

By Alfred Tennyson

Poem was penciled with a bit of shorthand by Frank Krueger on the backside of an envelope.

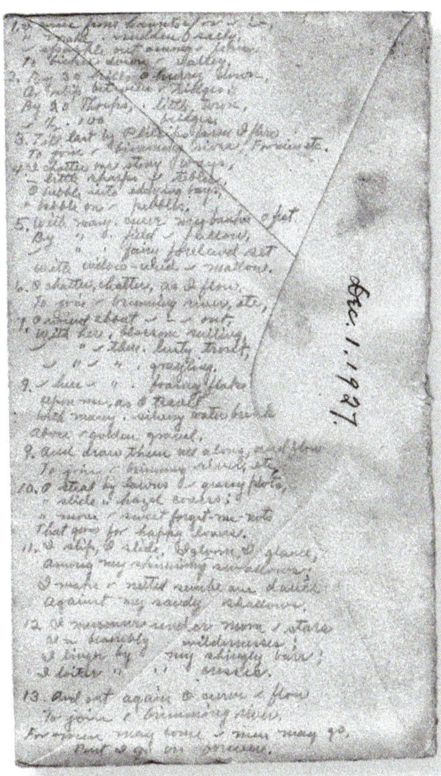

In the spring of 2012, I visited the Krueger home with my friend, Viki, thanks to the generosity and kindness shown by present owner, Roger Wallace. The home has been well maintained, and it still carries the aura of beauty that Frank Krueger intended it to. The beautiful woodwork, built-in china cabinet and hardwood floors speak for themselves. Although the elevator is not used, it is intact and Mr. Wallace thinks it could be workable. The glass doors of the china cabinet still bear the wounds of the bullets that were fired upon Caroline and Frank as they sought refuge during the shootings. One can still see where bullets penetrated the wall above the staircase and riddled the door between the dining room and kitchen. Thankfully they were preserved as a reminder of the day the world stopped turning for the Krueger family back in 1918.

ROGER WALLACE RESIDENCE, FORMER HOME OF THE KRUEGER FAMILY (AUTHOR'S PHOTO MAY 24, 2012)

| Sources |

Clark County Clerk of Courts: Transcript of Krueger Murder Trial, March–April 1919

Clark County Register of Deeds: Krueger Land Records

Clark County Registrar in Probate: Louis Krueger Probate File

The Clark County Journal, Withee, Wisconsin

Milwaukee Journal

Milwaukee Sunday Sentinel

Neillsville Times, Neillsville, Wisconsin

Sheboygan Press, Sheboygan, Wisconsin

The Wisconsin News, Milwaukee, Wisconsin

Utah Death Certificate, Carbon County, Utah

1900 Federal Census, Wisconsin, Clark County, Town of Longwood

1920, 1930 Federal Census, North Carolina, East Bend

Wisconsin Marriage Records Index pre 1907

Krueger Family Photos (author's collection)

Krueger Family Letters and Notes (author's collection)

Northwestern Report, July 9, 1920, Volume 177: Results of Court Appeals

"The Brook" by Alfred Tennyson (1809–1892)

Kay Scholtz was born in Neillsville, Wisconsin. She lives in Clark County with her husband in a little log cabin in the woods. She enjoys surrounding herself with nature in all seasons. Her interests include antiquing, genealogy, archeology, painting, quilting, and writing. Kay is treasurer of her township, and has worked in the cranberry fields for many years. She holds a special interest in preserving family and local history. This is her first book.